THE UNIVERSITY OF WINCHESTER

In the
tion, H
make
and le
ness of
educat

This in
centur
ers hav
theatre
as: how can theatre education
the political landscape of the twenty first ....es and
principles of theatre speak to different generat...ns. ...cring diverse illustrations of
practice from around the world, Helen Nicholson draws on much personal experience
and expert knowledge to demonstrate how cutting-edge performance practices continue to engage young people today.

HELEN NICHOLSON is Professor of Drama and Theatre at Royal Holloway,
University of London. She is the author of *Applied Drama: The Gift of Theatre*,
Theatre & Education and co-editor of *Research in Drama Education: The Journal of
Applied Theatre and Performance*.

Also by Helen Nicholson:

Applied Drama: The Gift of Theatre
Theatre & Education

Theatre, Education and Performance

The Map and the Story

HELEN NICHOLSON

palgrave
macmillan

First published 2011 by
PALGRAVE MACMILLAN

Palgrave Macmillan in the UK is an imprint of Macmillan Publishers Limited, registered in England, company number 785998, of Houndmills, Basingstoke, Hampshire RG21 6XS.

Palgrave Macmillan in the US is a division of St Martin's Press LLC, 175 Fifth Avenue, New York, NY 10010.

Palgrave Macmillan is the global academic imprint of the above companies and has companies and representatives throughout the world.

Palgrave® and Macmillan® are registered trademarks in the United States, the United Kingdom, Europe and other countries.

ISBN 978–0–230–57422–9 hardback
ISBN 978–0–230–57423–6 paperback

This book is printed on paper suitable for recycling and made from fully managed and sustained forest sources. Logging, pulping and manufacturing processes are expected to conform to the environmental regulations of the country of origin.

A catalogue record for this book is available from the British Library.

Library of Congress Cataloging-in-Publication Data

Nicholson, Helen, 1958–
    Theatre, education and performance / Helen Nicholson.
        p. cm.
    Includes bibliographical references and index.
    ISBN 978–0–230–57423–6 (pbk.)
        1. Theater and society. 2. Drama in education. 3. Theater and society – Great Britain. 4. Drama in education – Great Britain. I. Title.

PN2049.N55 2011
792—dc22   2011008067

10   9   8   7   6   5   4   3   2   1
20   19   18   17   16   15   14   13   12   11

Printed and bound in Great Britain by
CPI Antony Rowe, Chippenham and Eastbourne

Contents

List of Illustrations

Acknowledgements

Perhaps all books involve other people – certainly my writing is always inspired by conversations I have remembered and theatre I have witnessed – not all of whom can be acknowledged here. First, formal acknowledgement is due to the Arts and Humanities Research Council (AHRC) who funded the research leave that enabled me to complete this book. Thanks are also due to my colleagues in the Department of Drama and Theatre, Royal Holloway, University of London, who covered for my absence and offered intellectual and practical support in all kinds of ways. As she has now moved on, I would like to thank Kate Haines at Palgrave Macmillan, who has been kind enough to support me in the process of writing three books, and whose patience, good judgement and astute editorial guidance has been an inspiration.

The insights of many scholars and practitioners have been immensely helpful and encouraging, including all my colleagues on the editorial board of *Research in Drama Education: The Journal of Applied Theatre and Performance*, and especially Tony Jackson, Jenny Hughes, Kathleen Gallagher, Sally Mackey, Baz Kershaw, Shifra Schonmann, Gay Morris, Anton Franks, Colette Conroy, James Thompson and Joe Winston. Colleagues in the Department of Geography at Royal Holloway invited me to think about performance in different ways, particularly in planning the workshop and network grant, *On the Go: Mobilities, Settlement and Performance*, also funded by the AHRC. Students past and present – including Selina Busby, Wan-Jung Wang, Tina Muir, Louise Keyworth, Simon Parry and Martin Heaney – have introduced me to new ways of thinking. I am also grateful to Fred Inglis, who may recognize that early chapters benefitted from his wisdom and good-humoured teaching, and to Michael Anderson, Penny Bundy, John O'Toole and Peter O'Connor and the artists in Everyday Theatre for generously sharing their ideas and practice and for welcoming me so warmly to Australia and New Zealand. Jan Fredrickson, Rachel Betts, Ros Bird, Zola Bikwana, Sue Arthur and the teachers in the Masiphumelele Primary School, Khayelitsha inspired me with their integrity and creativity in Slough and South Africa. Thanks to Kaori Nakayama and her teams in Osaka,

Tokyo, Hiroshima and Mihara, and to Flic Minsall, Ashling McGee and Liz Bemment who were great companions in Japan. And to all the young people in Japan, South Africa, New Zealand, Southall, Slough and Hammersmith in the United Kingdom and in many other places who shared their work with me, my thanks. I should like to take this opportunity to thank my sister, Judith, for her immense kindness and support. But the last thanks go to my father, who liked reading maps, and always told great stories. This book is dedicated to his memory.

Helen Nicholson

 Arts & Humanities
Research Council

1

Mapping Stories

Beginning journeys

I am beginning this journey into theatre, education and performance in Slough, close to London's Heathrow Airport, which is not the most prepossessing town in England. Slough has the dubious accolade of being maligned in three consecutive centuries. In the nineteenth century Charles Dickens housed his mistress in Slough, mainly because it was so unfashionable that no one from his London circles or the moralizing public would detect his relationship with the woman he loved. In the twentieth century it was best known for a poem by the snooty John Betjeman, whose line 'come friendly bombs and fall on Slough' summarized upper-class prejudice towards industrialized towns in the 1930s. Poor Slough has recently achieved notoriety among a new generation as the setting for the BBC spoof documentary *The Office*, starring Ricky Gervais as the hapless paper merchant manager David Brent. Exported worldwide, this TV show has been blamed for the empty floors of brand new office space that no one wants to rent, falling property prices and a further lowering of civic pride. Slough may not be the prettiest of towns but, unlike its near-neighbour Windsor, it is very culturally diverse, with over 40 per cent of the population being of South Asian heritage (particularly India, Pakistan and Bangladesh). It is home to the highest percentage of Sikh residents in the country and its proximity to Heathrow means that it continues to receive many refugees and asylum seekers from different parts of the world. This lively cultural mix means that it makes a great place for research, sometimes to the amusement of my colleagues who prefer the more seductive charms of London's West End.

On this occasion my journey to Slough had taken me to a school on a housing estate that was built in the 1950s to accommodate Londoners whose homes had been lost in the Blitz. When I arrived, three classes of children aged 7 and 8 were waiting patiently in the school hall. This cavernous hall had been transformed by a few lights and reconfigured with the audience on three sides, giving the children plenty of room to move in a large central space. The atmosphere was calm, but the children were excited and ready for action. They had been 'doing' Pompeii, and this performance represented their creative responses to the story of its destruction. Two children stepped forward. They introduced themselves as Pacquio Proculo and his wife, and told us the date, 24th August 79 AD. The next line chills. 'This is the day we die', they say, and leave the space. From that moment, we had all left Slough.

The performance that followed wove together many different forms of learning. The story the children told is familiar – the unexpected volcanic eruption of Vesuvius that destroyed a Roman town and left many of its inhabitants dead. The theatrical composition, however, breathed new insights into this catastrophe. The everyday actions of baking and bathing had been researched, and the children's mimes were precise and witty. A boy ran through them carrying a large black bird-puppet, a symbol of death, which soared over their heads like a threatening dark cloud. The theatrical metaphor continued as the inhabitants became trapped, caught in death's giant game of cat and mouse in which escape was blocked by huge poles. One of the most moving moments was when the fire took over, represented first through the children's choreography and then through animation. Projected onto a billowing screen were self-portraits the children had drawn, each of which gradually singed and burned. When the animated portraits had crumbled, two children carried the empty fabric of the screen to cover the bodies, representing the shroud of ash that allowed the city to remain undiscovered for hundreds of years. This final image insisted on an empathetic response to history; it invoked both the sadness and the gift of Pompeii. The tragedy of the loss of life felt close, but remnants of the everyday lives of these people had been preserved and fragments of their stories awaited generations to come, including these children in Slough in 2009.

The children's dramatic representation of the Pompeii catastrophe invoked my own memories of visiting the ruins of Pompeii as a tourist some years previously. My imagination had been caught more by the ordinary objects of life than by the official Roman history, by the kitchens, the baths, the pots and pans. I was particularly taken by the graffiti, written in what my guidebook called 'vulgar Latin', a vernacular language unlike the Latin of official documents. I know the exact date I was there – 19th July 1994 – the day after Italy had lost to Brazil in the soccer World Cup final, and Italy was in mourning. I had arrived at Pompeii early to avoid the crowds, and in the quiet cool of the morning groups of men gathered on the ancient street corners to discuss the match. It was clear they thought Italy had been robbed. I remember writing a postcard to a friend, who likes his football, and telling him that I felt I had glimpsed a different time. For a moment it was easy to imagine the city was alive again, not with tourists or archaeologists, but with people just carrying on with their everyday lives and arguing about sport. This insight theatricalized my experience of Pompeii, allowing me to picture the streets and lanes before they were ruins, a process on which imaginative engagement with heritage sites depends.

Witnessing the children's performance in Slough, I could identify the complex layers of learning and teaching that had taken place and, perhaps more particularly, how the collaborative processes of making theatre had supported the children in developing an empathetic understanding of history. The Pompeii project had involved a partnership between the children, teachers and two theatre education practitioners, Tina Muir and Rachel Betts, all of whom brought different experiences and expertise to the work. The teachers' knowledge of the children's development combined with the theatre-maker's understanding of dramatic metaphor and produced a structure that supported the children's learning. The children themselves, central to the project, understood how dramatic form and curriculum content came together, and the aesthetic of the performance helped them to make the story their own. The school had been generously funded by government policies that encouraged creative approaches to learning, particularly in areas of social deprivation such as Slough, and this performance was given added significance because it was attended by Ed Vaizey, a Conservative MP who was at the time shadow Secretary of State for Culture. Although the Labour government had supported creativity in education during the early years of the twenty-first century, the worry was this policy would change if a Conservative government came to power in the 2010 elections. Inviting this high profile Tory to see the children's work was part of a strategy to convince him of the quality and value of this form of learning in the hope that, if he were to gain power, funding would continue. At the time Mr Vaizey seemed impressed, cheerily declaring himself 'gobsmacked' in the kind of upper-class accent John Betjeman might have been surprised to hear in Slough. His use of the colloquial term 'gobsmacked' to describe his enthusiasm led me to muse on the hours I had spent encouraging children to develop a critical vocabulary with which to evaluate drama, and I wondered what kind of educational role model this politician presented. Sadly, the children's efforts were in vain, when Mr Vaizey gained power in the elections in 2010 and became Minister for Communication, Culture and the Creative Industries, funding that sought to encourage creativity in schools was swiftly axed.

This book is about the contribution that professional theatre practitioners make to the education of young people. It is a book about why theatre matters, and how its practices, principles and policies speak to different generations. It is also a book about the cultural environments in which theatre and learning meet, and about how the educational concerns and artistic inventiveness of people living in different times and places have inflected theatre and changed education. In a morning, the Slough children's performance had reminded me of the ways in which theatre and education had converged in the past, and its continued vibrancy today. The work was both a beneficiary of, and vulnerable to, government's educational and cultural policies, and the presence of a member of parliament served as a reminder of the power of changing political climates on children's lives and learning. The children's learning processes were evident in the product, and illuminated the pedagogical complexity of work when teachers, theatre practitioners and children learn together. It showed the aesthetic power of transforming the school hall into a theatrical space, and the ways in which performers and audiences share and shape its meanings. The performance itself reminded me of the educational significance of narrative, memory and place, and the importance of interpreting history and animating cultural heritage. The school's history and location in Slough was also significant, as a former industrial town, it had received funding for regeneration through the creative industries and investment in creative learning in schools. These are all central debates in this book. My journey to Slough had been worth it.

Theatre and education

This book was inspired by seeing theatre and performance for, with, and by young people that is both artistically innovative, educationally effective and socially engaged. One way or another I have been involved in theatre education since the early 1980s when I became a drama teacher, and over the years I have seen some theatre in educational practices that is stunningly good and, to be honest, some pretty mediocre fare. At worst, I have seen young people subjected to the kind of performance satirized by the BBC comedy show *The League of Gentlemen* in which the earnest Legz Akimbo Theatre Company tour plays to schools about 'issues'. I remember being very amused by the sketch depicting Legz Akimbo's performance of *Everybody Out!* (a play about homosexuality) when it was aired in the 1990s, but watching it again on youtube I found myself cringing with recognition. Its sharp satire was built on the observation of every imaginable theatrical cliché – the patronizing use of direct address, unsubtle still-images to demonstrate social attitudes and untalented actors who were trying far too hard be matey with their school audience but would really rather be doing 'proper' theatre. The young people, of course, were not fooled, and part of the comedy lies in their bemused looks and their reluctance to participate. Judging by the comments on the youtube site, I am not alone in finding the familiarity of Legz Akimbo's approach to theatre education funny, but also rather depressing. Critics of theatre education seem to have this kind of unimaginative work in mind; the playwright David Mamet famously described theatre education as 'joyless' and a 'waste of time' (1994, p. 24), and the experimental British playwright Howard Barker was even more critical, arguing that a theatre that is designed for education 'diminishes its particular powers, poetry, the spoken voice, the hypnotism of the actor' (1997, p. 146). But there is good and bad theatre everywhere, in all forms, styles and genres, and part of my ambition in this book is to demonstrate that The League of Gentlemen's witty satire of theatre education represents, thankfully, only a very small part of the story.

One of my intentions in writing this book was to try to capture some of the spirit of innovation that has long characterized the most inspiring theatre education. There have been various ways in which theatre education has been defined over time, but the broad description that I am using in this book is that it involves professional theatre-makers working with young people, often in partnership with teachers in schools or other educational settings. Theatre education is not, interestingly, primarily concerned with actor training or teaching students to work in the theatre, but in encouraging young people to find points of connection between lived experience and theatrical representation. This means that theatre education often illuminates the cultural significance placed on theatre in society; investigating why, at different periods in history, theatre was considered to be an important element in children's education often reveals the social priorities of the day. Throughout the twentieth century, theatre education was allied to new developments in child psychology and provided a practical pedagogy for those interested in democratizing education. A history of theatre education, therefore, not only demonstrates how theatre became allied to educational and social reform, it also illuminates how childhood has been valued, conceptualized and understood at different times. In common with many others, I am drawn to the political idealism associated with theatre education, an impulse that has brought together theatre-makers, social reformists, political activists and educationalists to develop theatrical pedagogies that are designed to make a difference to young people's lives.

To find connections between life and art, theatre education practitioners have always undertaken radical experiments in theatre form, and this has led theatre-makers to break the boundaries between actors and audiences and develop dramatic methodologies that encourage participation. Contemporary practitioners are indebted to their twentieth century predecessors for their vision of participatory performance, and new performance vocabularies are now filtering into theatre for children, theatre education and public engagement programmes in response to changing social circumstances. In the process of researching this book I have encountered practices that are at the cutting edge of contemporary theatre, including site-specific performance, installation and autobiographical performance as well as provocative new plays written for young audiences and actors. There are new political challenges, too, as the boundaries between education and tourism, learning and leisure are blurred by an increasingly commodified and mediatized culture and in a climate in which creativity is regarded as an important attribute for monetary success in knowledge-based economies. This re-visioning of theatre education is demanding a re-conceptualization of which forms of learning theatre might address, a redefinition of the spaces and places in which learning happens and a re-imagining of the role of theatre-makers in educational settings. This book is intended to make a contribution to that process.

The Map and the Story

Theatre often relies on metaphor to engage audiences in matters of importance, and so I have invoked a metaphor to help me to articulate

some of the conceptual questions that have recurred in the process of writing this book. The subtitle of the book, The Map and the
Story, comes from a much-quoted sentence in the French philosopher
Michel de Certeau's book, *The Practice of Everyday life* (1984), 'what
the map cuts up, the story cuts across' (1984, p. 129). In de Certeau's
elliptical essay, the map and the story represent two different ways of
knowing; the map represents knowledge that is official, disciplined
and objective, whereas the story is associated with everyday moments
of creativity, ways of knowing that are practical, embodied and spontaneous. The metaphor has proved alluring to those seeking to describe
theatre and performance studies, notably Dwight Conquergood, for
whom the opposition has political resonance as well as epistemologi-
cal and ontological consequences. Conquergood used the metaphor
to critique the history of Western thought that separated theory from
practice, casting rigid boundaries between critical analysis and creativity. In this Enlightenment project, he argued, objective knowledge
was privileged over local, vernacular and community-based 'know-
how' and this forged hierarchical distinctions between officially
sanctioned forms of knowledge and ways of knowing which are more
'active, intimate, hands-on participation' (2004, pp. 311–12). Using
this metaphor, he makes a persuasive case for performance studies as
a 'radical intervention' within the academy because it has the potential to bring together these two domains of knowledge, and includes
both written scholarship and creative practices (2004, p. 318).

The radical history of theatre education chimes well with
Conquergood's analysis of different forms of knowing in theatre and
performance studies, and finding a productive negotiation between
creative practice and critical thought has preoccupied theatre peda-
gogues for many years. But I should also like to stretch this pliable
political metaphor into a slightly different shape. The metaphor can
be used to invoke the bureaucratic functionality of education and the
playful narratives of theatre, and thus serves to clarify how theatre-
makers have, at times, perceived their relationship to educational
policy-makers and institutions. When the 'story' of the unpredictability of dramatic practice is juxtaposed against the 'maps' of official education policies and political agendas, it can illuminate what
Jean-Francois Lyotard called the postmodern 'condition' of knowledge (Lyotard, 1984). Lyotard's concern was to question the status
of knowledge and analyse the 'grand narratives' of legitimation both
within education and beyond. He was particularly critical of the commodification of knowledge in education where there is an emphasis

on teaching the kind of skills needed 'designed to tackle world competition' and to maintain the social system as it is (1984, p. 50). Formal
education is always on some level an Instrument of State Apparatus,
to use Althussur's Marxist phraseology, and theatre-makers who
were drawn to work in educational contexts have often been, historically, inspired by oppositional politics, regarding themselves as
independent-minded cultural critics rather than uncritical agents of
government policy. This means that although theatre education has
sometimes benefited from government intervention, there have sometimes been tensions between the demands of official policies and the
ways in which theatre-makers have perceived their roles and shaped
their practices. I am interested in using the metaphor of the map and
the story to explore how theatre-makers working in educational settings have animated official policies, subverted the commodification
of knowledge and challenged outdated educational structures, and
where they have found a dynamic negotiation between their complementary ambitions and interests.

The metaphor works in other ways, too. Both maps and stories are
representational and, although the map may have claimed greater
objectivity, both are an illustration or an abstraction of the world from
one point of view. As the anthropologist Gregory Bateson describes,
the paper map is a 'representation of what was in the retinal representation of the man who made the map' (1972, p. 460). Bateson's
quest was to redefine ways of thinking about the mind as an ecological system rather than series of oppositions, and it is in this context
that the metaphor of the map illuminates the relationship between
the place of learning and knowledge production. Subsequent scholars
have built on his theories of the mind as an ecology, and developments in a range of disciplinary fields, including cultural geography,
science studies, aesthetics and architecture are shifting the terms in
which the authority of knowledge is conceptualized and situated. This
has implications for theatre and education, both as separate cultural
activities and when they work in partnership. Rather than seeing the
world in terms of different domains of knowledge, in which objective
knowledge is privileged over subjective feeling or local know-how,
there is an increasing search for ways of thinking and learning that
acknowledge their interdependence.

Pedagogically, this way of thinking invites a re-assessment of the
significance of what the US educator Elizabeth Ellsworth calls the
'materiality of learning'. In her book *Places of Learning* (2005) she
recognizes that the physical environment, the place of learning, and

the movement of bodies in space are integral to the experience of learning. She argues that when knowledge is packaged as a commodity, as something to be learnt and attained rather than something to be experienced and understood, it is dead. She makes a powerful case for re-examining the history of thought that has separated mind and body, reason and emotion, and advocates a pedagogy that acknowledges that understanding is created not individually, but spatially, through 'a complex moving web of interrelationalities' (2005, p. 24). It is the idea of inter-relationality that is particularly pertinent to theatre education. On the one hand, it rehearses the familiar idea that we all learn best by doing, but Ellsworth's emphasis on the centrality of place and embodiment also offers new ways of thinking about the significance of history and the imagination in all learning processes:

> Learning never takes place in the absence of bodies, emotions, place, time, sound, image, self-experience, history. It always detours through memory, forgetting, desire, fear, pleasure, surprise, re-writing. And, because learning always takes place in relation, its detours take us up to and sometimes across the boundaries of habit, recognition and socially constructed identities within ourselves. Learning takes us up to and across the boundaries between ourselves and others and through the place of culture and the time of history. (2005, p. 55)

This not only challenges deeply held assumptions about the individualization of learning that bind most Western education systems, it also suggests that knowledge is not fixed, but always mobile, fluid, created and re-created through dialogue and in relation to others.

Applied to theatre, education and performance, Ellsworth's perception of the materiality of learning and Bateson's idea that the mind is structured ecologically offers a way to re-conceptualize the interactivity of its aesthetic and pedagogic traditions for the twenty-first century. Theatre is ephemeral as well as material, and performance always exists in the present tense. Attending to questions of performance and representation in theatre education demonstrates that understanding is not always articulated in language, and that the materiality of the body and the ephemerality of memory hold meaning as well as words. Ric Knowles makes this point clearly when he argues for a 'politically engaged analysis of *how meaning is produced*' in theatre and performance, suggesting that it involves both the material conditions of production and the more ephemeral semiotics of reception (2004, p. 11. Italics original). Related to theatre education, this analysis suggests that the complexity and messiness of theatre-making can produce new patterns of knowledge, unexpected insights as well as creative moments of unknowingness and confusion.

Mapping histories and geographical stories

One way to conceptualize the dynamic between the materiality of learning and the ephemerality of performance in theatre education is to reflect on ways in which history and geography have influenced its practices and pedagogies. Different educational and theatrical histories converge in theatre education and, by acknowledging their historical and geographical specificity, I hope to construct a performance genealogy of the past that illuminates the present and might inform the future. Rather than offering a geographical survey or detailed history of theatre education, my aim in this book is to draw on an embodied repertoire of memories, practices, events, documents and archives to explore why theatre education matters at different times and in different places. Learning is never linear, and ideas and practices have been revisited and revised over time, particularly as new networks of exchange have facilitated debate and conversation.

The cultural historian Jonathan Arac has offered a way of thinking about the political relationship between the past, present and future that is instructive. A critical genealogy, he suggests, does not involve searching for an authentic origin, but 'aims to excavate the past that is necessary to account for how we got here and the past that is useful for conceiving alternatives to our present condition' (1987, p. 2). Accounting for the process of cultural change, theatre historian Joseph Roach explains that social practices often evolve gradually, through a process of 'surrogation' in which substitutes (or 'surrogates') are found for innovators when they move on. This process, Roach argues, attends to 'bodies – to the reciprocal reflections they make on one another's surfaces as they foreground their capacities for interaction' (1996, p. 25). A critical genealogy of theatre education invites us to look at both the abstract ideas and the embodied practices that have become accepted as 'true', 'natural' or 'common sense', and it also draws attention to moments of rupture, observes countermemories, questions the gaps and absences, and considers how established patterns are disrupted and why orthodoxies are disturbed. It is also a methodology that is self-consciously aware of its geopolitical specificity and porousness; the critical genealogy of theatre education I have invoked in this book reflects Anglo-American traditions of theatre and the history of Western thought, but it also charts how ideas and practices have travelled over time and change as they cross continents.

One of the insights of this critical genealogy is, therefore, that the principles and practices of theatre education have been intimately connected to the places and space in which learning happens. Theatre education always involves a negotiation of different organizational structures, cultural practices and interpersonal relationships, and place and space have become increasingly important concepts through which to interrogate theatre and performance practices, as Sally Mackey's illuminating analysis of place in theatre education has revealed (Mackey, 2007). To understand how the materiality of place has articulated and shaped theatre education, I have returned to the work of the French cultural theorist Henri Lefebvre, whose study *The Production of Space* was written in 1976 and translated into English in 1991. Lefebvre was critical of the Enlightenment history of thought that separated subjectivity from objectivity, ontology and epistemology, materiality and ephemerality, and his central thesis is that space is always actively and socially produced. Lefebvre did not see space as a gap between places, a 'blank sheet', to use the cultural geographer Yi-Fu Tuan's phrase, and he argued that a 'transparent, "pure" and neutral space' is an 'illusion' (Tuan, 1977, p. 292). Instead, Lefebvre insisted that space always holds different and sometimes contradictory meanings that change over time and according to context and circumstances. These meanings are neither fixed nor objective, but continually negotiated in and through social practice.

Lefebvre introduced three key concepts to differentiate between spatial narratives. 'Representations of space' refers to the structures and patterns of society that are coded and conceived spatially, particularly by professionals and bureaucrats such as architects, urban planners and government officials. This 'conceived space' draws attention to how the ideological structures of society are made tangible in the built environment and experienced physically. 'Representational' or 'perceived' spaces are more abstract, and relate to feelings and the imagination; they have a playful and symbolic quality that subverts the bureaucratic order of conceived spaces. According to theatre historian David Wiles, theatre occupies a representational space in which 'established practices and conceptualisations may be contested' (2003, p. 10). The third of Lefebvre's categories, 'spatial practices', disrupts the binary of material/ imaginary that exists between conceived and perceived space. Spatial practices are social, they relate to the structures and patterns of society and everyday life. They include pathways, routes and networks of interaction that bind people together and ensure social cohesion and continuity (1991, pp. 38–9).

Although the categories of conceived, lived and perceived spaces necessarily blur and interact, they provide a helpful way of thinking about how meanings are made in theatre education. Institutional spaces, such as schools, prisons or hospitals, might be thought of as conceived spaces designed by educational authorities. Theatre introduces representational space into the conceived space of education, where the orderliness of its structures might be disrupted through symbol, image and metaphor. Taking account of the spatial practices of the people who work in institutions – including teachers and students – would involve looking beyond the institutional environment they occupy and into their wider social networks of family, friendships and community. The triangulation of all three of Lefebvre's spatial narratives provides a starting point opportunity to look at theatre education from different perspectives, therefore, and to consider how it relates to other social practices. But in turn, Lefebvre's spatial theories also need to be historicized and the complexity of his argument should be set in context in order to avoid simplistic stereotyping of conceived spaces as malevolent and authoritarian, and other forms of spatial practice as liberating and emancipatory. Both Lefebvre and de Certeau were writing in the 1970s, when the contemporary spirit of counter-culturalism led artists and writers of the political Left to make a hero out of the subversive nomad in ways that now seem limited and contradictory. Sometimes I have heard versions of this narrative rehearsed by theatre-makers working education whose idealization of the nomadic trickster has led them to make judgements about the conservatism of teachers and schools on very flimsy evidence. I have found myself bristling with indignation on these occasions, as the presence of theatre-makers in schools is often due to enlightened and creative teachers who want to offer new opportunities to the children with whom they work on a daily basis. Notwithstanding, Lefebvre's critique of the dialectics of space still offers a way to recognize space as an embodied practice which is produced and reproduced through social relations and physical encounters, and this adds weight to the argument that learning is inherently relational and contextual.

Making tracks: The story of this book

The education of young people is always orientated towards the future, but it also builds on the knowledge of the past. Early accounts of theatre education were generally written to persuade, often with a sceptical audience in mind, and the processes of readership inevitably involve an act of interpretation. I am, therefore, indebted to the work of other scholars, particularly Anthony Jackson (1980; 1993; 2007), John O'Toole (1976) and Kathleen Gallagher (2003; 2007) who have, in different ways, taken interdisciplinary perspectives on theoretical material and accounts of theatre education in practice. As a way of building on this intellectual history, I have arranged this book in two parts. The first part, *Looking Back: Histories and Landscapes*, examines ideas and practices from the twentieth century that inform twenty-first century theatre education. In turn, the second part of this book focuses on contemporary practices in theatre and education. Structuring the book in this way has given me the opportunity to examine how educational principles and dramatic practices have been revisited, recycled and re-conceptualized, and it is interesting that similar concerns surface at different stages in the book. By drawing attention to the landscapes which this narrative of theatre education maps, I also hope to reflect on the cultural specificity of its practices and, at times, to question how my own ecology of mind has been shaped and defined by the cultural, artistic and educational practices I have inherited and assimilated. My intention is to illuminate a corner of theatre practice that is geographically and culturally situated, and created by pedagogies, values and beliefs that are rooted in the West. As Lefebvre described, nowhere is an empty space and no place carries universal meanings, and this means that I have a political responsibility to be alert to the specificity of my own speaking position rather than claiming that my pedagogic principles are universally shared. I hope that this book will open a conversation with the past, the present and the future, therefore, by questioning the values that have been deeply interwoven in theatre education that are informed by the Western history of thought. I began this process in miniature in *Theatre & Education* (2009b), and I have allowed myself here a more expansive canvas on which to paint a bigger picture.

In the first section of the book I have chosen to tell three inter-related histories as a way of illuminating some of the social, political, artistic and educational narratives that converge in theatre education. Chapter 2 examines the history of social reform in the early part of the twentieth century, in which the arts were regarded as an antidote to the moral and material deprivations of industrialization and the dystopic urban landscapes it created. Chapter 3 explores the idea of a rural, artistic and educational utopia in which drama and theatre found a new place in children's playful learning in the first half of the twentieth century. In Chapter 4 I address the political questions that defined and shaped the twentieth century theatre-in-education movement and the participatory pedagogies with which it was associated. The second part of the book recycles some of the central thematics that pre-occupied twentieth century practitioners, and revisits geopolitical questions of home, nationhood and intercultural dialogue in order to ask how they have acquired new meanings in the new millennium, at a time in which creativity has become a valued commercial commodity. Taken together, I hope that these narratives of theatre education show how innovative theatre-makers inform the values of education as a whole.

There have been moments in history when the success of theatre education meant that it was promoted as a specific genre, art-form or discipline in its own right, and its practices were codified, disseminated and refined. This may have the effect of extending good practice but, as Raymond Williams observed, as soon as audiences become aware of the conventions of dramatic performance they have already become stale. Mindful that some of the humour derived from the Legz Akimbo sketch is that audiences can see through the embarrassingly old-fashioned use of theatre form, I have chosen not to recommend particular sets of conventions or practices in this book. On the contrary, I am interested in celebrating how theatre-makers have experimented with bringing new forms of theatre to education in ways that both challenge young people's cultural expectations and reflect contemporary structures of feeling. It is this negotiation between the familiar and the new, Williams argues, that creates new forms of theatrical expression (1992, pp. 12–16). His insight into how theatre cultures change has encouraged my interest in the educational potential for *all* theatre, whether it was devised for young audiences, produced in partnership with young people or whether it addresses creative approaches to plays that were not written with education in mind. Given the richness and diversity of practices that are available to young people, the decision to include some of my own practice was not easily made. It is not offered as an example of the most innovative artistic practice, but it is an important part of the research methodology, as working as a practitioner allowed me to encounter and question the unexpected moments in the process that challenged ways of thinking that I had taken for granted.

The cultural geographer David Harvey comments that 'imagined Places, the utopian thoughts and desires of countless peoples, have ... played a vital role in animating politics' (1996, p. 306). Harvey is interested in how 'utopias of spatial form' are created and re-created differently in response to specific historical moments, and how images of utopia are often redistricted by social processes. The places that are invoked in this book, whether real or imaginary, often represent contemporary ideas of utopia. But as Lefebvre pointed out, 'Utopia is never realised and yet it is indispensible to stimulate change' (Latour and Combes, 1991, pp. 18–19). I am interested in what happens when the imaginary of Utopia comes into contact with practices of everyday life, and how it adjusts and compromises. To borrow Walter Benjamin's words, there is always an 'inescapability of imperfection' inherent in all human endeavour, and in many ways it is the messiness and unpredictability of theatre practice that is celebrated in this book.

Part One

Looking Back: Histories and Landscapes

2

Spaces to Imagine: Theatre and Social Reform

This history of theatre, education and performance begins at the end of the nineteenth century when the effects of industrialization had become a matter of serious concern. The nineteenth century had brought wealth to the middle class who had profited, either directly or indirectly, from the strength of manufacturing industry in the great industrial conurbations. Some members of the newly formed middle classes used theatre to demonstrate their own cultured tastes, and distance themselves from the working classes, and they regarded the theatre as a place in which to show the refinement of class rather than a place of learning. Mrs Julia Dewey, a self-appointed teacher of etiquette writing in New York in 1888, typifies this pretention. Her book *How to Teach Manners in the School Room* offers this piece of advice to young people who might wish to attend the theatre:

> In going to a place of amusement or entertainment, it is not polite to performers or audience to arrive late…Nothing should be done to attract attention. Eating candy, nuts, or anything else at a place of entertainment is not in good form. (1888, p. 81)

She makes no comment on the reasons why her pupils might attend the theatre, nor what they might see when they got there, and her instruction was solely concerned with how to adopt good manners even if 'the entertainment does not prove interesting'. Mrs Dewey's manual provides schemes of work for teachers that offer instruction in all kinds of social pitfalls that await members of the newly aspirational middle class, including the right way to drink water with a meal and the appropriate way to address acquaintances in the street. But Mrs Dewey's bourgeois cultural consumption was not the only way in which theatre extended its audiences; the end of the nineteenth century also saw a far more radical alliance between theatre and social reform, in which the arts became associated with education, health, public morality and social cohesion. This chapter will explore, at least in outline, how and why this happened, beginning with two stories that might begin to animate this history.

The first is a delicious story told by Jane Addams, a pioneering social reformist working in Chicago at the beginning of the twentieth century. She describes gangs of boys who became thieves so that they could afford to buy tickets for the theatre. They were carrying out 'all sorts of pilferings, petty larcenies, and even burglaries', Addams comments, 'to procure theatre tickets' (1912, p. 80). She recalls the sad case of a girl brought to the juvenile court on the charge of stealing artificial flowers to decorate the hat she wanted to wear to the theatre to impress her boyfriend. Although Addams obviously did not approve of the thefts, what really shocked her was not so much their dishonesty but their taste in theatre. The young people were choosing to attend Chicago's popular five-cent theatre which, according to Addams, offered a theatrical diet of 'vulgar' songs and stories of passion, murder and revenge. Her sternest criticism was reserved for the 'amateur night' talent shows – the *X Factor* or *American Idol* of its day – which attracted long queues of children who were keen to take part. Good acts might be rewarded with a contract to perform again, but unsuccessful young entertainers were jeered and pulled off stage by a long hook (1912, p. 86). Addams worried that this 'debased form of dramatic art' was harming young people's moral development and that the excitement caused by this entertainment was prompting criminal activity and even 'mental disorder' (1912, p. 92).

The second story relates to the professional theatre, again in the United States, where the influential critic on the New York Tribune William Winter worked from 1865 to 1919. Writing in 1908 towards the end of his career, Winter lamented the effects of the commercialization of theatre on artistic standards. Commercial theatre not only had low standards of artistic output, Winter argued, it was also contributing to a more general moral decline in which audiences were encouraged to become passive consumers of pre-packaged products rather than thoughtful appreciators of dramatic art. Winter's contempt for commercial theatre was primarily directed towards the new breed of managers – 'sordid, money-grubbing tradesmen' – who staged entertainment that Winter considered to be superficial. These 'department-store' managers, he scoffed, were 'dispensing dramatic performances precisely as vendors dispense vegetables'. They treated actors as commodities rather than artists with the result that their acting was 'about as interesting as sawing wood' (1908, pp. 206–8). Winter, in common with Addams, argued that the theatre should focus on making art rather than providing superficial gratification, and he particularly admired actors who could inspire audiences to feel 'deep human sympathy' (1908, p. 67). Winter thought that the imperative to make money was degrading audiences as well as actors, who were now 'composed of vulgarians, who know nothing about art or literature and who care for nothing but the solace of their common tastes and animal appetites' (1908, p. 306).

These two historical narratives illustrate some of the themes in this chapter. At first glance, both examples seem to demonstrate the pretensions of the middle class, in which the theatre was associated with upholding establishment values and iniquitous systems of privilege. Both authors show disdain for popular entertainment, and each posits a cultural hierarchy that places their own judgements of taste as morally superior. In this respect, both Addams and Winter anticipate Pierre Bourdieu's perception that artistic tastes are shaped by distinctions of social class and education and, under capitalism, by the unequal relationships between them (1984, pp. 52–60). According to Bourdieu, aesthetic preferences reflect the emotional dispositions and *habitus* of the cultured élite; Winter's judgements of taste, as a professional theatre critic, illustrate Bourdieu's thesis that intellectuals have particular class-bound preferences. Writing about the cultural hierarchy of theatre in this historical period, Richard Butsch suggests that theatre critics considered theatre to have a public duty not only to 'cultivate, but also to socialise people and, by extension, to prevent social disorder' (2008, p. 68). Winter favoured the attentiveness of middle-class audiences (possibly those who had followed Mrs Dewey's advice) and, as Butsch notes, this suggests an unequivocal conservativism in which forms of theatre judged to be high art were also charged with upholding the disciplinary system of the powerful. That is, of course, a legitimate reading.

There is, therefore, a more sympathetic and perhaps more nuanced reading of the contribution made by those who held an idealistic vision that theatre should be both morally uplifting and artistically challenging. Jane Addams, in common with other reformists on the political Left, was interested in encouraging members of the working classes

:ipate in making theatre and becoming active audiences for
___: art. Although the language in which she articulates attitudes
towards high art and commercial theatre rehearses the class prejudice
of the time, it also disguises a philanthropic and altruistic interest in
improving the conditions of the poor and benefiting society. Poverty
was regarded as a serious threat to social cohesion, and the culture
of consumerism that emerged in the period was held responsible for
the exploitation of the vulnerable. Popular entertainment, governed
by the capitalists that Winter so despised, was regarded by social
reformists of the political Left as morally and politically corrosive,
sanctioning the kind of licentiousness and lack of inhibition that was
considered inherently corrupting. The art form of theatre, by contrast,
was charged with providing spiritual uplift and was therefore seen as
socially and personally beneficial. The reasons why the arts, rather
than popular culture, became harnessed to social change in this period
is instructive, not least because they cast light on more general ideas
about the role of aesthetic education to create an equitable society.
Two nineteenth century thinkers serve to illuminate this history of
Western thought, both of whom were influenced by Romantic beliefs
that the arts have redemptive qualities. The first is Matthew Arnold
(1822–88), an English poet and school inspector whose liberal ideas
about the 'civilizing' effects of 'great art' provided a persuasive argument for including the arts (including some theatre) in educational
and social reform. The second influential figure is William Morris
(1834–96), also British, who was a socialist, artist and political writer.
Morris followed John Ruskin in questioning the élitism of 'great art',
arguing instead that it should be replaced by traditional rural arts and
crafts which would be found not in galleries nor theatres, but in the
everyday practices of life. In different ways, Arnold and Morris influenced the ways in which the arts came to be associated with social
egalitarianism and the links they made between politics and culture,
creativity and equality, can still be traced today.

An education in culture

The idea that the arts provide a liberating space away from the corrupting influences of urban life emerged in response to philosophical,
social and attitudinal changes during the nineteenth century. High
art had once been the sole preserve of the rich, but Victorian philanthropists regarded it as their social and Christian duty to make
the arts more available to the public as part of their programme of

civic reform. From the nineteenth century onwards social reformists were concerned that the material conditions of the urban poor were leading to social fragmentation and moral decline, and they turned to the arts to contribute to their programme of improvement. The urban industrial landscape was impoverished, and the arts provided an optimistic space that promised social cohesion and personal freedom. The cultural historian Raymond Williams commented that, in the nineteenth century, the work of artists was seen to offer 'that ideal of human perfection' that would overcome the 'disintegrating tendencies of the age' (1992, p. 42). Politically radical reformists, influenced by this perception, believed that the arts provided a refuge from the alienating effects of industrial capitalism, a view that had been by popularized by the Romantics in the nineteenth century.

The new social order required a revised set of moral principles by which to live, and during the mid-nineteenth century Arnold developed a theory of education in which culture, as the 'best' of humanity, would play a major part. He recognized that industrialization was changing the structures of society, and understood that the newly emergent middle class would play an increasingly important role in civic life as the power of the aristocracy waned. Arnold was a school inspector, and a great advocate of State-funded education, but he was concerned that education was becoming too narrowly focused on equipping young people to make money, and he argued that the moral health of the nation rested on balancing economic need with an education in culture. In his book *Culture and Anarchy* (1860), Arnold was critical of the middle-class culture of consumerism, self-interest and wealth production that he observed at the time. He suggested that the future of society depended on an aesthetically educated middle class, and argued that the goal of a liberal democracy might be achieved if people of all classes turned their minds to higher things by cultivating their inner emotional lives. To achieve this, Arnold made a sustained case for the study of culture as one way to resist the excesses of consumer capitalism:

> If culture, then, is a study of perfection, and of harmonious perfection, general perfection, and perfection which consists of becoming something rather than having something, in an inner condition of the mind and spirit, not in an outward set of circumstances. (Collini, 1993, p. 62)

Arnold saw education as a process of *becoming* rather than *having* and it is significant in this context that he saw perfection in terms of human emotions; Arnold's 'best self' echoes Christian virtues – humanity, love, sincerity, honesty, humility. It also invokes a familiar theme of the Enlightenment and Romanticism: great art would educate the inner mind to reach perfection, which in turn would bring about social harmony. As Terry Eagleton has convincingly argued, Arnold had a 'sensitive preoccupation with the whole quality of life' rather than a 'formulated code or ethical system' (1983, p. 27).

The space occupied by the arts in Arnold's liberal education was oppositional; it was diametrically opposed to the culture of individualism and consumerism that he witnessed in the period. He regarded culture as a means of uniting society, of establishing 'common bonds' both between the classes and between individuals because he believed it educated the 'best spirit of humanity' that exists in everyone. His comments on a national culture, and on establishing a place for culture within state education, were designed to promote social harmony. Knowledge of the nation's culture was not seen as an accomplishment, nor as conservatism, but as a means to achieving a more united society:

> By giving to schools for these classes a public character, it can bring the instruction in them under a criticism which a stock of knowledge and judgement in our middle classes is not of itself able to supply. By giving to them a national identity, the arts would confer on them a 'greatness and a noble spirit, which the tone of these classes is not of itself at present able to supply.' (1993, p. 19)

By allying aesthetic education to creating a national identity Arnold accepted that, by transforming the values of middle-class children from selfish individualism to a sense of shared moral duty, the future of the nation would be in safe hands. Arnold's liberal belief in the civilizing power of high art did, however, reassert the conventional perception that aesthetic experience occupies an essentially private symbolic space, independent of other social or cultural influences. In more practical terms, however, it also generated a profound belief in the importance of greater public access to the arts and culture both as a leisure activity and in formal education.

The study of culture was, for Arnold, a serious business of uniting the inner mind and sensibilities with the highest spiritual truths. Following Kantian aesthetics, the study of culture was 'disinterested' rather than self-interested, a term he used to imply its separateness from the everyday 'ordinary self' of commerce and industry:

> Its business is ... simply to know the best that is known and thought in the world, and by its turn making this known, to create a current of true

and fresh ideas. Its business is to do this with inflexible honesty, with due ability. (1993, p. 37)

The idea that culture might create 'fresh ideas' and 'inflexible honesty', rather than business and commerce, represents a political ambition. As Stefan Collini points out in his essay on the Arnoldian legacy, 'disinterestedness' in Arnold's vocabulary, does not signify a lack of concern with social and political realities (1993, p. x). On the contrary, he thought that educating the children of the prosperous middle class would lead them to treat the nation's working classes more humanely when they assumed leadership roles in adulthood. Arnold thus elevated the study of culture to a form of education for democratic freedom albeit from a position that left this class-bound social order in tact.

Creative communities and the arts in everyday life

Arnold's liberalism represented a significant shift of thought. William Morris, however, added another dimension to this history by envisioning an alternative society in which creative practice, rather than the study of culture, would be integrated into daily patterns of life. Morris' utopian vision was that society would be sustained by craft workers who would earn their living by making things that were both useful and beautiful. Social equality, he argued, was dependent on a combination of good living conditions, happy leisure time and satisfying work. Morris' economic system rejected capitalist divisions of labour, in which the product was not only separated from its producer through the marketplace, but was made on a production line that alienated the worker from the satisfaction of making a complete artefact. It was the process of manufacture, therefore, as well as the product made, which Morris saw as central to a socialist democracy. Critical of the 'Intellectual arts' which had, under capitalism, become the preserve of a professional élite, Morris redefined both the style and function of the arts. Anticipating Theodore Adorno's condemnation of a consumerist culture, Morris argued that the arts had become misused – ugly symbols of urban prosperity rather than integral to a more egalitarian economic system. He castigated the 'unhappy rich' for their materialism, and he suggested that they had not only exploited the working class, but had distanced themselves and others from the simpler traditions of a rural past. In his polemic *Useful Work versus Useless Toil* (1886), Morris offered an alternative to the 'unhappy life forced on the great mass of the populace' by suggesting that a system of labour based on traditional crafts would engender 'variety, hope of creation and the self-respect which comes from a sense of usefulness' (Morton, 1973, p. 67). To further this utopianism, Morris formulated principles for learning that was based not on the individualism and hierarchies he associated with an education system that served industrial capitalism but on the productivity of an egalitarian community of craft workers.

Morris' principles for education depended on his belief that creative labour – making as well as thinking – leads to the kind of humane sympathies required to sustain an egalitarian community. His attitude to education is perhaps best summed up by his famous dictum:

> I do not want art for a few, any more than education for a few, or freedom for a few. (1973, p. 54)

The arts were a means of integrating soul, mind and body, and Morris hoped this would lead more readily to an 'organic' society that would be free to exist without class divide. This involved a new style of education that would train the imagination, which he regarded as a reflection of the collective traditions of humanity rather than a sign of individual talent. He suggested that, in turn, the imagination would benefit both the individual and society:

> It would raise them at once to a higher level of life, until the world began to be peopled, not with commonplace people, but with honest folk not sharply conscious of their superiority as 'intellectual' persons now are, but self-respecting and respecting the personality of others, because they would feel themselves to be useful and happy. (1973, p. 203)

Morris' simple life was busy; his political theories and educational principles derived from a belief that a happy life is one in which everyone works together, combining activity with humanity. Freedom, in Morris' description, was defined by the productive relationship between useful labour and collective ownership. As the cultural historian E. P. Thompson pointed out, Morris combined aesthetic theory with public principles because he identified 'the relation of the artist to his society from a social, rather than individualist, standpoint' (1955, p. 769).

The significance of Morris' aesthetic theories to theatre education lies in his emphasis on the practice of arts as integral to socialist democracy. However, while his opposition to 'high art' indicated his dislike of the artificial refinements of class, Morris missed the contribution artists make as social critics. In emphasizing the decorative qualities of the arts, their aesthetic rather than intellectual appeal, he failed to recognize that the content of the arts may be both educative and emancipatory as E. P. Thompson identified:

> Morris has not emphasised sufficiently the *ideological* role of art, its active agency in *changing* human beings and society as a whole, its agency in man's class-divided history. (1955, p. 763)

For Morris, the educational purpose of the arts lay in the pleasure of craft and enjoyment of aesthetic form and his theories never fully resolved the balance between innocence and critical self-awareness. In Morris' socialist collective the practice of craft was firmly linked to the patterns and spatial practices of everyday life. In the process, however, he also underestimated the symbolic power of the arts and their subversive quality, thereby ignoring the social significance of the imagination and the political role of artists as social critics.

In similar terms, Arnold and Morris regarded the commodification of the arts as part of a wider malaise in society, and a symbol of moral decline. Arnold described how the 'worship of wealth' had corrupted society (1993, p. 66), and Morris explained how art had been 'crushed to death by the money bags of competitive commerce' (1973, p. 66). In broad terms, the kind of society both these thinkers described indicates their antipathy to industry and a self-seeking culture of individualism; their ideal was an 'organic' society of like-minded individuals who had reached moral consensus and shared values. The organic societies each advocated are, however, predicated on two persuasive visions; Morris' pre-capitalist utopia and Arnold's idealized myth of coherent nation sympathy. Terry Eagleton explains the significance of the meaning of the word 'organic' in social and political theory:

> Organic societies are just convenient myths for belabouring the mechanised life of modern industrial capitalism. (1983, p. 36)

Despite differences of inflection, both Arnold and Morris succeeded in linking arts education to social equality and personal fulfilment. It was this aspect of their work that captured the imaginations of the more radical educationalists and social reformists of the 1890s. In the following two sections I shall address how their ideas began to be translated into practice, first focusing on the role of arts in social reform in the early twentieth century, and then examining the educational place of theatre in uniting fractured societies during the same period.

The arts and urban regeneration

The idea that art-making creates a libertarian space was symbolic of wider ideas about society, childhood, education and family that took root in the early twentieth century and endured, in different configurations, throughout the century. Theatre occupied a rather more ambiguous place in this history than the visual arts, not least because the commercial theatre was associated with the kind of public entertainment of which the principled educationalists and social reformists of the nineteenth and early twentieth century did not always approve. Morris' and Arnold's ideas about the social role of the arts spread among the educated middle class in both Britain and North America, and this is testament to a widespread anxiety about the social effects of poverty at the end of the nineteenth century. Some radical reformists of the period, including Jane Addams in Chicago, responded by rejecting the bourgeois society that both Arnold and Morris despised, in favour of dedicating their lives to improving the living conditions of the poor. By choosing to live, as well as work, in urban environments, these reformists sought to bridge the ever-increasing inequality in housing, education and cultural provision between wealthy and poor areas. A particularly good example that serves to illustrate how the arts became integrated into social reform might be found in the University Settlement Houses, a movement which began in the East End of London in 1884, spread quickly to the United States, and arrived in Australia in 1908 when the University of Sydney Settlement House opened. The movement provides an insight into how Morrisonian principles of communal living were combined with an Arnoldian vision of the power of the arts to unite society.

Settlement Houses were conceived and founded by Samuel and Henrietta Barnett, who had moved to the East End of London when Samuel became vicar of St Jude's Whitechapel in 1873. They were Christian Socialists who were influenced by the works of Matthew Arnold and Karl Marx, and they counted William Morris among their circle of radical friends. They believed that social change would only be possible when the material conditions of the poor improved. Part of this involved increasing access to culture and education, and the practical solution the Barnetts found was to build the first Settlement House, Toynbee Hall in the East End of London, where men and women from universities lived among the poor in order that both social groups might learn from each other. Samuel Barnett echoes

Morris' principles of communal living in his description of the first settlement:

> A settlement is simply a means by which men or women may share themselves with their neighbours; a club-house in an industrial district, where the condition of membership is the performance of a citizen's duty; a house among the poor, where residents may make friends with the poor. (1898, p. 26)

In the early days the settlers made a significant contribution to working-class education in the local area, organizing courses, debates and a range of cultural activities. Combining a Morrisonian communal life and an Arnoldian interest in cultural education, Barnett exhorted the university settlers to share 'their best with the poor and learn through feeling how they live' (1884, p. 272). For many of the university students, the experience of living in Toynbee Hall was life-changing; the Liberal MP William Beveridge, the architect of the Welfare State in Britain, maintained a lifelong interest in the Settlement House and the future Prime Minister Clement Attlee, who implemented The Beveridge Report in the 1940s, is said to have become a Labour party member as a direct result of his work in the East End in the first decade of the twentieth century.

Although the material conditions of life were perhaps the most pressing concern for these British reformers, they valued the arts, particularly the visual arts, for providing a space for reflection and contemplation away from the squalor of the slums. The wealth generated in the industrial revolution had led to a programme of art gallery, concert hall and museum building that not only represented the municipal pride of the newly wealthy middle classes, it also increased public access to the arts. The National Gallery in London, for example, was founded in 1824 with the 'refinement' of the 'lower classes' as one of its stated intentions.[1] Although the philanthropists' motives had been undoubtedly benign, and they genuinely regarded public galleries and concert halls as libertarian spaces, the imposing and perhaps intimidating architecture of many of these public buildings quickly came to symbolize the values of the powerful. The Barnetts and their followers recognized that galleries needed to be situated in deprived areas and linked, where possible, to Settlement Houses if they were to provide the kind of enlightenment they sought to encourage. The 'Pictures for the Poor' initiative, a radical experiment that took works of art to socially deprived areas in the 1880s and 1890s, was a brave attempt to put aesthetic and cultural theory into practice. It led directly to

Samuel Barnett founding the Whitechapel Art Gallery in 1901, which still has a lively education programme that encourages local people to participate in the arts.

The initial motivation for these galleries was to spread Christian socialism, and specifically to promote social responsibility and caring for others. The Reverend Barnett accepted that East Enders infrequently attended church, and put his faith in the arts to make his parishioners receptive to religious values, as his wife recalled in his biography:

> Culture which opens men's minds to the enjoyment of art and literature – whence they see the lives of those who on earth have done the will of their father in heaven. (1918, p. 76)

Culture was not seen to dissolve economic boundaries, nor offer material improvement, but to enrich the spiritual health of the poor. 'The want of clothes' Henrietta Barnett commented, 'does not so loudly call for remedy as the want of interest or culture' (1918, p. 76). For many reformists, spiritual and physical health were closely linked. T. C. Horsfall, who founded the Manchester Art Museum alongside the Manchester University Settlement in 1895, was concerned with sanitation and the arts in equal measure; the first would improve conditions for the body, the other would restore the soul. He acknowledged that the urban conditions of the working class had very little aesthetic appeal and founded the gallery precisely to enable the poor to discover beauty. Horsfall intended not only to improve their behaviour and fill their leisure time with more morally uplifting pastimes than drinking, but he also provided some aesthetically pleasing works of art which he hoped would go some way to compensating for the ugliness of the built environment. Horsfall, like Barnett, argued that the 'tastes and habits' of the poor might be educated through the fine arts. In developing a scheme to loan paintings to schools, he accepted the contemporary orthodoxy that moral sensibilities and aesthetic education are related, but also asserted his interest in showing alternative ways of living to children accustomed to the squalor of urban housing.

> The children would begin to be dissatisfied with the miserable surrounding of their own homes, and it would further have a good effect on their moral characters. (1885, p. 129)

Horsfall's conference in 1885, 'Education under Healthy Conditions' discussed cheap school meals, rainy children's playtimes, overcrowded housing and the arts. The inclusion of the arts in a conference otherwise devoted to children's physical health reflects the beliefs of the time; the arts would provide moral and spiritual nourishment. In this, they were not only following Matthew Arnold's description of culture as 'sweetness and light' but also adapting William Morris' premise that the arts might contribute to a whole way of life.

Theatre and social cohesion

The Barnetts themselves seem to have had little time for theatre, preferring the contemplative space of the art gallery to the liveness of theatre. This was very much in the spirit of the times; not only were there concerns about the unruliness of the audiences for popular theatre in the nineteenth century, the working conditions and education of children acting in commercial theatre had caught the attention of social reformists, and this added to the perception that the theatre was a morally ambiguous place. Anne Varty's excellent study *Children and Theatre in Victorian Britain* (2008) documents the campaign in the 1889s and 1890s to provide adequate education for theatre children, a protest that was strongly supported by social reformist Mrs Millicent Fawcett, who was also a leader in the suffrage movement. Fawcett built her case on new employment and education legislation, and she used the Factories Act that prohibited child labour under the age of 10 and the Education Acts that required children to attend school from the age of 5 to 13 to strengthen her argument. Children had become valued cultural commodities in an entertainment industry where they were expected to portray roles that sentimentalized childhood innocence, but staging this confection simultaneously exploited their labour. This double standard appalled social reformists on both sides of the Atlantic. Alice Minnie Herts, who built on her work in the Settlement Houses and founded the Children's Educational Theatre of New York in 1903, stated in an article in the New York Times in 1911 that 'to commercialise the imagination of the child seems to me to be a terrible thing' (1911, p. 7).

Theatre did, however, become embedded into the Settlement Houses of the United States through the work of Jane Addams (1860–1935). Addams visited Toynbee Hall in 1888, and returned to Chicago to found Hull House in 1889. From the beginning, Addams turned particularly to the theatre, rather than art galleries, to encourage the working classes to engage in cultural activity. Addams was interested in improving the lives of urban young people, particularly those from immigrant families. She observed that many felt isolated in their new surroundings, and she realized that pastimes needed to be sociable as well as edifying. In her persuasive book *The Spirit of Youth and the City Streets* (1912), Addams makes a case for including theatre as part of this process of social integration. Echoing William Morris' nostalgia for an organic society, Addams comments:

> The public dance halls filled with frivolous and irresponsible young people in a feverish search for pleasure, are but a sorry substitute for the old dances on the village green in which all the older people of the village participated. (1912, p. 13)

As well as being scandalized by these 'frivolous' dance halls, Addams noted that young people were drawn to the five-cent theatre to hear the 'the most blatant and vulgar songs' (1912, p. 19). Although she condemned its morals, Addams recognized that popular theatre offered a shared experience that had social benefits – she conceded that even this form of theatre had potential to show deprived youngsters other possible worlds. She recounted the appeal of theatre to one girl she encountered, 'the blankness and greyness of life for her had only been broken by the portrayal of a different world' (1912, p. 81). Addams sought to turn young people's enthusiasm for popular theatre into an interest in dramatic art, understanding that 'the theatre is the only place they can satisfy that craving for a conception of life higher than that which the actual world offers them' (1912, pp. 75–6).

In common with both Arnold and Morris, Addams was critical of working-class entertainment and she considered that a diet of popular forms of theatre such as melodrama, music hall or vaudeville would ensure that the working class remained emotionally, culturally and socially malnourished. The work of 'great' dramatists, by contrast, might serve to elevate hearts and improve minds. Describing theatre as 'a house of dreams', Addams set up a programme of theatrical activity at Hull House that involved young people as actors as well as audiences for the newly formed Hull House Players. The repertoire of Schiller, Shakespeare and Molière showed her general consistency with Arnold's ideas about the value of a cultural education, although Addams' claims that young people were clamouring to learn their 'stiff' lines stretches credulity. It was, perhaps, the social element that the young people valued, as Shannon Jackson notes in her extensive historical analysis of Hull House, *Lines of Activity: Performance, Historiography, Hull-House Domesticity*

(2001). Jackson draws attention to the ways in which the processes of theatre-making 'generated unique affective bonds among tentatively formed social groups', and offers significant evidence that these rehearsals also 'served a pedagogical function' for those who were committed to take part (2001, pp. 216–17). Furthermore, Jackson notes, the level of community participation and the production values changed over time, particularly when the Hull House Dramatic Association was formed (2001, p. 222). Addams' own accounts of the efficacy of the arts and effects of industrial labour on children was written to persuade; *The Spirit of Youth and the City Streets* is peppered with emotive stories about children who showed both moral fortitude and creativity, including a starving Russian girl who was writing a novel, a girl who saved all her money from washing up to have singing lessons and a particularly brave boy with cork legs who refused monotonous work in favour of more interesting labour even though he found it exhausting. It is interesting that alongside her programme of dramatic art, Addams also encouraged playground games, festivals and pageants that carried moral messages from the immigrants' traditional home cultures. Linking public festivities to national unity was an idea that had originated in the eighteenth century with Jean-Jacques Rousseau, and Jane Addams regarded these activities on the one hand as meeting the 'recreational needs' of the socially isolated immigrant communities, and on the other as a way of integrating society by introducing shared cultural activity and local pride into civic life (1912, p. 101). Her justification for including theatre in her social reforms relied on mixing an Arnoldian education in feelings and a Morrisonian sympathy for traditional communal activities as a way of binding society.

Whereas the English reformers were primarily concerned with overcoming class division, settlers at Hull House and other US Settlement Houses thought of theatre and other performative events as part of a process of Americanization. Plays and pageants not only brought people together in shared activity, they also fulfilled a moral imaginary of nationhood. The dream of American democracy, for Addams and her followers, was dependent on both celebrating the diverse cultural heritages of immigrant communities and cultivating shared moral sympathies. Theatre and performance, therefore, contributed to forging a new national identity. Addams had the insight to look forward, and she saw that a new generation of Americans were unlikely to relate to the traditions of their immigrant parents' 'fatherland'. Young people were more attracted to contemporary popular entertainment than 'old world' traditions, and it is significant that she saw the dangers of too much of this kind of freedom in nationalist terms:

> Unless we mean to go back to these Old World customs which are already hopelessly broken, there would seem to be but one path open to us in America. That path implies freedom for the young people made safe only through their own self-control. This, in turn, must be based upon knowledge and habits of clean companionship. (1912, p. 45)

The virtues Addams espoused for this new democracy were primarily social and communitarian rather than individual, and she used theatre to teach young people from immigrant families how to become 'good' American citizens. By combining the values of 'clean companionship' and social respectability, Addams furthered an ideal of American democracy that invoked Morris' domestic practices of craft and folk arts, and was also indebted to Arnold's moral cultivation of the nation's 'best selves' through the study of culture.

The theatrical work of Hull House, and other social reformist organizations that sought social integration through performance, might easily be read as an example of how the middle classes imposed their values on others. This way of working is generally interpreted as an illustration of how immigrants were expected to assume a new national identity by adopting an image of America that reflected white middle-class values and norms. Theatre scholar Jan Cohen-Cruz, writing about the mass street pageants directed by Percy MacKay around 1915 that aimed to encourage immigrants to become Americans, points out the uneven power relations in this cultural ambition, in which 'immigrants were the object, not the subject' of the performance which sought to 'mold them into seemingly uncritical citizens' (2005, p. 18). Richard Butsch comments in a similar vein on the work of Hull House and the Little Theatre Movement, suggesting that their work was intended to move the self-cultivation of the middle-class drawing room into the public sphere (2008, pp. 72–8).

On the one hand, this is, of course, a fair criticism. On the other, however, the social reformists' interest in theatre and performance does need to be read in the context of wider political ideas that were circulating at the time and a more nuanced understanding of the processes of theatre-making. Shannon Jackson explicitly challenges the assumption that theatre at Hull House was primarily concerned with this kind of cultural assimilation. Her account of the cosmopolitanism of theatre at Hull House describes how, when Greek immigrants performed classical Greek plays, there was an 'ambivalence and complexity of cosmopolitan exchange around "the best" of each culture' (2001, p. 230). The rehearsals required co-operation between people of different backgrounds, a process that inevitably troubled boundaries between the social and the cultural. Furthermore, she points out, many of the Hull-House Players were Irish and maintained strong links to the Abbey Theatre in Dublin, thereby asserting their Irish-American identity (2001, p. 233). What I would like to add to Jackson's detailed history of theatre at Hull House is a reading of the history of ideas that inspired the Settlement House movement on both sides of the Atlantic; the reformists' emphasis on public and civic virtues, however dated and élitist they may seem today, were informed by a genuinely radical attempt to improve the lives of those who lived in poverty and social isolation.

'Civilising' spaces: Theatre, nationhood and social reform

Whereas English social reformists saw the arts as offering a space for reflection on an existing national heritage and for healing class division, in the United States theatre was seen as a place in which nationhood might be created and imagined. This is consistent with Benedict Anderson's perception that nation is 'an imagined political community' whose sense of identity is built on an abstract 'image of communion' that circumscribes its moral and cultural territory (1991, p. 6). Although the political agenda has changed, the idea that the arts might help create social and national cohesion has endured in various forms since this period of social reform.

Matthew Arnold's idea that high art is inherently 'civilising' now seems dated. The word 'civilised' is easily and rightly criticized; it begs questions about whose civilization is valued and which cultures are ignored or undermined in the process. But, as Norbert Elias points out in his book, *The Civilising Process* (1978), however problematic the word seems now, the term 'civilisation was, at the moment of its formation, a clear reflection of ... reformist ideas' rather than an image of cultural superiority through education or privilege (1978, p. 38). Furthermore, as Raymond Williams observed, Arnold had a 'commitment to extending popular education' (1980, p. 5). Arnold, Morris and their followers resisted the commodification of the arts and opposed an education system that was orientated toward money-making and self-centred individualism. Over time, of course, the social meanings of the theatrical space and the political reasons why the arts were included in an education evolved and changed; and Morris' socialist ideals found a new articulation in progressive education, as I shall discuss in the next chapter.

Although the language may have altered, the idea that the arts can make a positive contribution to urban regeneration and the lives of those who are experiencing poverty has endured across two centuries of change. This is testament to some remarkable people, many of whom were women, who dedicated their lives to social reform. The reformist spirit of the early twentieth century is perhaps best symbolized by the continuing work of Hull House and Toynbee Hall in the twenty-first century. The Jane Addams Hull House Association offers support and training for people and communities who are underserved by other agencies, and the association still brings together creative activities with social welfare provision. Toynbee Hall similarly offers practical support to local people, and it still relies on teams of residential and non-residential volunteers to implement their ambitious programme of projects that aim to improve the lives of those who are experiencing poverty. Active citizenship lies at the heart of Toynbee Hall's mission statement, and the arts, including theatre, are integral to capturing the imaginations of young people.[2] Both organizations remain an inspirational demonstration of their founders' visions by maintaining their traditional commitment to social justice, and by adapting their work and their working methods in response to the times.

3

Spaces to Play: Childhood, Theatre and Educational Utopias

The effects of industrialization were felt not only in urban cities, but in Victorian schools. The institutional spaces of school, for many English children and teachers at the end of the nineteenth century, were imposing red-brick buildings with high windows designed to prevent children from being distracted from their lessons by looking outside. The architecture maintained a sharp distinction between places outside school and the enclosed institutional space. School buildings of the period, still a familiar sight in England, are a good example of Lefebvre's description of conceived spaces as the public and material articulation of bureaucratic principles. The buildings were put up in response to the 1870 Elementary Education Act which made primary education compulsory for the first time, necessitating a rapid building programme. School architecture was influenced by E. R. Robson and J. J. Stevenson, architects to the London School Board, whose gabled buildings reflects official attitudes to education at the time. Inspired by vernacular Dutch architecture, these non-sectarian state schools were designed to suggest their distinctiveness from Church schools, but children were still contained within high walls, girls and boys were often segregated by different entrances, and classrooms laid out so that children could sit in rows facing the teacher whose authority was emphasized by positioning the desk on a small raised platform. Adornment on the walls was discouraged; punishment was often corporal, and learning was by rote. Schools were intentionally disciplined spaces in which artistic creativity had very little place.

Just as social reformers reassessed the potential for the arts to contribute to a democratic society, radical educationalists began to address the shortcomings of an educational system based on discipline and punishment. For drama and theatre to secure a space in schools depended on both social and educational reform, and their introduction and development during the twentieth century was part of wider and radical shifts in cultural practice and pedagogic thought. There had been two related developments during the nineteenth century that were particularly influential on the changing culture of education, both of which afforded theatre education a place in the curriculum. First, technological knowledge about children's physical and cognitive development had increased rapidly during the nineteenth century, and this information was beginning to be shaped into psychological theories of play and child development. Second, artistic and literary representations of children as symbols of natural beauty, purity and innocence became embedded in the popular imagination and, following the Romantics, childhood was characterized as a period of freedom and play. Both perceptions contributed to an understanding of how children and childhood were constructed and understood in the newly professionalized discipline of education in the early twentieth century. It was this revised conceptualization of childhood that allowed children to become active learners rather than passive recipients of knowledge, and this made space for creative approaches to drama and theatre in educational settings.

Debates about childhood turned on how constructions of nature and naturalness were understood. Industrialization had forced children into factory labour, and this meant that fictionalized conceptions of childhood as a time of natural innocence took on a new political radicalism when the exploitation and physical maltreatment of little children in factories was commonplace. The power of the imagination was popularized in children's literature and theatre, where the inner beauty of children, and their redemptive qualities, were represented in rural and domestic narratives such as *Heidi* (1881) and *Little Lord Fauntleroy* (1885). The dominant, albeit implicit, message in these plays and novels is that virtuous children are those with nuclear families in bourgeois homes who have the added advantage of the freedom and liberty afforded by a rural life. This replaced the idea of the child as savage with the angelic stereotype of the innocent child and, as historian Peter Coveney has argued, this Romantic idealization of childhood became personified as an idealized child of nature:

> In a world given increasingly to utilitarian values and the Machine, the child could become the symbol of the Imagination, the Sensibility, a

symbol of Nature set against the forces of a society actively de-naturing humanity. (1967, p. 31)

Children were considered to be naturally imaginative and innately playful, and the freedom of a rural life was regarded as most conducive to children's development. Contrary to the actual experiences of many children, the social imaginary of childhood was one of pastoral simplicity and, as Coveney argued, this indicates a political critique of the economic and social circumstances of the day. This perception of childhood led some educational reformists to follow William Morris by suggesting that simple living, close to nature, was a certain route to both personal happiness and social equality. This vision inspired action, and in response the social reformist Ebenezer Howard started the Garden City Movement at the turn of the century in order to build cities that provided healthy housing in a reordered society. Henrietta Barnett was also involved in this practical politics, and was instrumental in developing the Hampstead Garden Suburb in north London. Some altruistic Victorian educators found ways to offer deprived urban children country holidays based on the reasonable belief that children would thrive better in the open space of the countryside rather than in a polluted city; Samuel and Henrietta Barnett founded the Children's Country Holiday Fund in 1884, a charity that still organizes holidays for children experiencing deprivation today.[1]

The cult of childhood was a convenient romance and a projection of adult anxieties. It is noticeable that, while the ideal of a carefree childhood was gaining symbolic currency, there was also a programme of building schools with high brick walls to contain potentially unruly pupils. In her book *Strange Dislocations* (1995) the education historian Carolyn Steedman traces this history, suggesting that the nineteenth century brought together literary constructs of sentimental child-figures and scientific, technological knowledge about children:

> Real children (children observed, children described, children remembered by the adults they became) fuelled the imaginative constructs that in their turn interpreted and explained – for instance – the 'child-life' of industrial conurbations, the statistics of child labour, or the physiological bodies of children. (1995, p. 5)

Steedman argues that this powerful combination of fiction and the technologies of child development led to the twentieth century preoccupation with the interiority of the self, and to the idea that a good childhood is a major source of happiness in adulthood. Early twentieth century science introduced normative theories of children's physical and emotional development, and Darwinian theories of natural selection became enmeshed, in different ways, with ideas of children's play, psychological stages of development and models of instinctive behaviour. More poetically, the image of the garden became associated with happy children, rehearsing Morris' Arcadian vision of egalitarian simplicity. Steedman explains this synthesis of concepts, suggesting that ideas of 'natural growth' formed the basis of much scientific investigation into child development, where nature, tamed by horticulture and shaped into a garden, provided education with a glowing image reaching back to Eden, and forward to Utopia:

> [They] evolved an education system for young children based on a notion of the human being as an organic unity, with the human mind as a spontaneously formative agency. The 'child-garden' would allow the developing child to be active in a fitting way, and activity would permit the flowering of inborn capacities. (1990, p. 82)

According to sociologist Chris Jenks, it was in this period that the natural and the social became conflated, and the arts became valued for their power to reveal children's purity, emotional warmth and natural goodness (1996, p. 7). However this history might be interpreted now, at the time this utopian childhood paved the way for educational reform that would include drama and the arts as part of a process of democratizing learning.

This chapter is focused on how conceptualizations of childhood created a utopian space for drama in schools and created new ways of thinking about an educational theatre for young audiences. No one set of principles is ever imported wholesale into educational or artistic practice, and creating the conditions for an ideal childhood required a workable pedagogy, and it is here that theatre and drama (or creative dramatics as it was known in the United States), became increasingly firmly integrated into the practice of education. This poetic pedagogy that promoted childhood as a time of freedom was not, however, universally well received. Consistent with Yi-Fu Tuan's perception that too much space can be threatening (1977, p. 52), conservative commentators regarded libertarian teaching methods as a threat to moral order, arguing that self-discipline, obedience and authoritarian teaching practices were a more reliable route to virtue. Put simply, whereas traditionalists required children to know their place, progressive reformers invited them to find a space. As the geographer

Tim Cresswell points out, the word 'progressive' is associated with speed and mobility and this emphasis on activity and the energy of the body in progressive pedagogies meant that, for traditionalists, progressivism was perceived to be socially disruptive (2006, p. 36). Notwithstanding this continuing controversy, the arts became symbolic of a new progressive pedagogy; creativity, self-expression and play were to replace authoritarian structures of learning and the arts were charged with creating happy and democratic spaces to learn.

Progressive education

By the beginning of the twentieth century educationalists were beginning to explore approaches to teaching and learning that took account of new conceptualizations of childhood based on the emergent field of child psychology. As these theoretical principles were turned into educational practice, they were shaped into a coherent pedagogical method that became known as Progressive Education. There were many notable figures whose work influenced this movement, including Friedrich Froebel (1782–1852) whose book the *System of Infant Gardens* (1855) first brought the image of the garden to child psychology, and Jean Piaget (1896–1980), although the American philosopher John Dewey (1859–1952) remains its leading figure. It is significant to this history that Jane Addams helped shape Dewey's ideas. He had worked at Hull House from its foundation and served on its board of directors, and it was there that he observed the social benefits of disrupting conventional hierarchies of learning. It was central to the ethos of Hull House that people from different socio-economic and cultural backgrounds have much to learn from each other, and this was essential to their project of social change. Dewey recognized that working together artistically can create a democratic space for learning and, through his influential book *Art as Experience* (1934), he can be credited with providing one of the first theoretical justifications for including artistic experiences in education.

Experience is an important concept in Dewey's philosophy. As a Darwinian, Dewey believed that all life, including human life, constantly changes and evolves. Education should equip young people to adapt to new circumstances and he concluded that education should not be isolated from society but integral to it. This led him to believe that children's learning should take place within the context of their environment and everyday experiences so that they might learn to interact productively with the world around them. Dewey's pedagogy aimed to encourage children's 'natural' curiosity and he developed ways to use their interests to promote constructive learning. In his book *Experience and Education* (1938), he offered a clear summary of the differences between traditional and progressive education. He describes traditional education in terms of its isolation from other institutional contexts:

> The subject matter of education consists of bodies of information and skills that have been worked out in the past; therefore the chief business of schools is to transmit them to a new generation ... [T]he general pattern of school organisation (by which I mean the relations of pupils to one another and to teachers) constitutes the school a kind of institution sharply marked off from other social institutions. (1998, p. 2)

It is interesting to note that Dewey comments on the spatial organization of learning, and suggests that the ordered institutional patterns that dominated traditional schools (timetables, classroom layout and so on) differ substantially from the domestic spatial practices of the family. Progressive education, by contrast, aimed to encourage links between the domestic, the vernacular and school life.

Dewey's philosophical pragmatism led him to challenge the premise that teachers were the authority of all knowledge. He argued that knowledge was not always based on abstract principles that could be learnt by rote, but new knowledge was acquired through a combination of new experiences and repetition of past understandings. Shannon Jackson describes this in performative terms, suggesting that his pedagogy anticipated 'contemporary performance theories attention to repetition, citationality and the restoration of behaviour (2001, p. 16). Dewey himself described progressive education as a series of questions about how meaning is constructed:

> What is the place and meaning of subject-matter and of organisation *within* experience? How does subject-matter function? Is there anything inherent in experience which tends towards progressive organisation of its contents? What results follow when the material of experience are not progressively organised? (1998, p. 7)

These questions underline Dewey's belief in a prepared, progressive approach to learning. He has been erroneously associated with advocating anti-authoritarian and unstructured teaching methods but, by 1938, he was already distancing himself from those who thought adult intervention was 'an invasion of individual freedom' and he was careful to acknowledge the importance of history and established learning in his pedagogy (1998, p. 9). By questioning the authority on which knowledge is built, however, Dewey secured a place for experiential learning in schools in which the mantra 'learning by doing' signalled a new and democratic interest in the epistemology of knowledge, the spatial organization of education and the social dynamics of learning. He believed that education is an instrument of social change, and the relational aesthetic of his experiential learning defined a social role for the arts, in which learning by doing was expected to encourage co-operation, shared understanding and public spiritedness.

Dewey advocated artistic practice in his pedagogic philosophy, not as a way of encouraging children to become professional artists nor to demonstrate the refinement of class, but as a means of encouraging the growth of perception. Following his naturalist philosophy, Dewey suggested that both aesthetic experience and the processes of art-making are active, sensate and embodied. An aesthetic experience, he argued, involves interactivity between art object and audience. Rather than having an intrinsic value in its own right, he argued, an art object is empty of meaning without the perception of the audience. This idea was enthusiastically turned into practice by avant-garde artists in Black Mountain College in North Carolina, an educationally innovative space in which John Cage and his collaborators produced 'found art' and 'Happenings' that relied on the audiences to make meaning. Educationally, the appeal of Dewey's aesthetic theory was that it promised to integrate the inner realm of feelings with the exterior world of objects. Unlike the followers of Matthew Arnold, who assumed that 'great art' would cultivate the children's 'best selves', Dewey stated that 'receptivity is not passivity' but the arts are perceived actively and emotionally (1934, p. 52). He consistently argued that experience of the arts, whether as audiences or artists, would unite thought, feeling and action. In the final chapter of *Art as Experience* Dewey endorses Shelley's belief that the imagination is 'the chief instrument of good', and suggests that artistic experience not only allows for empathy between individuals, but also claims that art is 'more moral than moralities' (1934, p. 348). Dewey's liberalism led him to unite freedom, virtue and self-development and, following Darwin, he considered individual change to be a continual and natural process of evolution.

Drama in schools: Childhood and play

Drama in schools was shaped by the principles of progressive education, although it was teachers, rather than professional theatre-makers, who first recognized its potential to contribute to experiential learning processes. Harriet Finlay-Johnson was the inspirational headteacher of an English village school in Sompting, Sussex, from 1897 to 1909, and she developed a revolutionary methodology that placed drama at the centre of children's learning. Finlay-Johnson's teaching methods were championed by local and national school inspectors, and the Chief Inspector for Schools, Edmond Holmes, persuaded her to write a book, *The Dramatic Method of Teaching* (1912), in which she documented how children integrated drama and play into their everyday learning. There is no evidence to suggest that she had read early accounts of Dewey's philosophy, but Finlay-Johnson also favoured active approaches to learning and considered drama to be the most appropriate medium through which children's natural curiosity might be stimulated. There are several reasons why Finlay-Johnson's work caught the imagination of educationalists keen to further progressive approaches to education. She offered a practical demonstration of new theoretical ideas about teacher-pupil relationships, active and experiential learning and she particularly valued outdoor spaces in which children might be free to play.

Although Finlay-Johnson does not acknowledge many of her influences directly, her enthusiasm for the simplicity of rural life and the happiness that drama can bring to children is clearly reminiscent of William Morris' busy community of craft workers. It is interesting that Edmond Holmes wrote about Finlay-Johnson's work in terms that are recognizably Morrisonian, thinly disguising her school as 'Utopia' and characterizing the 'Utopian child' as 'alive, alert, active, full of latent energy, ready to act, to do things, to turn his mind to things, to turn his hand to things, to turn his desire to things, to turn his whole being to things' (1912, p. 13). She used dramatic play to encourage problem solving and, as examples of her dramatic method, she recounted how children enacted Maori rituals, dramatized historical events, performed Bible stories and, on one occasion, built a shed in the lane by the school to house the fictional 'Tig', a prehistoric boy who was the central character in a favourite story. Her interest in providing a stimulating environment led her to re-conceptualize the spatial dynamics in which learning took place, and the children often worked outside the formal organizational structures of the classroom. She wrote:

> A great advantage of this new method of learning lessons by means of playing and acting them, lay in the fact that it was not absolutely necessary

to have the lessons in one particular room; they could as easily, or more easily, be played in the open air. Frequently we acted our history plays on the downs, in overgrown chalk pits, or just in our own school playground. (1912, p. 13)

The natural simplicity of this rural lifestyle and the active, experiential learning Finlay-Johnson described appealed to successive educators searching for an education based on democratic principles.

Finlay-Johnson's Morrisonian pedagogy was complemented by an interest in the role of the teacher, and in this respect her dramatic method anticipated Dewey's child-centred approach to artistic learning. This meant that, unusually for the period, she described her relationships with pupils as 'fellow workers, friends and playmates' (1912, p. 29). Not only did she wish to work alongside children in the outdoors, she also structured her teaching to suit children's 'natures'. 'It is more in keeping with child nature not to sit constantly as a "passive bucket to be pumped into"' (1912, p. 33) she remarked and, in a telling passage about the role of the teacher, linked nature study to children's dramatic play:

> Instead of letting the teacher originate or conduct the play, I must demand that, just as the individual himself must study Nature and not have it studied for him. The play must be the child's own. (1912, p. 19)

Drama and nature study were equally important to Finlay-Johnson's approach to teaching, implying that she accepted the Romantics' idea that that the exterior natural world and children's own inner natures are in harmony. This attitude is captured in Holmes' sentimental preface to her book, in which he describes her school as the place 'where children and teachers lived for a space in the world of romance and happiness' (1912, p. 14).

Finlay-Johnson's cultural tastes were eclectic. She admired literature and theatre, particularly Shakespeare, for their capacity to inspire an appreciation of beauty, although she encouraged the children to find their own 'original treatment and interpretations' of his plays in performance rather than treating his work with reverence (1912, p. 88). She also valued the vernacular, and she persuaded the children's mothers to practise Morris dancing and folk singing as well as perform their own plays. This meant that drama and performance occupied a central place in everyday life; the children's learning was not situated in a separate space within the school institution but affirmed a sense of belonging to their families, communities and other social groupings.

Finlay-Johnson's dramatic method was physical, performative and embodied, and she convinced social and educational reformists of the value of a healthy garden, in which learning was not static and constrained behind desks, but open, playful and mobile. Her work serves as a practical example of the radical reforms that were necessary to make schooling interactive and child-centred, and illustrates the potential for drama within this democratic project that was to endure beyond her brief career. Her interdisciplinary approach to curriculum planning influenced a succession of educators, as Gavin Bolton's elegant description of her work testifies (1998). Perhaps the most notable impact was on the British drama educator Dorothy Heathcote who developed a drama methodology in the 1970s and 1980s that inspired generations of teachers to integrate learning through drama into the school curriculum.

Mapping children's nature: The dramatic instinct

It was the social dynamic of drama and its capacity to promote happy and active learners within a rural environment that inspired Finlay-Johnson's dramatic pedagogy rather than a specifically scientific interest in children's development. Her work became well known internationally and, within months of the publication of her book, she was cited by scholars across the Atlantic. Part of the appeal of her work lay in her ability to paint a picture of an English pastoral arcadia, an image which seemed far removed from the urban environments of North America. Ellen M. Cyr, who wrote the preface to the American edition of *The Dramatic Method of Teaching* in 1912, praised the spontaneity within this child-garden but, interestingly, she primarily chose to emphasize the benefits of drama to children as individuals rather than its ability to build learning communities.

At the turn of the century North American psychologists had codified children's natures into a selection of individualized 'instincts', one of which was called the 'dramatic instinct'. The idea of the dramatic instinct had gained some currency on both sides of the Atlantic, but it was in the United States that it really took hold. The Clark University scholar Elnora Whitman Curtis published her book *The Dramatic Instinct in Education* in 1914, and although she cited the influence of Finlay-Johnson's Sompting School on her work, there were distinct social and cultural differences between their educational traditions that affected the two women's approach to drama. As a member of the middle-class intelligentsia, Whitman Curtis belonged to a very

different social background from Finlay-Johnson, who was the daughter of a house painter and trained as a teacher at evening classes. The
tone of Whitman Curtis' commentary on Finlay-Johnson's method is
faintly patronizing; she particularly disliked the talking flowers used
to teach the children nature study, which she described as 'taking
methods to extremes' (1914, p. 74). As a practising teacher, Finlay-
Johnson regarded drama as a *method*, and her interactive processes
of teaching and learning were rooted in classroom practice rather
than illustrative of scholarly research. Whitman Curtis, by contrast,
clearly saw this way of life as quaintly old world, and her academic
interest was in furthering technical knowledge about children's moral
and psychological development. Her study of contemporary social sciences convinced her that drama was an *instinct*, a way of thinking
that emphasized the growing culture of individualism within educational theory and, by implication, she rejected the utopian ideal of a
Morrisonian community of learners.

Whitman Curtis had been awarded a PhD which was examined,
significantly, by G. Stanley Hall the controversial child psychologist.
Stanley Hall believed that children's instinctive behaviour is based on
genetic memories of the 'primitive' phase of evolution during which
young children are instinctively drawn to play in mud and older children to form gangs (1904, p. 78). There is a question to be asked here
about whether Stanley Hall included girls in the primitive phase of
mud and gangs, and although Whitman Curtis similarly bases the
dramatic instinct on primitivism, this primitive instinct upheld the
traditional role of the arts as a 'feminising' influence. According to
Whitman Curtis, the dramatic instinct serves a unique emotional
need for young people to express their feelings and inner personali-
ties. To support their moral and emotional development she favoured
dramatizations of fairytales and middle-class theatrical confections
such as *Little Lord Fauntleroy*, thereby mixing fiction with scientific
ideas that were current at the time to justify a conventional faith in
the sanctity of the child. She cites Jane Addams' work at Hull House
approvingly, and her psychological reading of the unguarded passion
for popular entertainment in Chicago led her to believe that 'theatre
is a dangerous force when left to itself' (1914, p. 29). Writing about
children's literature of the period, Juliet Dusinberre has argued that,
by the early twentieth century, the interest in children's 'natural' creativity had become increasingly entwined with genetics and eugen-
ics; middle-class parents in Britain became interested in the work of
Ellen Key and Leslie Stephen, who believed that there was a direct

correlation between the level of children's imaginations and their 'natural' social superiority.[2] Primitive, natural instincts, on both sides of the Atlantic, clearly followed the cultural tastes and habitus of the educated middle classes.

Informed by the authority of the social sciences, the idea of the 'natural' child appears to promise equality but it disguised a way of thinking about children that, with hindsight, appears highly divisive. In a particularly chilling passage published in 1914, Whitman Curtis praises the way in which German scientists recommended outdoor play to counteract what they saw as the deterioration of the race (1914, p. 102). Stanley Hall, who advocated selective breeding and forced sterilization, wrote the preface to Whitman Curtis' book and he described the dramatic instinct as a 'corrective' that offered potential for 'psychic and moral orthopaedics' (1914, p. xiii). The use of scientific language seems to add weight to Hall's naturalization of childhood, and this raises further questions about the ideological construction of the 'natural' dramatic instinct. Whitman Curtis followed Addams in suggesting that theatre might 'convert members of our foreign population into good American citizens' (1914, p. 71), but her comments reveal a very different ideological position. The final paragraph of her book is instructive:

> Surely the function of the school is not only to utilise the dramatic instinct in the curriculum, but, by means of it, to train the faculty of criticism and appreciation, so as to produce a reaction against *all* degenerate tastes, and to work towards the general uplifting of public morals. (1914, p. 224)

Quite what is meant by 'degenerate tastes' is unclear, but it is disturbing to see how Arnold's liberal idea of a nation united by a common culture had been adapted to support a very different political position. Although it would be misleading to suggest that Whitman Curtis herself represented the extreme Right, and her authorities are eclectic, it is important to recognize that the idea of a 'natural' childhood that emerged in this period filled an ideological space that was later turned, terrifyingly, to official use by the Nazis.

In his analysis of how the 'nature' of children was socially constructed in the nineteenth and early twentieth centuries, the geographer Stuart C. Aitken argues that psychological theories required children's development to be mapped in ways that reveal the dominant values of the time (2001, p. 35). Of course, as Aitken points out, most theories of 'natural' child development supported the liberalism of Dewey's progressivism, but one of the effects of codifying instinctive

patterns of behaviour and development is that an increasingly bureaucratic education system began to turn its professional gaze on children's physical and emotional well-being. These interpretations of the
nature of childhood focused attention on the children themselves, and
their physical and emotional progress was described, monitored and
regulated as part of a theorized process of naturalizing child development. Michel Foucault memorably described this form of surveillance
as panopticism, in which the disciplinary power of experts is internalized by the object of their gaze who 'instinctively' learn to conform to
their ideas (Foucault, 1991). In some ways this is an ironic inversion of
Dewey's democratic intensions; the emphasis on normative, linear or
stage-related patterns of learning signalled a move away from addressing the material conditions in which children were living which had
so occupied nineteenth century social reformists, and focused on the
interiority of children's minds and imaginations as representative of
their inner natures. When it no longer seemed practical (or possibly
politically desirable) to escape from the morally corrosive effects of
urbanization into the natural environment of William Morris' socialist imaginary, the arts were charged with providing a space in education through which children might learn to connect with their own
inner natures. This either creates a culture of conformity, in which
children internalize the dominant disciplinary values of the day or,
more optimistically, it offers them the opportunity to find happiness
within the aesthetic space of the self.

Child art and child drama: Modernist aesthetics

The Victorian idealization of childhood as a source of goodness paved
the way for modernist constructions of childhood as a way of thinking about selfhood and creativity. Although the sanctity of the child
is perhaps most associated first with Romanticism and secondly with
Victorian sentimentalism, the sanctity of the artist was also a potent
symbol of modernism. In the period following the First World War
artists and intellectuals across the Western World forged a radical
reassessment of the traditional values of patriotism, duty and honour
which, they recognized, had led to slaughter and carnage on a horrify-
ingly unprecedented scale. If obedience to authority had taken millions
to their deaths, trusting one's own instincts seemed a more optimistic
alternative to following the 'heroic' leadership of 'great' men. To fuel
this break with the past, both theatre practitioners and educationalists turned to the newly emergent fields of anthropology, psychology

and psychoanalysis to counteract the repression of individuality that
had been inflicted by the moralizing society of the nineteenth century.
Freedom, they believed, would not come from adhering to standards of
behaviour that were externally imposed but would be found inwardly,
in the interiority of the self. Carolyn Steedman observed that it was
during the twentieth century that the idea of the child acquired new
meanings across the Western world, and one's own childhood became
'the means for thinking about and creating a self ...: an interiority'
(1995, p. 20). Theatre practitioners and educationalists contributed to
this shift in perspective in their separate fields, but their shared interest in the sanctity of the self created the conditions for a sustained
dialogue that would shape the future of theatre education.

In the turmoil following the First World War the simplicity of child-
art had been enthusiastically embraced by modernist intellectuals,
including the Bloomsbury Group, who valued its instinctual purity. The
success of the Bloomsbury Group lay in their insistence on aesthetic
individualism; the arts were regarded in both social and psychological
terms, as the expression of, in Clive Bell's words, the 'soul of mankind'.
As enthusiasts for the abstract work of Cezanne, Matisse and Picasso,
Roger Fry and Bell admired the simplicity of the artists' vision because
they symbolized emotions, according to Bell (1914), from the 'depth
of man's spiritual nature' (1976, p. 76). In their post-Freudian world,
Raymond Williams conceded, they regarded 'civilised individualism'
as the radical alternative to the 'spiritual famine' and emotional repression which had characterized Victorian and early Edwardian society
and led to the 'herd instincts' apparent during the 1914–18 war (1980,
p. 154). It was the soul of humanity, and not society, which was thought
to be, in Virginia Woolf's words 'pure, uncontaminated, sexless as the
angels are said to be sexless' (1979, p. 75). As such, the practice of the
arts, which revealed the depth of the soul, was necessarily socially liberating. Art, for Fry, was a symbol of the unseen energy of imagination,
'the greater cleverness of its perception, great purity and freedom of
its emotion' (1981, p. 17); to extend this image of emotional purity to
children's art-making was a logical development of thought. In one of
the first serious considerations of child-art as a genre, Fry found in children's painting the evidence he needed to suggest that abstract art is a
representation of an innate and common humanity:

> Children, if left to themselves, never, I believe, copy what they see, never,
> as we say, 'draw from nature', but they express, with a delightful freedom
> and sincerity, the mental images which make up their own lives. (1981,
> p. 15)

Fry's emphasis on 'freedom and sincerity' in this passage is significant; he elides self-expression with moral and aesthetic individualism. The implication, in the work of Woolf and Fry, is that social freedom naturally stems from individual consciousness, and that society might be united by those with the greatest freedom of spirit.

The idea that childhood simplicity generated the most authentic art, a view held by the Bloomsbury Group in the early modernism of the twentieth century, became potently assimilated into education theory and the popular imagination in the period immediately following the Second World War. In the theatre, consistent with Steedman's view that accessing childhood became the way to liberate the adult self, play became characterized as the rediscovery of the actor's inner child. Typical of this perspective is the US director Michael Chekhov's advice to actors who, writing in 1953, suggested that playfulness (in this case specifically clowning) 'will awaken within you that eternal *Child* which bespeaks the trust and utter simplicity of all great artists' (2002, p. 130).

Child-art, as a revelation of children's inner mental lives, was valued in education theory as a means through which children might, freely and naturally, adjust to the constraints of the external world. Child-art became recognized as a modernist genre, partly through the work of the Austrian educator Franz Cizek's interest in children's paintings and Herbert Read's book *Education Through Art* (1943) that received wide circulation. Child drama, by contrast, was not so widely recognized or understood. Peter Slade, whose prolific career included professional theatre for young audiences, educational drama in schools and drama therapy, was among the first to make theorized connections between play, theatre and children's drama. Slade founded the theatre company for children the Pear Tree Players in 1943, broadcast children's programmes on BBC radio and became Drama Adviser for Birmingham schools, but it is for his book *Child Drama*, first published in 1954, that he is perhaps best remembered. Slade's ambition in writing this book was to provide educationalists with a rationale for including child-drama in schools that paralleled the child-art movement. He describes child-drama as 'an art in itself', although his priority is children's emotional well-being, and he aims to create 'a happy and balanced individual' (1954, p. 105).

Slade made the link between psychological theories of imaginative play and children's creativity, and emphasized the importance of Sincerity and Absorption in their dramatic play (Slade capitalized words he regarded to be particularly important concepts). Slade describes Absorption as a state of 'being completely wrapped up in what is being done or what one is doing ... A strong form of concentration' (1954, p. 12). This emphasis on focused attentiveness anticipates the work of the psychologist Mihaly Csikszentmihaly, whose concept of creativity as 'flow' found favour in theories of creativity towards the end of the century (1996). Both Slade's Absorption and Csikszentmihaly's flow are regarded as pre-requisites for creative activity, because they are playful moments in which self-consciousness and fears of failure are diminished (Slade, 1954, p. 12; Csikszentmihalyi, 1996, p. 110). Slade finds Sincerity in Absorption because, he suggested, it is in this state that children are least inhibited by the constraints of the adult world. Looking back on his career in 1999, Slade commented that:

> It will be easier to understand the psychological importance of [drama education] and its value if it can be accepted that there is a child drama which is an art form in its own right, as with child art (see the work of Viola, Cizek, Herbert Read). It should be understood that years of practice in improvised acting (if taken seriously) leads also to the type of deep involvement and believability, which enriches all acting and leads to that beautiful, final civilised art we call Theatre. (1999, p. 254)

Consistent with modernist aesthetics, Slade's elision of psychological well-being with self-expression and 'civilised art' offered not only a powerful rationale for the emotional significance of drama in education, it also privileged those forms of theatre that were thought to be most authentic and sincere.

Although Slade was perhaps less successful in popularizing child drama as a genre than the visual artists, his ideas about the importance of the creative imagination echoed the modernist perception that individual and social freedom are intimately linked. Nonetheless, child drama informed two post-war initiatives; it inspired an increasing number of teachers to use improvised drama in their classrooms, and it generated new ways of thinking about the educational potential of professional theatre for children and young audiences. It is in the development of theatre for children, however, particularly during the middle years of the twentieth century, that the commercial, the psychological, the educational and the artistic were perhaps most delicately balanced. It is interesting, and perhaps seems paradoxical, that many progressive educationalists and social reformists had an antipathy to the theatre as a cultural institution. In the first half of the twentieth century, as I have described, the commercial theatre was regarded with suspicion, at best a shallow confection and at worst morally corrupting. It was a view that Slade himself supported. But the modernist idea of child drama created an ethical and aesthetic space that allowed a new form of theatre for children to emerge. Writing in 1948, Slade made a veiled attack on commercial theatre for children, arguing that theatre for young audiences should connect with children's inner worlds rather than represent adult nostalgia:

> For Children's theatre is a LAND not a building. It is the land of the Imagination and Emotion set in an Empire of Dreams. If we do not realise this, or worse, if we do not want to realise this because of our own blind adult conceptions, we shall get the wrong sort of theatre and it will not be a children's one at all. There is a danger of its becoming merely a sentimental symbol of those who are no longer young. (1948, p. 4)

It is interesting that Slade described his theatre in spatial terms, and his suggestion that theatre provides children with a safe place to escape from material realities into the unconscious world of dreams is entirely consistent with the times. His emphasis on child drama and on creating theatre that reflects children's perspectives rather than an adults' point of view influenced fellow theatre-makers including Brian Way, who founded the Theatre Centre in London in 1953, and Caryl Jenner who had been a member of Slade's Pear Tree Players, and established the Unicorn Theatre in London 1956. In her history of theatre for children in the United States, Ellie McCaslin also notes that, by 1958, there had been a revolution in theatre for young audiences led by The Paper Bag Players in New York. Unlike other theatre companies who presented familiar stories and fairytales on stage, The Paper Bag Players developed their own material using everyday objects that children use in their own play (1971, p. 195), a methodology that continues to inspire theatre for young audiences today.

The relationship between children's own creative involvement with drama and acting in commercial theatre had been perhaps more readily accepted in the United States than in England. Creative dramatics, as it was known in the United States, was a movement that aimed to encourage children's playfulness and imaginative development through improvised drama. Its inception is most associated with Winifred Ward, who also started the Children's Theatre of Evanston in 1925. Ward saw no conflict of interest between creative dramatics and children performing professionally, and she saw creative dramatics as part of children's actor-training and as a staging post towards a professional contract. Ward insisted that all the child actors she employed professionally had undertaken creative dramatic classes and, Isabel Burger reports, by 1958 this view was replicated among directors of theatre for young audiences across the United States. Burger cites the director Constance Welsh who states that the 'permissive atmosphere of the creative dramatics group' encourages children to become sensitive actors (1983, p. 186). This echoes the move in the professional theatre towards greater emphasis on spontaneity and the use of improvisation, but it also returned children to the commercial stage as potential commodities.

'Humanising' spaces: Theatre and the nature of childhood

Theatre-makers who work in educational settings often negotiate a utopian dynamic between place and space, and one of the enduring themes that derived from this period of social change is that the physical space of theatre and the processes of making drama enable a negotiation between the interiority of the self and the social imaginary of other possible worlds. This idea developed at a time when the newly emerged discipline of child psychology led theatre-makers to assume that particular forms of imaginative play were instinctive and natural. The Froebelian idea that children were natural organisms, like any other creatures, who needed space and liberty for healthy growth offered an explicit challenge to the repressive moralizing of the Victorian era. This way of thinking was memorably fictionalized by Frances Hodgson Burnett in her children's novel *The Secret Garden* (1911) in which two children, the colonial Mary and the wealthy but sickly Colin, escape the repressive environment of a dark Victorian mansion into the light of a forgotten garden where they play with a working-class country boy, Dickon, who was depicted as close to animals and nature. This natural environment enables Mary and Colin to grow freely and become emotionally, spiritually and physically healthy. This illustrates how the link between child psychology and nature captured the popular imagination at the time, and its emphasis on playfulness further contributed to the democratization of learning.

The modernist perception that an education in the arts enables children's natural development marked a significant shift in thought away from the Victorian idea that an education in culture is civilizing, and towards the belief that the engagement with the arts is inherently 'humanising'. What a critical genealogy of this idea reveals, however, is just as the Victorians held a particular view of civilization, so too did the modernists have in mind a peculiarly Western view of humanity. At the time, this idealization of human nature was thought to open up new possibilities for social action but, according to the sociologist Pierre Bourdieu, this was a way of thinking that ascribed 'quasi-magical powers' to the arts which served to legitimate the values of the educated élite (1996, pp. 229–31). Carolyn Steedman further points out that the idealization of childhood is a trope, an adult projection of how they would like human subjectivity to be:

> The idea of the child was the figure that provided the largest numbers of people living in the recent of Western societies with the means for thinking about and creating a self: something grasped and understood: a shape, moving in the body ... something *inside*: an interiority. (1995, p. 20. Italics original)

The idealization of child-nature is based on an abstract ideal of human nature and the belief that goodness is to be found inwardly, in the sources of the self, to borrow Charles Taylor's memorable phrase (Taylor, 1989). At the time this emphasis on the 'humanising' qualities of the arts provided a welcome move away from the idea that they are 'civilising', but this position still constitutes an evaluative judgement about what, or who, is regarded as 'human', and who is, by implication, excluded.

This history underlines the ways in which *all* theatre for children is delineated by a specific set of ideologies, principles and aesthetic values, whether or not they are explicitly declared. Western idealizations of childhood did not always travel well, however, as Manon van de Water's brilliant book *Moscow's Theatres for Young People* (2006) reveals. He describes how an early attempt in the 1920s to integrate Stanley Hall's theories of the dramatic instinct into Moscow's theatre for children was short-lived, and the plays soon evolved from 'fairy tales, to politicised fairy tales, to Marxist propaganda plays with the main objective being the ideological education of the young Soviet citizen' (2006, p. 49). Theatre for children in Moscow remained an instrument of ideological education, in various forms, until the liberalization of the cultural environment that accompanied Glasnost and Perestroika in the 1980s. Soviet theatre had a different vision of utopia, and their communist principles made the idealization of the child-garden and the aesthetic purity of children's imagination as 'natural' look decidedly bourgeois. And although Muscovite plays for children did not journey easily to the West, the revolutionary politics of Communist theatre had a profound influence on the history of theatre education. It is to the interaction between political activism, progressive education and the theatre that I shall now turn in the next chapter.

4

Places to Learn: Activity and Activism

Any history of theatre education would be incomplete without a discussion of the Theatre-in-Education movement which began in England in the 1960s, a period of political radicalism and educational change that created the first real opportunities for professional theatre-makers to work in schools on a sustained basis. Theatre-in-Education (often abbreviated to TIE) reflected the counter-cultural spirit of the time, and sought to extend the participatory pedagogies of progressive education to theatre as a medium of political activism. In this chapter I shall map some of the significant elements of this historical narrative, and tell the story of a theatre that was committed to political revolution rather than social reform. Distinctions between social reform and revolution were not only political, they were also aesthetic and educational.

In the previous chapter I suggested that one of the reasons why principles of social reform through the arts turned so seamlessly into a more individualized aestheticization of selfhood was that reformists who followed the work of William Morris and Matthew Arnold underestimated the role of artists as social critics. Their reformist principles were based on a yearning or nostalgia for an integration of self and place that never existed – a social imaginary of a homogeneous nation and the utopia of an organic rural community – and this meant that they were more concerned with affects of aesthetics and the social leveller of craft-making than with the politics of dramatic form or the ideology of theatrical content. Equally importantly, middle-class social reformists had a dismissive attitude towards working-class

57

culture, and, despite their egalitarian intentions, over time this had the effect of privileging middle-class values and tastes which became increasingly individualized and internalized as an ideal of selfhood. This created a space for activists on the political Left, particularly in the period following the First World War, to explore ways to use theatre as a tool to articulate their anti-capitalist sentiments more explicitly.

The focus of this chapter is the history of theatre that happened in public places – on the street, in factories, in pubs and subsequently in schools – which sought to address questions that were deemed relevant to the working classes and which aimed to revolutionize class politics. In the social upheaval following the First World War, the Bolshevik revolution in Russia and the Wall Street Crash, socialist theatre became increasingly linked to international movements that summoned a new relationship between theatre and politics. At the centre of many debates which contributed to the political and artistic revolution which began in the 1920s, and lasted for much of the century, were questions about the social and educative purpose of theatre, and its political philosophy. The social historian Raphael Samuel has pointed out that it was in the 1920s and 1930s that theatre became increasingly used as a weapon of political struggle, in which revolutionaries roundly rejected all forms of bourgeois theatre, and developed new theatrical languages to appeal to different audiences. This spirit was central to the International Workers' Theatre Movement in the 1920s and 1930s, the politics of Brecht's theatre and the civil rights and counter-cultural movements of the 1960s, all of which made their mark on the TIE movement. Taking theatre to the people, particularly to places where the working classes lived and worked, had been seen as a subversive act in the 1920s and 1930s, and this political philosophy informed the development of TIE. Taking theatre into schools, encouraging active learning and energetic debate, allowed radical young theatre-makers to engage with the politics of both theatre and education.

This revolutionary theatre placed importance on its social effectiveness and on the political impact of the work. This led to new, highly experimental theatrical languages designed to capture an audience's attention by engaging with popular culture and encourage their involvement. It is also characterized by a move away from the social imaginary of William Morris' pastoral aesthetic, and instead stressed the significance of the urban environment and identified the factory as the place of workers' power. In common with previous theatre education initiatives, TIE opposed the commercialism of mainstream theatre, and its practitioners developed a new theatrical pedagogy through which the more conventional meanings of both schools and theatres as conceived spaces and cultural institutions might be opposed and transgressed.

Theatre and the class struggle: A futurist dream

Looking back over twenty years after the fall of the Berlin Wall in 1989, it is perhaps difficult to imagine that there were political activists who, for much of the twentieth century, believed that a workers' revolution that would overthrow capitalism might actually happen. There were, however, many different groups of political activists who sought to use theatre as a means of communication and debate in order to mobilize the working class and politicize their audiences. Although similarly critical of the capitalism of commercial theatre, unlike the social reformists they sought to connect working-class culture to oppositional politics and use performance as an instrument of class struggle. In his history of workers' theatre 1880–1935, Raphael Samuel describes the changes of the period in the following terms:

> It was a crystallisation of a self-consciously proletarian aesthetic, of a futuristic dream in which socialism was no longer an escape from the proletarian condition but rather a realisation of workers' power. Instead of deference to high culture, there was an iconoclastic desire to break with it. (1985, p. xix)

This 'realisation of workers' power' led to a re-conceptualization of the instrumentalism of theatre, leading to performance styles that aimed to accentuate class difference in order to mobilize the workers into taking political action against the ruling classes.

At the centre of this activist movement lay a Marxist critique of capitalist society, and although Marxism was interpreted differently by theatre activists, there was an enduring belief that an oppressive class system had become accepted as a social inevitability endured throughout the twentieth century.[1] This analysis created an interest in how the working classes were complicit in holding an economic system in place that not only failed to serve their needs, but also actively exploited their labour and furthered a long history of iniquitous social relations. Marxist ideas were circulated through debate and discussion, and contributed to the formation of the Workers' Theatre Movement (WTM), an international movement committed

to furthering the cause of Communism which had branches in the United States, Japan, Australia, Russia and across Europe. Their intention was to politicize and mobilize industrial workers in their own environments, and this involved a range of tactics, including agitating local disputes, travelling to support striking communities and furthering class solidarity through political debates on a local and international scale. The British WTM was an umbrella organization, founded in 1926 during the General Strike and the period of mass unemployment, and it gathered together different socially committed theatre companies. It had been influenced by European propagandist companies including Blue Blouse (Russia) and Red Megaphones (Germany) and their names – Hackney Red Radio, Deptford Red Blouses, Lewisham Red Players – announced their allegiance to both 'red' communist politics and to the urban environments in which they worked. Tom Thomas, one of the leaders of the WTM, described how his visit to Germany in 1931 had inspired an interest in taking theatre to places in which working-class people lived and worked. It is interesting to note that, looking back on his work in 1977, Thomas regarded the politics of place and dramatic form mutually as embedded:

> We were full of enthusiasm for the ideas of groups who could create their own repertoire, and talk to the people directly on the streets. We rejected the idea of playing to friends and families, which was the basis of most amateur dramatics, or of asking people to come and pay money, which was the basis of commercial theatre ... Instead of a theatre of illusion ours was to be a theatre of ideas, with people dressed up in ordinary working clothes. No costumes, no props, no special stage. 'A propertyless theatre for the propertyless class' we called it. (1985, p. 89)

There are a number of connections Thomas makes between Marxist politics and theatre form that are worth underlining here. Thomas' primary interest is in mobilizing the working class by shaking them out of the passivity that he held responsible for keeping capitalism in place. For this reason he is particularly critical of a theatre of illusion which he saw, in Marxist terms, as responsible for the false consciousness that obscures social reality. By stripping away the spectacle and artifice associated with bourgeois theatre, Thomas aimed to show the capitalist exploitation experienced by urban factory workers and to use theatre to debate socialist ideas on the street. Significantly, most performers were working class themselves and were dressed in boiler suits to mirror the audience's own clothes, thereby suggesting not only solidarity between workers of different trades, but also representing visually the possibility of collective action.

The success of this form of theatre-making lay not in its aesthetic appeal, but on its ability to persuade. There are two published accounts of successful performances during the cotton workers' strike in 1931, both given by Ewan MacColl, and although the details are differently remembered they offer an insight into the activists' motives and intentions.[2] MacColl recalled that his Manchester-based company the Red Megaphones (later Theatre of Action) frequently performed only to a handful of people at a time, and that they were often arrested for breaching the peace. But on the day of a strike ballot in Wigan a large crowd of around two hundred people gathered in the market place to witness their performance on an empty coal-cart. It proved so popular that that they had to repeat their entire repertoire twice, including the short play *The Fight Against the Eight Looms* that dramatized the issues the strikers faced. MacColl's obvious delight when one of the strikers raised a red cloth, a symbol of Communism, suggests not only that the message had been heard, but also that the excitement generated by the performance had encouraged a sense of belonging to a wider political struggle:

> While we were performing, one of the blokes in the audience climbed the central lamp standard and tied a piece of red cloth to it. And a great roar went up from the crowd. When we'd finished, we said, 'Well, that's all we know.' And they said, 'Do it again,' so we did it again. We didn't actually get through it a second time because the police came. They were very polite on this occasion because the crowd was a big one; when there was only a few people around they would come up and say 'Piss off,' but here they were quite polite, just moved us on, it was a great day. (1985, p. 236)

No doubt the heightened atmosphere of the strike favoured the audience's receptiveness to the company's political message, and their parodies of popular songs also suggest that there was an element of audience participation that may have contributed to capturing their attention.

MacColl famously declared 'to hell with art', and although this suggests that activism was prioritized over theatre aesthetics, members of the WTM had extended debates about the most appropriate and effective styles of performance for their work (Goorney and MacColl, 1986, p. xxxvi). Propagandist scripts such as the New York Shock Troupe's *Newsboy* (1933) and Odet's *Waiting for Lefty* (1935) travelled across continents, and performance methodologies including the iconic Living Newspapers spread between countries. Every script and performance was open for change, and it was expected that they would be continually adapted and reshaped to respond immediately to local circumstances. The WTM was disbanded in 1936 due to the changing cultural climate, including a more stable industrial economy with higher employment, and the rise of Fascism brought a broader alliance between revolutionary Communists and the Independent Labour Party. Theatres of the Left also became increasingly profes-sionalized, bringing a greater concern with production values and developing more subtle forms of political theatre. In the United States, the Federal Theatre Project briefly continued its grass-roots activism, and included theatre for young audiences and, notably, provided new opportunities for black writers, designers, directors and performers.[3]

Part of the professionalization of political theatre was offered by Bertolt Brecht, the most influential single dramatist within the Marxist tradition, whose work became widely known after the Second World War. Brecht's interest in Marxist dialectics, in learning to think in ways that challenged the status quo, defined his theatrical output and was to influence British political theatre of the Left throughout the century. Brecht's alienation technique, which is often misunder-stood as discouraging audience's emotional engagement, provided a theorized understanding of how real life events can be dramatized for political effect. He furthers this view in *The Messignkauf Dialogues*:

> The alienation effect consists in the reproduction of real-life incidents on the stage in such a way to underline their causality and bring it to the spectator's attention. This type of art also generates emotions: such per-formances facilitate the mastering of reality, and it is this that moves the spectator. (1965, p. 102)

Emotional engagement with the 'reality' of situations rather than with individual characters offered a new way of thinking, and this polit-ical aesthetic particularly appealed to British activists. By contrast, Brecht's approach was less widely adopted in the United States where, as North American theatre academic Janelle Reinelt has observed, the culture of bourgeois individualism dominated the theatre (1994, p. 3).

There are, however, a number of ways in which the Marxist trad-ition of revolutionary theatre influenced a politicized TIE movement. Marxism gave a political dynamic to the progressive education's active and participatory approaches to child-centred learning. It also raised materialist questions about the social implications of the place of performance, suggesting that theatre should be relocated into the urban crucibles of capitalism, and performed in factories, pubs, and on the streets where people lived and worked. Taking theatres into schools was a logical extension of this political thought. Marxism also offered a way to theorize the content of performance, demanding audiences to engage in contemporary concerns rather than using theatre as a means of escape. 'Nothing comes from nothing' as Brecht famously stated, and this political landscape provides the context for the development of the movement that became known as TIE.

Transgressing place: Theatre in education

It is significant that TIE began in Coventry, an industrial city in the English midlands that had been badly bombed in the Blitz. In November 1940 the city centre had been almost flattened overnight; several hundred lives were lost, more than half the houses destroyed and its medieval cathedral had been ruined. The feelings of loss and disorientation experienced by the residents, some of whom recalled being unable to find their way round the devastated city, meant that the post-war process of redevelopment had a particular symbolism for Coventry's inhabitants. The City Architect Donald Gibson took the opportunity to completely redesign the city's streetscape, and Coventry became one of the first post-war examples of a modernist city with shopping precincts and utilitarian concrete buildings with clear architectural lines. As geographers Phil Hubbard and Lucy Faire point out, the post-war reconstruction of Coventry articulates Lefebvre's idea of conceived space, in which urban planners drove forward their vision of modernization but failed to address the personal symbolism and cultural capital of memories associated with the residents' everyday practices of living.[4] Gibson was, however, alert to the need for public places of entertainment, and the Belgrade Theatre Coventry was the first new civic producing-house theatre to be opened in post-war England in March, 1958. This modernist building is now listed, and it stands as a testament to the enduring faith in the role of the arts in official policies of urban regeneration.

Although the term theatre in education had been widely used in the 1940s, it acquired a new energy in the 1960s when it became associated with the Belgrade Theatre's educational provision for young people and was shaped, over time, into a genuinely innovative theatrical methodology. In his chapter on the early days of TIE in Tony Jackson's book, *Learning Through Theatre* (1980), Gordon Vallins credits Anthony Richardson, the artistic director of the Belgrade during the 1960s, with recognizing the social and civic importance of the theatre for Coventry as a city. Richardson's vision was that the theatre would develop active links with all aspects of the community:

> Our discussions at the time centred not merely on the education services but also on the civic authority. We envisaged theatrical performances on the problems of administering a city, the city authority's ritualistic roots; involving industry where production, managerial and shop-floor problems would be examined in a theatrical context. (1980, p. 8)

Vallins' list of possible subjects for theatrical treatment went on to include law making, the moral and spiritual role of the cathedral, links with local cinemas and, of course, an education programme for local schools. This emphasis on using theatre as an instrument of civic governance not only has resonances of the WTM's attitude to industrial dispute and local politics, it is also indebted to Brecht's political theatre in which topical issues were open for debate and, incidentally, anticipated the Brazilian theatre director Augusto Boal's Legislative Theatre by several years. It also suggested that Belgrade Theatre's education programme was conceived as part of a wider cultural ambition to place the theatre at the centre of civic life.

The Belgrade Theatre's cultural and education policies addressed some of the existential issues faced by inhabitants living in a newly built city, particularly one in which collective memories were lost when its buildings were destroyed and further obliterated by the modernist principles that informed its redevelopment. One of Lefebvre's central claims is that modernist architecture and urban planning emphasize its visual impact rather than the embodied, multi-sensory experience of living, reducing its ' "iconological" forms of expression (signs and symbols) to "surface effects" ' (1991, p. 106). He criticized the astringency of modernist architecture, describing it as a 'repressive space' because its open plan designs exclude the possibility of intimacy and privacy within its public buildings (1991, p. 147). Monumental spaces, by contrast, contain all three of Lefebvre's spatial practices – conceived, perceived and lived – and physically experiencing monuments confirms a sense of belonging:

> Monumental space offered each member of a society an image of that membership, an image of his or her social visage. It thus constituted a collective mirror more faithful than any personal one. Such a 'recognition effect' has far greater importance than the 'mirror effect' of psychoanalysis'. (1991, p. 220)

Lefebvre specifically identifies cathedrals as offering these multiple 'horizons of meanings', in which official power is rehearsed and personal meanings are inscribed and embodied. Seen in that light, it is not difficult to imagine what it might it have meant to citizens living in Coventry in the 1960s that their most famous historical monument was a derelict cathedral that had been destroyed by enemy bombs. Tim Cresswell describes place as 'the raw material for the creative production of identity' (2004, p. 39) and this insight suggests that the task of re-building the city was not just about constructing new buildings nor providing civic amenities, but about asking deeper questions about the inhabitants' civic identities and their emotional connections to places they had known well. The process of reconstruction also involved looking to the future, and asking questions about what kind of society they wanted to build, and how its values, its politics and its stories might be articulated in and by its new public spaces. In an echo of the earlier twentieth century social reformists, the theatre offered itself as a focus for forging a new collective identity in an increasingly secular society.

It is interesting, but perhaps not surprising, that it was a promenade performance about the Coventry Blitz, *Out of the Ashes*, performed by the newly formed Belgrade Youth Theatre in 1965 that showed the potential for theatre to contribute to education. Vallins describes how the process brought the oral history and vernacular languages of local people onto the public stage of a city that had already been transformed, literally, beyond recognition. Young cast members interviewed their parents and grandparents about their experiences of living through the Blitz, and their improvisations added to a script developed with a local writer. The performance brought together the past with contemporary world events and was structured, according to Vallins, 'around music hall turns drawing on the "pop" culture that surrounded us: the television show, the "pop" concert, the wrestling match, bingo, film and "pop" song' (1980, pp. 7–8). The use of popular culture to tell a local story and the promenade performance was symbolic of a wider commitment to connect with the people of Coventry; by taking over different spaces in the theatre, members of the community added not only their collective memories to the drama, but created the sounds, textures, smells and images of live performance within a relatively new building. This transgressed modernist idealizations of theatre as an abstract or empty space, removed from other social meanings, and although this way of working now seems familiar, it should not be under-estimated how innovative and radical this approach was in the mid-1960s.

The devising process for *Out of the Ashes* emphasized the social dynamic of participation, the immediacy of improvisation, the significance of vernacular stories and used the energy of popular culture, all of which became important principles within the TIE movement. The impetus for developing new ways of engaging young people in theatre came when Vallins realized that his visits to schools would be better if they involved children in 'doing theatre rather than listening to me chat about it' (1980, p. 8). This dissatisfaction with his own teaching methods, coupled with his belief that the theatre should be at the centre of civic life, led directly to discussions with headteachers about a scheme that would involve theatre-makers working with teachers, as Vallins describes, to 'use techniques of the theatre in the service of specific education objectives (1980, p. 13). Fully funded by the local education authority, this work demanded strong local partnerships with schools and a willingness on the part of both teachers and theatre-makers to develop theatrical pedagogies that would encourage children's participation and active learning. To realize this ambition, Vallins recruited theatre-makers who were also educationalists in order to 'turn the two dimensional experience [of teaching] into a three dimensional one' (cited in Redington, 1983, p. 46). This approach marked a first step towards shaping a coherent methodology for TIE and defining the social and pedagogical role of professional theatre-makers as 'actor-teachers' in formal education.

It is important to recognize that TIE grew out of Britain's postwar reconstruction, and that the 1960s brought a period of economic expansion that offered generous State funding for the arts in redevelopment projects. Although TIE companies accepted local government funding, actor-teachers did not consider themselves to be instruments of civic authority. On the contrary, many actor-teachers aligned themselves with the alternative theatres of the political Left, and built on the traditions of the WTM and Brecht's anti-illusionist theatre by considering theatre to be an agent of social change, a voice of social criticism and a means through which the class struggle might be strengthened. This meant that they often regarded themselves as part of the spirit of rebellion and anti-authoritarianism that fuelled civil rights protests, prompted the flower power generation and led to the student unrest that began in *les évenements* in Paris 1968 and spread across the Western world. Schools as place-bound institutions were essentialized as rigid and authoritarian, demonstrating a familiar modernist narrative of places as 'stuck in the past, overly confining, and possibly reactionary' to borrow Cresswell's words (2006,

p. 26). Transgressing the official and bureaucratic meanings of place (or conceived space, in Lefebvre's terms), whether they were found in the disciplinary structures of schools or theatres, was integral to both their theatrical pedagogy and their political armoury.

Participation in a theatre of ideas

The sense of change in the 1960s and 1970s provided fertile ground for a new theatrical pedagogy, and the methodology that began in Coventry spread quickly. TIE companies did not perform shows, they devised programmes that often lasted a full day, and the emphasis on participation meant that they were difficult to capture in print (videos and DVDs had yet to be invented). Nonetheless it is significant that TIE was well documented at the time, suggesting that there was an appetite for grappling with its theories and practices. John O'Toole offered the first account of its educational potential in *Theatre in Education* (1976); Tony Jackson's edited collection *Learning Through Theatre* (1980) defined the field and his second edition in 1993 illustrated the international dynamic of the movement; Ken Robinson's collection *Exploring Theatre and Education* (1980) captured energetic debates between theatre-makers and educationalists; Christine Redington's thorough analysis of TIE addressed the question *Can Theatre Teach?* in 1983, and collections of scripts edited by Redington and by Pam Schweitzer were published in the 1980s by Methuen. All these interventions, as well as related conferences and training courses, helped to shape an understanding of the educative potential of TIE.

Although variously inflected by different companies at different times, the primary objective of TIE was to develop a vigorous theatre of ideas that would encourage young people to learn actively and think dialectically. In this respect TIE combined Dewey's liberal progressive pedagogy and Brecht's Marxist anti-illusionist theatre, and it worked best when the two approaches complemented each other. Radical theatre and progressive education both valued action and activity, and sought to encourage children to solve problems and think for themselves. David Pammenter, one of the first actor-teachers at the Belgrade Theatre Coventry, identified the significance of 'newly adopted education theory' which promoted 'learning by doing' (1980, p. 38). He further suggested that TIE companies should be the responsibility of theatres rather than schools in order to achieve political independence and artistic freedom, in his words, to 'counter-balance the pressures and demands of an institutionalised system of education' (1980, pp.

38–9). Pammenter's political commitment to the transgressive qualities of theatre led him to develop methodologies that would pose 'real'
questions for students, and to devise elements of performance that,
somewhat controversially, took a political perspective on the dramatic
content. He defended his position in terms that invoke Brecht:

> Because the work is being devised and the devisers have a *de facto* bias,
> it is bound to be there. The question is, is it a useful bias? If the team has
> something important to raise, uncover and explore in the forum of a pro-
> gramme, then they must have some kind of a perspective on it. Learning is
> a dialectical process and the true dialectic can only exist if *real* positions
> are taken. (1980, p. 44)

Dialectical thought is principally associated with Marxism, which
Brecht turned into theatre in the *Lehrstück*, usually translated as
'learning plays'. Learning to think dialectically, in ways that challenged the accepted ideology of capitalism, was one of the central
tenets of the *Lehrstück* and this principle became embedded in many
TIE programmes. It led actor-teachers to develop working methods
that focused on the dynamic between performance and participation,
and to create dramaturgical structures that drew the young people's
attention to the performance's own theatricality.[5]

Significantly, in the *Lehrstück* Brecht experimented with working
in non-theatrical spaces, but although he encouraged audience participation his strategies for this remained undefined. Brecht's social
gestus provided inspiration for the dramaturgical structure of many
TIE programmes, but actor-teachers can be credited with developing
new participatory strategies that are now very familiar – the dramatic
action was frozen or halted to enable students to judge the actions,
read an image or address questions raised by the performance, sometimes by working in role or by hot-seating particular characters. In
terms of content, TIE programmes frequently investigated contemporary social issues or historical themes, often with local significance.
In participatory work, students were often positioned ideologically to
challenge orthodox interpretations of history or resist conventional
solutions to contemporary social problems. This coheres with Brecht's
Marxist view that historicizing the past has the potential to disrupt its
meanings:

> We must drop our habit of taking the different social structures of past
> periods, then stripping them of everything that makes them different
> so that they all look more or less like our own, which they acquire from
> this process a certain air of having been there all along, in other words of

permanence pure and simple. Instead we must leave them their distinguishing marks and keep their impermanence always before our eyes, so that our own period can be seen to be impermanent too. (Willett, 1964, p. 190)

Published examples of programmes that addressed historical themes include Belgrade Theatre Coventry's *The Price of Coal* (1980) about the local history of coal mining, and M6 Theatre Company's *No Pasaran* (1980) that addressed questions about the rise of Fascism. Contemporary issues about town planning were raised in Bolton Octagon TIE company's *Holland New Town* (1980) and Belgrade TIE's *Lives Worth Living* (1983) explored contemporary attitudes to disability. In the introduction to her collection of TIE scripts, Christine Redington comments on the socio-political quality of the scripts, and observes that 'TIE is about opening up a wider world for the pupil than just home and school, leading the pupils to question what they see and hear' (1983, p. vi).

A good example of a TIE programme that took its influence from Brecht's *Lehrstück* to illuminate a historical event is Greenwich Young People's Theatre's programme, *The School on the Green* (1985, published in 1987). This programme tells the celebrated story of the longest running strike in British labour history, held at a village school in Burston, Norfolk from 1914 to 1939. The dramatic action is narrated by Dossy, an elderly resident of Burston, who invites the children to witness the story of the school and learn how teachers Tom and Annie Higdon were unfairly dismissed for demanding better conditions for the children. The central part of the programme is structured around a series of backstories, in which the events that led up to the dismissal are opened for critical questioning. Each scene, therefore, offers a mixture of scripted performance that demonstrated a particular element of the story, and provides opportunities for children to discuss the issues raised as if they were investigating the past. The movement between documentary and commentary (or action and reflection), a central feature of Brecht's *Lehrstück*, holds the play's political dynamic. In one scene for example, the class work in role during Annie Higdon's lesson on astronomy on the village green at night, and her dialogue turns into a documentary account of Galileo's wrongful imprisonment by the Pope for views that turned out to be justified. The actor-teacher invites the children to comment on the scene's content; the aims of the questions offered in the script underline the programme's politics:

1. To explore the notion of change and resistance to change
2. To challenge the notion of 'important people' always being right.

3. To encourage the pupils to think about 'the order of things' in the village of Burston. (1987, p. 78)

I remember seeing a demonstration of this programme at Dartington Halll in 1986, and I was struck by the clarity of the political challenge; participants were asked to question ideas that are assumed to be natural or true and they are given the power to make independent judgements about what they have witnessed. The choices were not, however, unambiguous. The dramaturgical structure aligned them firmly on the side of the striking children, their parents and the Higdons, who were consistently presented as caring and kindly towards the village poor and their children. The ruling classes, however, conform to conventional stereotypes; Farmer Fisher is autocratic and rude to Annie Higdon, and the Reverent Eland is sanctimonious and unyielding. In its structure, form and characterization the programme offers a vehicle for discussing wider questions about power, knowledge, trade unionism and progressive education, in which the participating audience are invariably positioned on the political Left, against conventional forms of authority and on the side of the working classes. This is the paradox of many TIE programmes. The drama exerts its own discipline, and although the programme may appear to offer the opportunity to transgress the social meanings of a didactic educational space, it still expects participants to conform to its own internal ideological structure. The representation of controversy is, of course, one of the most important functions of drama, and representing balance is likely to be theatrically bland. The question at stake is not whether the work showed political bias, but is how far, and in what ways, the participants were given the tools to understand how these dramatic effects had been achieved.

Although TIE programmes seemed to lay bare the illusion of theatre by actors changing character on stage and so on, there is scant evidence that the process involved opening the mechanics of production for critical scrutiny. There is another dramatization of the Burston story which started life in 1975 as a performance in a school, and was published as a script in 1992, which raises different pedagogical questions. The published version of Roy Nevitt's *The Burston School Strike* differs both in form and content from *A School on the Green*, although it also explores the power of trade unions, workers' rights and the social role of education. In many ways what makes the Burston story so rich for dramatization is that these issues are embedded in the story, thereby offering theatre-makers a chance to portray a moment of labour history in which sustained collective action success-fully caused social change. Whereas the Greenwich Young People's Theatre's programme was heavily fictionalized, however, Nevitt's play was researched in detail as a piece of documentary theatre. The play was constructed using the oral history testament of the Burston village children, by then in old age, and original documents about the strike. Documentary theatre, as Alan Filewod explains, runs in the tradition of MacColl, Brecht and Piscator, in which the 'actor is not a surrogate but a mediator whose command of artistic vocabulary embodies a critical attitude to the actuality it presents' (2009, p. 60). In Nevitt's play, the tradition of socialist theatre-makers is upheld not only by the choice of subject matter, but also by the critical attitude towards the form. The linear structure tells the story clearly and allows audiences to follow the argument as it unfolds; songs of the period that punctuate and historicize the action allow actors to mediate the events and encourage moments of reflection. The well-crafted dialogue allows young actors to position themselves in relation to the subject matter, and invites them to question how far they identify with the motives of individual characters they embody and to consider their dramatic function within the play as a whole.[6] Working on the dramatic realization of the script both offers young people an opportunity to consider the complex issues raised in the play *and* develop their understanding of the aesthetic of the production.

These two dramatic interpretations of the Burston story, both from the political Left, illustrate the ways in which participating in theatre can ask wider social questions. One of the strengths of TIE lay in its inter-disciplinarity, and a good programme would provide a focus and a catalyst for learning in many different areas of the curriculum, particularly in primary schools. During the 1980s the place of drama became increasingly secure in the school curriculum, particularly at secondary school level, where there were more drama graduates who had been trained to teach drama and theatre to examination level. Writing about the demise of TIE in 1992, Nicolas Whybrow commented that the introduction of drama at examination level had led to 'the increasingly misapplication of companies' work, with students being told by teachers to take notes about its formal aspects – set design, acting style, and so on' (1994, p. 274). He added that learning about theatre 'runs the risk of giving rise to different forms of élitist (class-based) stigmatisation' (1994, p. 277). Teaching children about theatre-making had never been the purpose of TIE, and some actor-teachers continued to regard most forms of theatre as bourgeois and inherently conservative, and they were resistant to changing focus. Furthermore, the political energy that had inspired the counter-cultural movement of the 1960s dissipated following the collapse of the Berlin Wall in 1989. The rise of the political Right with the election of Margaret Thatcher in 1979 and Ronald Reagan in 1981 had put the political Left in disarray, and their neo-liberal monetarist policies and conservative education agendas were incompatible with progressive pedagogies. In Britain many TIE companies bore the brunt of financial cuts to education and to theatre and this meant that local partnerships that had been built up between theatres and schools over many years were eroded, and the quality of newly formed touring companies became unreliable. TIE had served a particular historical moment and, by the 1990s, the idea that TIE companies might inhabit a transgressive counter-space within theatres and schools seemed increasingly less likely.

Despite early promise, unlike the WTM, TIE had never become an international movement. Some interest in TIE had been generated in the United States, particularly by the Creative Arts Team in New York which was founded by Lynda Zimmerman in 1974. With the support of Chris Vine, who came to New York in 1993 with the experience of working in TIE with Greenwich Young People Theatre in London, the Creative Arts Team gained enduring respect. Despite the success of individual companies, however, TIE did not become a major cultural force in schools across the United States. Radical theatre-makers had consistently been more attracted to the neo-avant-garde than Brechtian social realism, and politically motivated companies such as The San Francisco Mime Troupe (founded in 1959) and Bread and Puppet Theatre (1961) were more likely to disrupt the bourgeois gaze through use of giant puppets and visual comedy than the social realist dialectics of TIE. This cultural climate was not fertile ground for TIE, which was criticized for its poor production values and a lack of aesthetic integrity. The influential critic Lowell Swortzell, despite subsequently supporting the work of the Creative Arts Team, stated a clear preference for the less ideologically driven Theatre for Children over TIE (1993, pp. 239–50). It was through the work of the Brazilian theatre director Augusto Boal that issue-based theatre later gained currency in the United States, and although the strategies and politics of Theatre of the Oppressed (TO) and TIE have some striking parallels, TO is more widely associated with addressing social questions, particularly in community settings, than animating the school curriculum (Cohen-Cruz and Schutzman, 2006).

Elsewhere, there were different reasons why TIE did not gain a lasting hold. In Australia, John O'Toole and Penny Bundy also noted that TIE lacked magic and artistry and observed that, although many Australian theatre-makers shared the oppositional politics of British TIE practitioners, an increasingly strong sense of post-colonial identity led them to reject TIE on the basis of its association with a former colonial power (1980, pp. 135–6). By the late 1980s many Australian TIE companies had been replaced by youth theatres or professional theatre companies that toured shows to school audiences. Mary Ann Hunter's history of Magpie Theatre, which began in 1976 as a TIE company under the directorship of Roger Chapman, shows how the company moved from TIE to developing work with young performers and for young audiences as a way of encouraging a new generation of Australian theatre-makers (2001, pp. 73–4). Even in Britain, once separated from the oppositional polities that drove its aesthetic strategies, TIE was drained of its life and political energy and inevitably some programmes became predictable and formulaic.

What's Left?

So what's left of these radical and reformist histories? One of the insights of this critical genealogy is that theatrical experiments in educational settings have always been interwoven with the dramatic and educational innovations of their day, and this means that the practices of theatre educationalists offer insights into how it spoke to the culture and society of the period. Furthermore, it suggests that theatre education has always been delicately poised between the policy demands of State education and oppositional or reformist politics. This negotiation between public policy and the physicality of artistic practice has often been productive and inventive and, although education policy has been generally orientated towards economic prosperity and social stability, theatre education has often been integral to political movements that aimed to question and challenge established patterns of thought, feeling and action. It is perhaps unsurprising, therefore, that the two historical periods in which educational drama and theatre have been most energetic and innovative coincided with periods of significant economic growth and cultural change.

As part of this critical genealogy, I wanted to find a way to understand what's left of the radicalism of twentieth century theatre education by engaging physically and imaginatively with the cultural memories that inspired this history. My journey took me to Burston.

Re-reading the dramatized versions of the strike at the village school had captured my imagination, and I was intrigued to learn that Burston is still an important site of cultural memory for activists on the political Left. Each year on the first Sunday in September there is a rally on the village green to commemorate the strike and, as places of cultural performance such as theatres, market squares, churches and streets are particularly fertile sites of memory according to Joseph Roach, this seemed like an appropriate place to visit. The performance studies scholar Diana Taylor points out that memorializing events survive 'as long as people find them meaningful'. She adds that they promise to exceed knowledge that is captured in more tangible forms of documentation:

> Performance practices and behaviors offer an alternative history, one based on memory, events, and places rather than just documents ... Practitioners re-affirm their cultural identity and transmit a sense of community by engaging with these cultural behaviors ... Scholars can explore cultural communities, historical displacements, and erasures by relating modern-day performance to embodied practices that have been described in other media. (2008, pp. 101–2)

Armed with this insight, and keen to expand my understanding of what was left of the political principles that had informed theatre education in the past, I hoped my visit to Burston would act as an 'unofficial designated auditoria of cultural self-enunciation' to borrow Roach's words (1996, p. 27), that would illuminate this alternative history. The village website offered an invitation to 'celebrate the people who continue to fight for trade union rights, working class education, democracy in the countryside and international solidarity', and the speakers included the octogenarian socialist campaigner Tony Benn, trade union leader Diana Holland with entertainment provided by the performance poet John Hegley. The 2009 rally also commemorated the 50th anniversary of the Cuban revolution with a speech by Luis Marron from the Cuban Embassy in London and a salsa band. I imagined that those attending would have at least something common with the TIE activists who dramatized the Burston story and, with this in mind, I set off for a weekend in Norfolk. By bringing the past into the present, I hoped that this process would enable me to think what Roach describes as the 'otherwise unthinkable' about how this history has impacted on contemporary theatre education.

I arrived in Burston the day before the rally to visit the school, which is now a museum dedicated to the strike. The school itself is a robust, sandstone building standing on the village green as I had imagined, very close to the church yard where the striking teachers Tom and Annie (Kitty) Higdon are buried. It looks tranquil and almost stereotypically English, perhaps more obviously associated with the conservatism of rural life than trade union activism. The school was built in 1917 with funds raised through public appeal, and names of its many benefactors are carved on its outside walls, recording donations from the Miners and Railwaymen trade unions, the Independent Labour Party and agricultural unions. The school serves as a symbol of socialist solidarity of the early twentieth century and, in terms of the history of education, it is a reminder that the child-centred teaching methods the Higdons favoured were seen as a threat to established authority. Although there is no evidence that the Higdons used drama in their teaching, the setting reminded me of photographs of Harriet Finlay-Johnson's school in Sompting. Children in both schools obviously played and learnt outside, and followed the socialist principles of William Morris by putting the school at the centre of village life. Education was representative of a wider commitment to social justice and child welfare. It is significant in this context that interest in the strike school's history was rekindled in the 1970s when the annual rally was revived by trade unionists and the school's local trustees opened it as a museum. Burston School is linked, therefore, with two periods of history when innovations in theatre education were particularly dynamic. Its various commemorations function as a way of bringing the past into the present, and also mark how, as Diana Taylor suggests, the meanings of cultural memory change over time and come to represent different perspectives and worldviews.

Having walked round the school (twice) on that September Saturday I tried the door. It was locked. I had travelled quite a long way to get there, and I felt decidedly grumpy. You would have thought – I said to myself – that someone would be there to open it on the day before the rally. Eventually, I peered through the window and the sign I saw caused me to reflect. Entrance was free, and I might find the key on a hook by the front door of a nearby bungalow. Feeling suitably chastened, I realized that I had come to assume that all museums are part of a commodified heritage industry. My perceptions of who owns history were challenged, and I spent some time in the school before putting money for my Burston Strike book and tea-towel in an honesty box and returning the key. The following day I cycled the five miles from the pub where I had stayed to the rally – giving a shamefully false impression of my green credentials (I had already driven two hours to get to Norfolk). The village green was festooned with colourful banners from different trade unions; stalls promoting political activity lined the perimeter and a man with a megaphone was trying to organize the march around the village that followed the route the striking children had taken in 1914. I dithered about, not sure how to join in. At first I felt I wanted to observe rather than participate, but as the banners were held aloft I found myself swept up in the performance. I walked the circular 'candlestick' route with an elderly gentleman wearing a boater, a lifelong member of the Communist Party who had attended Oxford in the 1930s. The Communists were particularly well organized as a group, marching in formation. There were many political movements represented, including teachers' unions and human rights lawyers, although the conversation around me was more about middle-class holiday destinations than revolution (Tuscany and the South of France seemed favourites). Nonetheless the rally took me back to the days when Margaret Thatcher was in power and I actively protested against apartheid, nuclear arms and education cuts. We were accompanied by the Easington Colliery Brass Band, whose presence seemed to invoke another era and the bitter industrial dispute before the coal mines were closed in the 1990s. Although the band maintained links with the Trade Union movement, in common with Grimethorpe Colliery Band whose story was told in the 1996 film *Brassed Off*, they are now available for commercial bookings. Perhaps the most moving moment for me was not the speeches, nor the band, nor the march, but the brief conversation I had with a local man who remembered the strike school. He was standing to attention as we passed his house, leaning heavily on his walking stick, and wearing a smart jacket and tie even though it was a warm Sunday afternoon. His presence offered an emotional link with the past, in which individual and cultural memory became intimately linked.

There was serious political commitment demonstrated by those who participated in the rally that September afternoon, but my overall impression was that the event represented a political climate that had largely disappeared. Solidarity and collective self-consciousness, described by the historian E. P.Thompson as 'the great spiritual gain of the Industrial Revolution' (1963, p. 913), had flourished in an industrialized economy and this political identity was re-asserted by the rally, but it seemed primarily a commemoration of past achievements and calls to future activism were muted. Taking part, however, allowed imagination and memory to converge, in Roach's terms, because it juxtaposed contemporary expectations against past struggles. I realized that I had learnt to take for granted a commodified heritage in a mediatized world, and I had forgotten that there is a social and political symbolism in the simple commemorative act of walking around a village to the sound of a brass band. The Burston rally also underlines many of the recurring themes that informed theatre education in the twentieth century: an enduring commitment to egalitarianism and social justice on a national and international scale; an interest in the values and 'vortices of behaviour' that are inherent in performing cultural memory and working-class social history; a commitment to child-centred education and to hearing the voices of children. As I left Burston, I wondered whether the globalized economy of the twenty-first century would achieve similar gains. The second part of this book represents my attempt to find out.

Part Two

Moving On: Theatre Education in the Twenty-First Century

Introduction: Traces and Places

Lessons from the past

My argument in the first section of this book is that all forms of theatre education – however construed – symbolize new ways of thinking about education, childhood and subjectivity, and it has been consistently associated with providing children an aesthetic space that is socially liberating. This genealogy also serves as a reminder that contemporary practice is built on many histories, of which the theatre-in-education movement, though influential, was only one small part. Learning lessons from the past sheds new light on the policies and practices that inform twenty-first century theatre education, and insists that we attend to the principles that inspired our egalitarian predecessors. In this introduction to the second part of the book, I shall summarize some of the ideas from the past that have been recycled to address contemporary concerns and which will, therefore, reappear in the chapters that follow.

There were strong moral and political imperatives that inspired the development of theatre education; the idea that great art is 'civilizing' and artistic practice is 'humanizing' seem elitist and prejudicial today, not least because it begs questions about whose idea of civilization is envisioned and who, or what, the Western ideal of 'human' excludes. They are both related to very specific values and belief systems, 'thick concepts' as Bernard Williams described them, that represent contemporary notions of goodness (Williams, 1973). More specifically, the integration of life and art was informed by the grand narratives of Liberalism and Marxism, where ideas about what constituted the good life were differently inflected. There was, however, some general agreement about specific aspects of cultural and social practice that shaped the development of theatre education in the twentieth century. There was a shared distrust of commercial theatre which was widely considered exploitative and morally degrading; it was generally believed that the arts would promote social cohesion, either by cultivating the nation in Liberal values or, in Marxist terms, that it would unite the working classes and mobilize the class struggle. Traces of both perspectives remain visible today; theatre still holds a place in urban regeneration in post-industrial societies, theatre-making continues to be charged with healing social division, and public access to the arts remains an important indicator of social capital and civic participation.

Each interrelated history on which theatre education is built shows how children's cultural geographies are defined by their material conditions of living and the places in which they live and learn. Educationally and artistically, there is a belief that participating in theatre, particularly in schools, should have a social role rather than fulfil a commercial function, reflecting the Arnoldian perception that an education should be concerned with *becoming* rather than *having*, and the Morrisonian perspective that making art promotes happiness, social equality and well-being. Theatre education continues to be associated with a sense of belonging, and it remains widely understood that both old and new forms of theatre have the potential to raise questions about identity, diaspora and nationhood in ways that the social and educational reformists would recognize. Of course, change is gradual, and no one would assume that everything suddenly transformed on the stroke of midnight at the end of the millennium; but this convenient temporal marker does allow us to reflect on how new social circumstances are demanding a response. So, what *has* changed?

From industrialization to globalization

If one of the central concerns for the nineteenth and twentieth century theatre-makers and educationalists was industrialization, the major challenge that faces their twenty-first-century successors is globalization. Of course globalization is not a new phenomenon – Marx and Engels identified that industrialization had introduced a world market in the *Communist Manifesto* in 1848 – but the process of extending capitalism beyond national boundaries is taking on a new momentum in the twenty-first century. Globalization has redefined the social implications of cultural policy, as Australian media scholar Terry Flew has observed:

> Creative industry sectors are key innovator sites and digital content production and distribution in an era of globalization and digital networked structures, where there is a premium being attached to creativity and innovation as sources of competitive advantage for the enterprises, cities,

regions and nations. This is different to the modernist paradigms of cultural policy as the preservation of a great tradition or the integration of citizens into a common national culture. (2009, p. 357)

Globalization has many definitions, but for the purposes of this argument I should like to isolate two aspects that are particularly significant for theatre education. The first relates to globalization as an economic development. Changing working patterns on a global scale mean that, in many Western economies, the production of ideas is more commercially valuable than the manufacture of products. These 'creative' or 'knowledge-based' economies, it is argued, require new forms of education that will enable young people to adapt to fast-changing world markets. The second is concerned with the cultural dimensions of globalization, and considers the social effects of a world that is increasingly interconnected through new technologies, where the imagination is manipulated by news media, where consumerism has become a leisure activity, and by which cultures are becoming increasingly homogenized.

Writing about the ways in which we are all implicated in globalization, Doreen Massey challenges the pervasive view that there is no alternative to globalized capitalism. She is particularly critical of the perception that countries which are not part of this globalized system are 'just "behind"' and they will eventually follow the West's lead. This is, she says, 'not a description of the world as it is so much as an image in which the world is being made' (2005, p. 5). My interest in the remainder of this book lies in investigating contemporary practices that challenge the perception that there is no alternative to the image of the globalized world. I am interested in how many of the ethical and artistic concerns that have long been associated with the egalitarian and vernacular practices of theatre education have been recycled, remoulded and recast in practice for the twenty-first century by teachers, artists, theatre-makers and young people. This raises questions about the challenges young people face in globalized societies, and where they are placed, both literally in their lived environments, and theoretically in educational discourse. The cultural geographer Stuart C. Aitken argues that the contemporary crisis for young people is not primarily sociological or psychological but spatial and temporal. He makes the case that Western constructions of childhood have been globalized, and argues that the moral geographies of childhood need to take greater account of their spatiality and locality if they are to recognize where children's identities are situated, and how they relate to contemporary structures of cultural and social power (Aitken, 2001).

The narrative of this book is defined by my response to the challenges of globalization and contemporary geopolitical concerns, and asks how theatre education is maintaining its traditional commitment to providing learning experiences that are artistically challenging, socially engaged and egalitarian in this climate. The structure of the second part of this book is shaped by this political imperative, and the examples I have chosen are intended to illuminate these questions. Chapter 5 offers an analysis of the ways in which twenty-first century theatre education has been affected by educational policies designed to support creative economies, in which, as Flew described, creativity and innovation are seen as 'a source of competitive advantage' and, therefore, as integral to the success of globalization. This commodification of creativity has placed theatre education in an ambiguous position, I suggest, not least because it has introduced new sources of funding into the sector and brought a renewed interest in creative approaches to learning. What is interesting, however, is that despite education policies that are instrumental and economist, theatre practitioners and educationalists are continuing to work together in ways that are both artistically, culturally and socially engaged and inventive. This story provides the map for the second part of this book.

Increased global interconnectedness is demanding a reconsideration of how the creative processes of theatre-making might contribute equitably to education. To address this new cultural landscape, I have organized Chapters 6, 7 and 8 around the political and cultural geographies of belonging. My geographical narrative is inspired by the work of Kwame Anthony Appiah, whose vision of equality depends not on simply privileging the local over the global but on understanding how human experience might be equitably conceived on smaller geographical scales. He envisions this interconnectivity as interlocking circles:

> It is because humans live best on a smaller scale that we should defend not just the state, but the country, the town, the street, the business, the craft, the profession ... as circles among the many circles narrower than the human horizon, that are the appropriate spheres of moral concern. (1998, p. 94)

To elucidate these 'spheres of moral concern' I have chosen to revisit questions of home, nationhood and intercultural dialogue that first preoccupied social reformists in Chicago's Hull House over a hundred years ago when Jane Addams recognized the loneliness of migrant workers. Chapter 6 reflects on dramatic representations of home, and considers how dramatizing the risks and security of life in families and on the street may both represent idealizations of home and promote social justice. The main case study in this chapter is a programme in New Zealand that explores contemporary issues of family violence by revisiting classic theatre-in-education methodologies, and my analysis of this sensitive work moves between an interpretation of artistic practice, the sociology of the family and cultural geographies of childhood. Chapters 7 and 8 reflect on my own practice-as-research project, *Performing Citizenship, Investigating Place* in three contrasting contexts, Southall, United Kingdom, Mihara, Japan and the Cape Flat townships in South Africa. In Chapter 7 I am interested in revisiting questions of theatre and national identity that preoccupied Matthew Arnold and the Hull House volunteers. In this practice, I investigated how third-generation British Asian young people are constructing their national identities by working with them on *The Tempest*. In Chapter 8 I examine questions of global citizenship by reflecting on two cultural exchange projects in South Africa and Japan. This practice, which differs from Theatre for Development in that it focused on the aesthetic, artistic and citizenship education of young people rather than addressing community issues, taught me to question my own horizons of expectation and cultural assumptions. This chapter is a response to Aitken's challenge to recognize the ways in which childhood is constructed locally, spatially and linguistically, and it is in this context that I revisit debates about progressive education raised in Chapter 3. The ninth chapter addresses questions surrounding the pace of technological change, and returns to metaphors of domestic life to raise questions about how scientific knowledge becomes poetic in theatre. In the final chapter I return to the aesthetic space of the theatre, and ask how theatre as a cultural institution is helping to shape forms of participation, and how theatre-makers are continuing to encourage children and young people both as artists and as citizens.

Moving in ever-widening circles from the home, street, nation and to the world and back full circle to domestic spaces, maps the cultural geographies that, Appiah suggested, relate to spheres of moral concerns within a globalized world. In each case, however, my intention is to show how they overlap and intersect rather than represent essentialized cultural identities. Within each chapter, therefore, although the starting point is provided by a specific social space, my aim is to contest any suggestion that cultural practices can be contained in a 'hierarchy of neatly ordered boxes' as Doreen Massey puts it (1998, p. 125). On the contrary, I am alert to the ethical and political possibilities of social interaction, both within and beyond the fictional and live spaces of theatre.

Moving on: Recycling and renaming

Before I move on, it is worth pausing for a moment to consider how the various practices associated with theatre education have been described. Tony Jackson provided useful definitions of different educational interventions made by professional theatre-makers and approaches to teaching drama in schools in 1993. His lexicon included simulation, education in theatre, educational theatre and young people's theatre, each of which have left significant and important traces in twenty-first century theatre education. New social circumstances bring new forms of theatrical expression and, in this respect, theatre-makers who work in twenty-first century theatre education are following their predecessors by bringing together cutting edge contemporary theatre and new educational ideas. In practice, I have found that although some people are finding specialist terms such as 'process drama' useful descriptors of educational practice, theatre-makers are more likely to discuss their work in terms of the theatre forms they are using – such as site-specific performance, installation, autobiographical performance, promenade performance, scripted plays or multi-sensory theatre – all of which are terms that are widely recognized both inside and outside educational settings.[1]

In addition to these descriptions of specific forms of practice, I shall use three generic terms to delineate specific domains of practice and divisions of labour – theatre education, drama education and theatre for young audiences. *Theatre education* involves professional theatre-makers working with young people in all kinds of educational settings and learning environments, including schools, hospitals, theatres, museums and heritage sites. This work may be undertaken by free-lance practitioners, or those who work for companies that specialize in theatre education or they may be part of a bigger theatre or cultural organization. *Drama education* is taken to refer to the teaching of drama in schools, whether this is undertaken by specialist drama teacher teaching to examination level in secondary schools, or by teachers as part of an integrated curriculum in primary schools or arts teachers who want to use drama to illuminate different subjects in imaginative ways. *Theatre for Young Audiences* involves professional performance that is particularly designed for children and family audiences within the cultural sector. It often has high production values and strong links with education, as Shifra Schonmann has rightly identified (2006, p. 26). Theatre for young audiences may be less instrumentally educational than some approaches to theatre education, but my decision to include it in this book is built on the view that all imaginative and challenging theatre extends children's cultural education, and the experience of seeing the work of professional theatre-makers contributes to their artistic development. Although each set of practices operates in different places and spaces, and each carries different traces of past methodologies, there is often considerable overlap, and the sharing of practices through established networks and informal partnerships enriches the conversation.[2]

In the chapters that follow, I will consider the ways in which twenty-first century theatre-makers are finding vernacular spaces for creative learning that Harriet Finlay-Johnson might have valued. I will explore the role of the theatre in providing equitable spaces to learn, and examining the ways in which theatre continues to create new insights through interdisciplinary approaches to learning. This process of recycling ideas and practices from the past troubles the contradictions and tensions between the official 'map' of educational and cultural policy and the embodied and vernacular 'story' of theatre practice. It recognizes both the complexity of place in creating a sense of selfhood, and the openness to artistic innovation, new imaginings and social change that a progressive idea of space affords.

5

Globalization and Regeneration: Re-branding Creativity

Post-industrial landscapes: From political movement to corporate brand?

One of the arguments in this book is that theatre education has always been responsive to contemporary social circumstances, and it has often led the way in developing new educational practices. Three landscapes symbolize the changing educational climate in which drama and theatre education developed and flourished, each of which signify a different pedagogical approach to theatre and education. The first is a cityscape of Victorian factories, where the labour of the urban poor was exploited in dirty and dangerous environments. This provided the impetus for a second image that is closely related to urban deprivation but represents its idealized opposite, a pastoral utopia, an organic community in which happy and healthy children roam free among the fields. For many people this rural idyll was more often imagined than a lived reality, but it inspired a whole way of thinking about the social, cultural and physical well-being of children in which the arts played a central part. The third represents a futurist dream which introduced the clean lines of modernist architecture to city planning; bombed towns and overcrowded cities were regenerated as an optimistic vision of a new age, and one that saw the introduction of high-rise living, open-plan schools and black-box theatres. The twenty-first century has brought a new urban landscape which is equally significant for theatre education. The great industrial conurbations in the West have been left without their traditional factory employment and, as disused factories became part of a decaying cityscape, they have been newly regenerated as cultural quarters to attract affluent consumers with designer tastes. Empty warehouses have been converted into fashionable loft apartments, derelict factories refurbished as new art galleries, museums and theatres with names that recall their industrial past such as The Tobacco Factory (Bristol, UK), The Custard Factory (Birmingham, UK) and The Power House (Brisbane, Australia). Contemporary urban design favours open spaces and the bare brick of former industrial buildings, and where there were factories and docks there are now places that are conceived, in Lefebvre's terms, to provide the kind of cultural activities favoured by the metropolitan class. These cultural activities include theatres as well as the more obvious consumerist pleasures of restaurants, farmers' markets, craft stalls and designer shops. This landscape not only marks changes in fashion, it also signals a significant shift in the economy which is making new demands on education.

I am writing this part of the chapter in a cafe in Bristol, a city in the South West of England. The writing is an excuse for a day out; I am fond of Bristol, partly because I lived here when I was a teacher in my twenties which was a particularly happy time in my life. As I write, I am looking at streets and buildings I once knew well and allowing a delicious mix of melancholy and nostalgia to surface as I reflect on how the distance between then and now has changed both the city, and me. Bristol still feels like home, and I have always enjoyed the edginess and buzz of the city, although when I moved here the centre of Bristol was rather more ramshackle than it is now. In 1980, the first year I lived in Bristol, increasing tension between the police and the black community led to race riots in the St Paul's district. The city was, and felt, socially divided but it was also counter-cultural, bohemian and politicized. The Oscar-winning animation characters Wallace and Gromit were conceived in what looked like a disused garage behind my flat, and I was told that when the Arnolfini art gallery moved to a semi-derelict tea warehouse on the docks in 1975 the staff was unimpressed by its location, not least because it was a well-known haunt for prostitutes. In the bleak days of the Thatcher government in the 1980s, however, the presence of the arty crowd in city centre venues seemed to increase social division rather than enabling public access to the arts. As a drama teacher in a large secondary school, I was determined that the young people I taught would experience the arts and I hoped they would learn to enjoy all kinds of cultural activities, but this involved breaking down their assumptions about who was 'allowed' into these spaces. The school had been built and opened in the 1950s, one of the very first designed for the modernist utopia of comprehensive education, and it flourished in an era of full employment in the local ice-cream, tobacco and jam factories. By the 1980s, however, the school buildings were showing their age, the factories were closing and employment and deprivation was high. I vividly remember accompanying a group of fifteen-year-olds on a history trip to the harbour, and I was surprised to learn that several of them had never ventured as far as the city centre, even though it was less than a twenty-minute bus ride from their homes. When I left Bristol in 1992, the city was still quite run down.

As I look around now, from my waterside cafe, it is a very different picture. I can see the layers of the city's history in the architecture, but my overwhelming impression is that it is designed to promote tourism, support the creative industries and provide leisure facilities. Heritage sites along the harbour such as Brunel's iron ship the S.S. Great Britain have been restored and revitalized, and there are trendy bars and organic restaurants that advertise themselves as 'family friendly'. What has changed, since I left Bristol, is that cities have been increasingly charged with providing the cultural infrastructure that supports twenty-first century creative economies. My purpose in this chapter is to find a way to think through some of the theoretical, political and sociological implications of these changes, and to consider what happens to theatre education when cultural and educational policies meet twenty-first century economic agendas.

Creative cities and creative economies

My walk round Bristol's regenerated harbour helped me to imagine how economic changes are mapped on the landscape. Cities symbolize how people's working and domestic lives change over time and, although it was the pastoral idyll that held the imagination of William Morris and his contemporaries, the new utopia for many people in the twenty-first century is the creative city. Urban regeneration through the arts is not, of course, a new phenomenon – Henrietta and Samuel Barnett brought the arts to the slums of the East End of London in the early twentieth century. But whereas the Barnetts turned to the arts for moral and spiritual enlightenment, twenty-first century urban planners are interested in the role of the arts in building economic capacity. Regenerated post-industrial environments with thriving cultural quarters are regarded as one way to attract the most creative thinkers, and this means that cities have become instrumental in supporting local creative economies. Business 'gurus' Richard Florida and Charles Landry both market themselves as authorities on creativity, and lecture worldwide on the post-industrial 'creative city'. In his book *The Creative City: A Toolkit for Urban Innovators* (2008) Landry describes creativity to be 'like a new currency that is more sophisticated and more powerful than finance capital' and suggests that redesigned and rebranded cities are the places to incubate this profitable 'culture of creativity' (2008, p. xxv). Florida has similarly argued that cities, creativity and prosperity are intimately linked. In his book *Whose Your City?* (2008) he asserts that those with the 'today's key economic factors – talent, innovation, and creativity' are sufficiently affluent to move between different cities and have the economic capacity to choose where they might live at different times of life (2008, p. 10). As a consequence, there is huge competition among 'place promoters' to become European City of Culture, for example, or to host the Olympics, in the expectation that this will provide an opportunity to promote their city's cultural assets as 'the place to be' in a globally competitive market-place. 'Cities are central to neoliberal globalization' Doreen Massey states, and in her criticism of the inequalities brought by globalization she suggests that 'the competition between them is both product and support of the neoliberal agenda' (2007, p. 9).

Stylish urban environments and new opportunities in the creative industries in the West are dependent, therefore, on a globalized workforce. A good example of the effects of globalization on manufacturing industry is offered by James Dyson, a British engineer and producer of vacuum cleaners. In The Richard Dimbleby Lecture in 2004, he explained why he had re-located the assembly of all his products to Malaysia, and identified the impact this has had on his labour requirements in Britain:

> The biggest problem was that we had no local suppliers. Our British three-pin plugs were made in Malaysia. Our polycarbon plastics came from Korea. Our electronics came from Taiwan. It was a logistical nightmare. We needed our suppliers on our doorstep so that we could drive them to improve their quality and keep pace with technology ... Our engineers and scientists are in Wiltshire. For a company that depends on innovation, that's what counts. The know-how is here. It generates money for the British economy. (BBC TV, 2004)

'Innovation' and 'know-how' are located in the hands of highly skilled, well-paid British employees, who 'drive' an apparently docile workforce in Asian factories to produce high quality goods at low costs. Local economies in very different parts of the world have become increasingly mutually dependent, therefore, though this is not based on an equal spread of capital but on highly differentiated patterns of labour and uneven levels of opportunity. As a consequence, electronic goods such as mobile phones or computers are made very cheaply and even appear 'free' to Western consumers provided that they sign up for an expensive service package designed by those with the 'know-how' in knowledge-based economies. The move from selling goods to selling ideas and services means that inventiveness and creativity – in any domain or field, including science, engineering, digital technologies as well as the arts – is now essential to Western economies, but this system is also dependent on inequality on a global scale.

What is at stake here is how the commercial re-branding of creativity as a marketable commodity impacts on the social role of theatre in educational settings. As an official policy, the relationship between creativity and the economy represents a significant shift in educational priorities which was evident not only in the Labour government in the United Kingdom in the first decade of the twentieth century, but was also enthusiastically adopted in knowledge-based economies across the world. This way of thinking about creativity marks a move away from the nineteenth and twentieth century idea that creativity and cultural practice provide an antidote to the dehumanizing effects of industrial labour. One of the twenty-first century inequalities is related to mobility, and although highly qualified creative employees may travel from city to city to seek new opportunities in different parts of the world, this apparently 'free' labour market relies on the cheap labour of others who are compelled to remain static, prohibited from crossing geopolitical borders by strict international controls. As Massey argues, globalization is contributing to social injustice and personal suffering on an international scale:

> And so in this era of 'globalisation' we have sniffer dogs to detect people in the holds of boats, people dying in the attempt to cross frontiers, people precisely trying to 'seek out the best opportunities'... Capital, the rich, the skilled...can move easily about the world.. Meanwhile the poor and the unskilled from the so-called margins of this world are both instructed to open up their borders and welcome the West's invasion and whatever form it comes, and told to stay where they are. (2005, pp. 86–7)

So, while creative types are drinking their lattes in the designer cafes housed in former factories, children in countries such as Bangladesh are tied to making anything from designer trainers, cheap t-shirts and electronic components in working conditions that would have horrified social reformists in the nineteenth and twentieth centuries. So where does this leave theatre education? Where is the ethical position from which to speak?

Mapping policies: Globalization and creative learning

There is, of course, a pragmatic balance to be struck between a critique of the inequalities presented by globalization and the need to educate young people in ways that will benefit their futures, and for that reason it is worth considering both sides of the argument. One of the most influential voices in this debate is the British educationalist Ken Robinson, who is an advocate of educating for the creative economy. Robinson has argued that twenty-first century schools are still based on a system that served the needs of nineteenth century industrialization rather than twenty-first century global capitalism. In his book *Out of our Mind: Learning to be Creative* (2001), Robinson points out that industrial economies required two distinct forms of labour, one academic and the other manual, with those destined to become members of the professional classes (doctors, lawyers and teachers, for example) following an academic education, and the rest – the vast majority of the population – trained as manual labourers. This division was evident in the different types of education available – one academic and the other technical – which replicated the class system. Furthermore, the structures of education that served an industrial economy were time-based, in which the curriculum was organized into fixed timetables and children's progression was standardized according to their chronological age. This mirrored manufacturing industry, where labour was paid according to hours worked rather than completion of the task. Robinson rightly observes that the pace of technological innovation will require twenty-first century employees to continually renew and develop their skills. To meet this need he advocates a radical change in educational priorities in which creativity and creative approaches to learning become central to children's education:

> The companies, communities and nations that succeed in future will balance their books only by solving the complex question of human resources. Our own times are being swept along on an avalanche of innovations in science, technology and social thought. To keep pace with these changes,

or to get ahead of them, we will need all our wits about us – literally. We must learn to be creative. (2001, p. 203)

Without a jobs-for-life economy in the manufacturing industries, it is argued, there is a need for an increasingly flexible workforce in which creativity is an economic imperative. Robinson's emphasis on creativity in education as a way to 'balance the books' represents a new way of thinking in which creativity is not an expression of personal fulfilment, nor a Morrisonian socialist utopia, but a commercially exploitable and marketable commodity.

Official educational policies that privilege creativity and creative approaches to learning have undoubtedly been motivated by economic instrumentalism and fluctuating employment prospects. At the turn of the century, the British Labour government explicitly acknowledged that their vision for creativity in schools was directly related to the effects of globalization on the labour market:

> The Government recognises that young people need to develop the creative skills needed in the workplace of the future. Fast-moving technology and global communications call for an ability to produce creative solutions to complex problems. Creative teaching practices can help develop and release pupils' creativity, increasing their ability to solve problems, think independently and work flexibly.[1]

Accompanying this changing employment culture there has been a new value placed on a new 'type' of creative worker. Richard Florida, an American economist, claims that there is a newly emerged 'creative class' which is made up of professionals in a range of fields, including business, law, engineering, science and the cultural sector, who are talented, unconventional, passionate about their work and highly paid. He describes the Creative Class as having a 'crucial economic role' because it is:

> the norm-setting class of our time. But its norms are very different: Individuality, self-expression and openness to difference are favored over the homogeneity and 'fitting in' that defined the organisational age. (2002, p. 9)

Business 'gurus' such as Florida argue that members of the creative class possess specific personal and cognitive qualities, which are variously summarized as the ability to think divergently, to be spontaneous, to be flexible, to take risks, generate new ideas and so on.

On the level of policy, the Creative Partnerships scheme in England which began in 2002 with initial government funds of £40 million (rising to £150 million by 2008) illustrates the relationship between the skills needed to extend globalized economies and creativity in education. Describing the United Kingdom as a 'creative hotspot', Creative Partnerships was designed to build sustainable partnerships between the cultural and educational sectors, particularly in areas of post-industrial social deprivation and, in the medium and long-term, to revitalize local economies by producing creative-thinking employees.[2] Their definition of creativity, offered on their website, is written as a corporate statement of belief:

> We believe that creativity is not a skill bound within the arts, but a wider ability to question, make connections, and take an innovative and imaginative approach to problem solving. These are skills that are demanded by today's employers.[3]

This is an instrumental justification for creativity which links 'today's employers' with global capitalism. One of the policy objectives of Creative Partnerships is to encourage creative entrepreneurship, and however innovative and egalitarian the funded practice has been, the underlying political agenda is clear. Creativity equals profitability.

Let us just imagine – just for a moment – that theatre education accepts the challenge to encourage the kind of creative entrepreneurship that might appeal to global capitalists. What might it look like?

We might set an assignment that asks young people to create a piece of theatre that would attract the biggest audiences (or largest number of participants). It should be branded and exportable. Extra points would be awarded for merchandise opportunities – mugs, DVDs or posters would be a bit obvious. Designer items – computer bags, or pet accessories for example – might attract a special bonus. The show should either appeal to the exclusive metropolitan classes or to a mass market. A franchise might be established for participatory work in the corporate or charitable sectors, and games and activities would be subject to copyright.

In other words, this pedagogy would favour a particular kind of theatrical product. It must have novelty, and it must fill a gap in the market.

The assessment might include an interview to ascertain which person had been most creative. Students would be encouraged to compete, perhaps by denigrating the contribution of their teammates (rather like the popular reality TV show 'The Apprentice' in which competitors battle for a highly paid job with a well-known business personality). We would follow Richard Florida's advice and award top marks to those with the personal and cognitive qualities required by the creative class, and we would measure children's ability to think divergently, to be spontaneous, to be flexible, to take risks, generate new ideas and so on. We would ask them to award themselves marks according to how risky or spontaneous they were.

It is a theatrical pedagogy that would cultivate and reward a particular 'type' of person, and train them to work in a particular kind of society.

This Darwinian approach to creative learning may seem farfetched, or at the very least a joke too far, but it is not too distant from some education policies to be unimaginable; I have already seen children in primary schools being told to give themselves and their classmates marks out of ten for the level of risk they thought they had taken in their drama lessons, on the pretext that it would encourage them to develop creative skills. Although educationalists generally refute the myth that some personality 'types' are more innovative or creative than others, there is a risk that the system rewards the cluster of skills or intelligences that are most readily recognized by knowledge-based economies in post-industrial capitalist societies. Jean-Francois Lyotard, of course, anticipated this postmodern commodification of knowledge when he predicted that educational institutions would be required 'to create skills, and no longer ideals' (1984, p. 48).

The twenty-first century emphasis on an education for skills has led to policies that are informed by theories of management rather than theories of learning. The management consultant Charles Leadbeater, for example, who describes himself as 'a leading authority on innovation and creativity' has developed an approach to education called 'personalisation' that found favour with the New Labour British government in the first decade of the twentieth century.[4] His ambition is for schools to mirror the environment of the corporate sector by encouraging young people to become self-motivated learners and, by extension, economically effective employees. Leadbeater is principally concerned with how schools organize learning, and advocates more flexible work schedules 'modelled on airports'. This has led to education policies in which young people are required to develop specific 'Personal, Learning and Thinking Skills', one of which is creative thinking. Predictably, creative thinking skills closely mirror Florida's description of the qualities required by the creative class such as generating ideas, asking questions, making original connections, trying out alternatives and so on.[5] The Tools of the Mind project in Denver, United States, is more robustly theorized than the British model of personalized learning, but it also extols the virtues of self-regulation, which is described as 'the development of executive function in the early years and beyond'.[6]

The British drama educationalist Joe Winston has convincingly argued that approaches to learning that are based on 'personalisation' are 'the latest in a series of projects to reform education that follow a rational, managerial, technical model, concentrating on system changes and structures to increase effectiveness' (2010, p. 7). Winston is particularly critical of the ways in which this system devalues the professional knowledge and expertise of teachers, whose 'passions, interests, hopes and dreams' are ignored and undermined. The US educationalist Megan Boler has identified similar problems in skills-led curricula that promote emotional literacy, and her advice has implications for personalized approaches to creative learning:

> Any one of these skills may be taught in a way that invites analysis of social and cultural context, or instead closes down discussion and teaches a skill in purely individualistic terms. (1999, p. 103)

This suggests that there is a need for further analysis of the cultural and social implications of creative learning, and calls for a more nuanced understanding of the political debates that inform education policies. Personalized and creative learning may seem to offer a contemporary alternative to systems of learning that sought to divide the professional and labouring classes, but without a secure set of pedagogic principles and social values it is simply replacing an ideology based on disciplinary structures of power with another that favours self-regulation. As educationalists Richard Edwards and Robin Usher point out in their book, *Globalisation and Pedagogy: Space, Place and Identity*, the demands of a globalised economy are met particularly well by an education programme that encourages 'the cultivation of the self as an individualised reflexive project' (2000, p. 131).

The cultivation of selfhood is central to the success of a globalized, knowledge-based economy and represents a shift from ways of working that were based on models of people as machinery and instruments of industrialization. A more flexible working culture expects employees to be sufficiently emotionally committed to their work to self-regulate their use of time. Florida suggests that the self-management of the creative classes in the 'no-collar workplace' is integral to profitability:

> While the no collar workplace certainly appears more casual than the old, it replaces traditional hierarchical systems of control with new forms

of self-management, peer recognition and intrinsic forms of motivation, which I call *soft control*. (2002, p. 13. Italics original)

Florida's enthusiasm for 'soft control' warrants critical analysis. Not only does it often generate a freelance culture in which contracts are short-term, employment rights are limited and jobs are insecure, it also relies on a specific idea of selfhood. In their book *Empire* (2000) Michael Hardt and Antonio Negri have observed how the 'immaterial labour' of the contemporary economy has formulated 'a new theory of subjectivity...that operates primarily through knowledge, communication, and language' (2000, p. 29). They describe this emphasis on self-cultivation as 'biopolitics', a word they use to conceptualize where power is situated in contemporary life. In a disciplinary society, they argue, authority was exerted on individuals from above through hierarchical institutions such as prisons, factories, schools and so on. By contrast, in today's 'society of control' the locus of power has shifted from social institutions to 'flexible and fluctuating networks' – the 'soft control' that Richard Florida approves. As part of this process, they suggest, the 'social forces of capitalism' have become internalized and embodied as part of people's personal aspirations (2000, pp. 23–5).

One of the implications of this way of thinking is that the process of creative innovation is not confined to designing goods and services, it also extends to a theory of subjectivity that emphasizes personal transformation, self-reflexivity and self-regulation as an 'executive function' even in early years education. If the social dimension of theatre education that was so respected in the twentieth century is to be revised and revitalized for the twenty-first, there is need for those who value its oppositional voice to find alternatives to the individualized theories of creative learning that, as Craft, Cremin and Burnard point out, dominate contemporary policy and educational research (2008, p. xxii). In broader sociological terms, Zigmunt Bauman suggests, the contemporary culture of individualism actively generates consumerism, encouraging people to continually re-invent themselves and to crave new products that reflect their new image. Without a jobs-for-life economy societies of control have created the circumstances in which people willingly re-invent themselves within 'flexible and fluctuating networks' to create new ways of living and adapt to changing patterns of employment (2005, pp. 10–11). Bauman describes this kind of fast-moving, consumerist and networked society as 'liquid', a term he uses to express the transitory qualities of this form of contemporary life.

Image and imagination

In *Liquid Life*, Bauman comments that children were always thought to be the nation's future, but they are now 'first and foremost tomorrow's consumers' (2005, pp. 112–13). From the perspective of education, which is still organized by nation-states, I would contest the detail of Bauman's view but it is the case that national *prosperity* rather than Matthew Arnold's ideal of national *cohesion* that is now shaping many official policies for creativity in education across the world. Bauman's argument that the idea of childhood has changed is similarly persuasive; he suggests that today's ideal image of childhood is not based on 'the (romantic) notion of innocence' but on children whose 'knowing, choosing self' indicates a culture of consumerism that is cultivated by increasingly nuanced and performative marketing strategies (2005, pp. 113–14). This puts pressure on children. Baz Kershaw has argued that today's society is constructed and governed by the globalized media images of late-capitalism, and this means that 'all human life has become theatricalised and dramatised' (2007, p. 12). This emphasis on the theatricalization of life in this globalized, world (dis)order raises new questions about the traditional role of artists as social critics, and how, and in what ways, theatre education might continue to provide a voice of opposition to the commodification of culture and childhood.

The debate turns on how the imagination is conceptualized and understood. In his study of the cultural implications of globalization *Modernity at Large: Cultural Dimensions of Globalization* (1996), Arjun Appadurai extends a spatial metaphor by arguing that the most significant component in the new global cultural order is the imagination. The 'image, the imagined and the imaginary' have acquired new social functions in the era of globalization, according to Appadurai, in which the construction of imaginary landscapes is no longer regarded as a means of escape from the monotony of industrial labour, nor is the imaginary associated with the pastimes of the social elite, nor with the emancipatory powers of the arts – positions that are all recognizable at different times in twentieth century theatre education. In contemporary social life the imagination has become a commodified social practice which transcends national boundaries, Appadurai argues, a process that is mediated by digital technology and the mass media:

[T]he imagination has become an organized field of social practices, a form of work (in the sense of both labor and culturally organised practice), and a form of negotiation between sites of agency (individuals) and globally defined fields of possibility. (1996, p. 31)

Appadurai describes the culture of globalization as a series of 'scapes' – including the *mediascapes* of electronic and digital communication and the *ideoscapes* of mediatized political imagery – which constitute an imagined world that is often deeply and personally felt. He suggests, however, that the fantasy of an imagined life that has been fuelled by the mass media is often painfully remote from actual possibilities. For those for whom conditions are harsh, he argues, the difference between their own lives and their imagined counterparts presents an 'ironic compromise between what they could imagine and what social life will permit' (1996, p. 54).

The idea that the imagination represents 'a form of work' suggests that one of the jobs for those employed in the commodified creative industries is to sell goods and ideas by appealing to consumers' imaginations. Maurya Wickstrom offers a contemporary example of how this 'ironic compromise' between the imagination and lived experience is exploited by homogenized globalized brands that particularly target young people. Wickstrom suggests that brands such as Disney and Nike have introduced creative forms of marketing that produce highly theatricalized shopping experiences, in which the consumer enters carefully managed store environments in which consumption and entertainment are intimately linked. The story of the brand is experienced spatially and at first hand, through which consumers come 'to embody the resonances of the brand as feelings, sensations, and even memories' (2006, p. 2). She describes this form of affective identification with consumer products as a *brandscape,* a term she uses to describe the ways in which the brand becomes 'performed' in ways that are very seductive and often hard to resist. Using the example of the experience of shopping for dolls at the American Girl Palace (a store in Manhattan), Wickstrom illustrates how the shop positions girls to identify with a particular form of Americanization. Each doll can be fashioned to match her owner's colouring, and the experience of shopping can include an hour long in-store musical *The American Girl Review* in which, according to Wickstrom, only those who accepted 'American values' are regarded as 'fully human' (2006, p. 149). Citing Hardt and Negri's concept of biopolitics, Wickstrom suggests that 'power in global capitalism depends on its ability to spread laterally, across geographical boundaries, through virtual space, and in the bodies and affective responses of human beings' (2006, p. 105). It is the affective responses to specific brands that make this marketing so effective. And looking at the American Girl Palace website, I have to admit that if I were still a little girl I would have badly wanted one of those dolls, especially if my friends all owned one. As Wickstrom confesses in relation to her own somatic responses to Niketown in New York City, brandscapes similarly exercise a powerful, personal and internalized imaginary.

Globalization is, therefore, not only homogenizing cultures by encouraging personal identification with global brands, it is also challenging faith in the moral authority of the imagination. Appadurai's insight that the imagination has become commodified, as a place in which power can be constituted and reproduced in the contemporary globalized world, has significant implications for the ethics and politics of twenty-first century theatre education. If brandscapes can create a collective sense of belonging through a shared affective and somatic experience, if the imagination has become a social practice and a site of consumer and political power, and if embodied learning can assimilate cultural memories of consumer products, it follows that identification with a performative event does not necessarily extend theatre education's traditional commitment to social justice. There are two questions that emerge for me from this insight. The first relates to the social responsibilities of theatre and theatre-makers in this era of globalization, and asks how theatre, as an art form and cultural practice, offers an ethical and aesthetic alternative to the commodification of the imagination. The second question is both pedagogical and political, and asks if there are other ways to conceptualize creativity that avoid the link between creative learning and global capitalism. My aim in asking these questions is to bring policy and practice more closely in alignment, and to find more robust ways to recognize the significant contribution that theatre practitioners, teachers and young people continue to make to an education that is both equitable and socially engaged.

Dramatizing the imagination: From arts education to creative learning (and back again)

My trip to Bristol prompted me to wonder what had happened to the young people we had taught, and if any had maintained an interest in the arts beyond school. Part of the vision for the arts faculty I had led was to invite artists into school to work alongside young people, and we scraped up money where we could in the hope that, by working with 'live' artists, the young people would begin to see them not as remote celebrities (or even dead!) but as everyday people who just happened to make their living from the arts. We also hoped that the young people we taught, some of whom came from deprived backgrounds, would consider careers in the arts (the term 'creative industries' had yet to be invented in the late 1980s and early 1990s). In some ways this anticipated the Creative Partnerships scheme that followed nearly twenty years later, which encouraged young people to consider creative careers. I spent some time trawling the web-pages of Friends Reunited to see what had happened to some of these young Bristolians, now in their early 30s. Reading their names and their short biographies was a moving experience, and I restricted my search to one year group, a class of around 350 students of whom 182 were listed on the site. Almost all still lived in Bristol, and many seemed to socialize with the same circle of friends. As I clicked on each name, I was surprised how many were still involved in the arts in some way or another, either through their leisure activities (playing in a band and painting were most often listed), or through their work. A significant number were working in the arts, following careers in TV or theatre in a range of roles, including carpenters, journalists and electricians, and one woman had left Bristol to become a community artist.

I wondered how far our teaching had influenced these young people, of course, but it also made me reflect on educational changes that had happened between then and now. At the time, the term creative learning was not in use and, inspired by Ken Robinson's work on arts education, we tried to make connections between different art forms. We did not find the idea of generic skills or similar creative processes across the arts particularly useful, but we did design a curriculum that allowed us to see how the arts illuminated each other sociologically, culturally and historically. I remember one particularly lively project about the 1960s, where the musicians learnt about rock music, the art department worked on pop-art, the dancers learnt about jazz choreographers and the twist and, in drama, we experimented with agit-prop street performance and 'Happenings'. Each was infused with an understanding of the culture and social history of the time, and the students were asked to consider why this explosion of counter-cultural creative energy had occurred across all art forms. It is here that the shift in terminology from arts education to creative learning is instructive. In policy terms, creative learning is identified with the acquisition of marketable skills which might be transferred to many different contexts, both commercial and leisure, whereas arts education adds the dimension of social engagement and cultural understanding which Megan Boler found lacking in a skills-led curriculum. In the 1980s and 1990s, despite some very heated debates about the ways in which drama and theatre might be taught in schools, we all took it for granted that the arts play a symbolic and ideological role in society, whether to maintain the Romantics' vision that artists have a role as social critics in the Western aesthetic tradition, or whether performative events represent, for example, community cohesion, ritual celebration or rites of passage. However construed, it is this interest in the social, personal and cultural dynamic of the arts that marks the distinction between creative learning that serves an economic agenda ('having' as Matthew Arnold described it) and theatre education that attends to 'being' and considers the social effects of culture in the twenty-first century.

Throughout this chapter I have been careful to stress that my questions about the politics of creative learning are levelled against official policy – the map of educational discourse – rather than the messier story of theatre education practice. Policies promoting creative learning may have been informed by global capitalism, but they have also introduced a new dynamic into theatre education, not least because the fusion of creativity and the economy has introduced much-needed new sources of funding into the sector which has enabled theatre-makers, teachers and young people to work together for sustained periods for the first time since the demise of TIE in the late 1980s. Teachers and theatre practitioners have always found inventive ways to respond to the prevailing social conditions, and these new partnerships have enabled them to make work with young people that is both artistically exciting and impressively socially aware. Within this context, the British government's decision to withdraw funding from the highly successful Creative Partnership scheme in 2010 is a retrograde step that will rob young people of the opportunity to develop artistically and acquire cultural capital, particularly in areas of social deprivation. Furthermore, theatre companies that occupy space in regenerated cultural quarters are often acutely sensitive to their privileged position and, as I shall investigate in Chapter 10, theatre professionals are working energetically to ensure that young people from many different backgrounds participate in their youth theatres and learning programmes. De Certeau's metaphor of the map and the story is particularly apposite here, and although the 'map' of official educational policies may seem to cut up theatre education's history of social engagement, the story of contemporary practice cuts right across this perception.

In times when government funding for the cultural sector and the arts in education is under threat, it is even more important to ask what might be lost when arts education is rebranded as creative learning. Well, there is a risk that the uncritical assimilation of creative learning agendas into theatre education will lead to the loss of theatre-makers' voices as cultural critics who use their knowledge of the art-form to shape new ways to imagine. It is interesting in this context that contemporary playwrights have offered a voice of opposition to globalization and, in a revision of the tactics of twentieth century political activists, anti-globalization protesters have used performance as a way of drawing attention to their views on the streets and in cyber-space. The Scottish playwright David Greig offers a clear articulation of one of the social roles of theatre in this political climate. He argues that the liveness, roughness and unfinished quality of theatre can present an alternative to the packaged manipulation of the imagination by the globalized mass media. Theatre, Greig suggests, offers a place to open up 'the multiple possibilities of the imagination' and enables audiences and theatre-makers to unfix packaged, second-hand and commodified images of the world (2008, p. 212). Echoing Appadurai, Greig comments that 'if the battleground is the imagination, then the theatre is a very appropriate weapon in the armoury of resistance' (2008, p. 219). Greig has dramatized his position in his play for young people, *Yellow Moon: The Ballad of Leila and Lee* (2006), in which the imagination is represented as a contested space which can be manipulated in consumer culture. *Yellow Moon* uses a mixture of action and narration to tell the story of Stag Lee, a troubled but charming teenager who makes a snap decision to leave home because he has murdered his mother's boyfriend. He takes Leila with him, a quiet, high-achieving Muslim girl with an obsession with celebrity and a propensity for self-harm which, she claims, makes her feel real:

> When Leila Sulieman cuts herself she feels like she is real. Like she's real like she's in a story. Like she's real like she's in a story. Like she's real like there's someone somewhere who wants to take her picture without her permission. (2007, p. 8)

This brief moment of reality Leila finds in self-harm fades quickly into self-loathing. Both Leia and Lee struggle to understand the difference between reality and their imagined worlds; Lee escapes from the unhappiness and brutality of his own world by imagining that his father is a gangster living in a large house in the Scottish Highlands, based on the flimsy evidence of one postcard. The incongruous pair travel from the city to the Scottish highlands in search of Lee's father, a journey that takes them into a dangerously bleak landscape from where they discover that Lee's father is not a wealthy landowner, but 'Drunk Frank' who makes ends meet, erratically, as a gamekeeper. Greig presents a landscape that is not a utopian child-garden but a dystopian threat – remote, barren and inhospitable – but it is also a place of self-discovery, captured by the repeated metaphor of a stag. Towards the end of the play, just before the last, painful dénouement of the plot, the narration builds the dramatic tension by refusing the three central characters the fantasy of a happy ending:

> We sit among the ash and smoke on two hot rocks by the stream and watch the sun go down.
>
> Please let that be the end. (2007, p. 48)

This beautifully crafted play acts as an essay about the imagination, its dangers, its comforts and its delusions, as each character grapples with how to tell – and write – the story of their lives.

Edward Bond, whose plays for young people similarly place characters at the extreme edge of danger, has commented that 'our corrupted imagination turns reality into a nightmare' (2000b, p. 57). Greig's play *Yellow Moon* dramatizes the tragedy of this corruption and, by drawing attention to theatre as a mode of storytelling, insists that audiences ask themselves about the ways in which the imagination is used, and how it can be commodified and abused.

It is because the imagination is subject to manipulation and abuse that a renewed case for theatricality in education must be made. Josette Féral, writing in a special edition of the journal *Substance* dedicated to Theatricality (2002), explains the social significance of the term in words that evoke Lefebvre. Theatricality creates a 'gap', Féral argues, 'between everyday space and representational space, between reality and fiction', and it is this gap that 'obliges us to see differently' (2002, p. 11). She describes theatricality in terms of its affects:

> It [theatricality] creates disjuncture where our ordinary perception sees only unity between signs and their meanings. It replaces uniformity with duality. It perceives the friction and tensions between the various worlds it observes, and obliges us to see differently. (2002, p. 11)

This suggests that, although creativity may be generated in the performance of everyday life, theatre frames and shapes everyday life into embodied, symbolic and aesthetic forms. In his book, *Theatre & Globalization* (2009) Dan Rebellato argues in similar terms that theatre has a particular ethical and aesthetic role in the globalized world of the twenty-first century:

> We will need to draw on theatre's particular mode of production – its gaps and complexities – to offer an arsenal of experiences that can help us to grasp the everywhere and the everyday. (2009, p. 85)

One of the challenges to contemporary theatre education, therefore, is how to use performative pedagogies to construct alternative narratives to contemporary biopolitical consumer culture that exploits the imagination. To borrow Wickstrom's words, this might be achieved theatrically and symbolically, by 'naming what threatens us' (2006, p. 12).

Creativity as spatial and cultural practice

Finding ways 'to grasp the everywhere and the everyday' requires a set of pedagogic principles that are politically different from the individualized theories of creative learning evident in many education policies. One way to conceptualize how creativity might be re-envisioned is to analyse the relationship between creativity and the materiality of place, thereby opening a way to explore the social and political dynamic of creative practice that has been missed by focusing on creativity as the skill-set of a particular type of person who generates a marketable commercial product. The social anthropologists Tim Ingold and Elizabeth Hallam have offered a spatial analysis of creativity that challenges the perception that creativity defines specific personal skills or indicates particular kinds of product. Using a theatrical metaphor, they contend that all aspects of life involve improvisation – 'there is no script for social and cultural life' (2007, p. 1) – and suggest that even daily routines and habitual patterns of behaviour are never repeated in exactly the same way. They suggest that creativity is integral to the flow of daily life:

> Creativity is a process that living beings undergo as they make their way through the world...It is that this process is going on, all the time, in the circulations and flows of the materials that surround us and indeed of which we make – of the earth we stand on the water that allows it to bear fruit, the air we breathe, and so on. (2007, p. 11)

In a strict sense, of course Ingold and Hallam are right that there is no script for everyday life, but there are repeated patterns of thinking, feeling and behaving that are repeated, often unconsciously, and this can serve as an obstacle to creativity. To understand creativity as cultural improvisation, as Ingold and Hallam suggest, is to understand that it is an embodied process that develops gradually over time. This way of thinking questions polarities between innovation and convention, suggesting that creative activity does not necessitate a break with the past nor does it assume that future patterns are inevitable. On the contrary, Ingold and Hallam acknowledge the importance of revisiting and reshaping past experiences which they see not as due to 'passive inertia but to its active regeneration' (2007, p. 6).

Conceptualizing creativity as part of the spatial practices of everyday life means that creativity is disassociated from the novelty-value of commercial products that, Ingold and Hallam suggest, characterize the discourses of modernity. They describe this paradigm shift in the following terms:

> Because improvisation is generative, it is not conditional upon the judgements of the novelty or otherwise of the forms it yields. Because it is relational, it does not pit the individual against either nature or society. Because it is temporal, it inheres in the outward propulsion from life rather than being broken off, as a new present, from a past that is already over. And because it is the way we work, the creativity of our imaginative reflections is inseparable from our performative engagements with the materials that surround us. (2007, p. 3)

The idea of performativity introduces the insight that living creatively is a fluid process that finds ways to negotiate the familiar and the new, and provides opportunities to re-imagine ideas, feelings and relationships with others as they shift and change over time. 'Social life is a task' they suggest, that relates to an entire set of relationships, both human and non-human (2007, p. 7). Citing Lebfevre's concept of rhythmanalysis, they suggest that all life's iterations and repetitions involve some form of cultural improvisation and movement. This means that there is an affective dimension to creative practice as new insights are generated in the light of new experiences. In some ways Ingold and Hallam's idea of creativity as cultural improvisation has resonance with Ervin Goffman's theories of the performance of everyday life, in which he argues that social roles are performed as a set of habitual behaviours (1959, p. 15). But instead of drawing attention to the multiple roles that people take in their everyday live, Ingold and Hallam focus their attention on ways in which the materiality of place shapes identities and sustains relationships.

In their book *Spaces of Vernacular Creativity: Rethinking the Cultural Economy* (2010), the cultural geographer Tim Edensor and his co-authors build on Ingold and Hallam's idea of creativity as cultural improvisation, and rehearse the argument that the concept of creative cities and the creative class privileges another set of middle-class tastes, and has re-branded artists as creative entrepreneurs. This new social distinction of taste, they argue, is articulated around a series of oppositions, some of which are described in spatial terms, such as local/global, suburban/ metropolitan, urban/ rural. Others hold implications about their consumerist appeal – cool/uncool, creative/ uncreative, commercial/ charitable and so on (2010, pp. 13–14). The ambition of the authors in Edensor's book is to identify and celebrate alternative, uncool or 'vernacular' spaces of creativity that are found in suburban gardens, for example, or community centres, garages and sheds. There has been some memorable experimental practice in 'found' spaces in recent years, and arguably the seriously 'cool crowd' are more likely to be seen at performances in semi-derelict spaces such as old swimming pools, disused factories and empty hotels than in more conventional theatre spaces. The idea of vernacular creativity, however, reasserts the value of creativity that has limited economic currency, and includes those who may feel excluded from the expensive cafés and designer spaces found in regenerated and gentrified cultural quarters. Re-focusing on the everyday and vernacular spaces in which creative activity happens allows a theorization of creativity to emerge that moves away from an uncritical acceptance of theories of learning designed to promote commercial entrepreneurship and rekindles discussions of value.

This emphasis on the vernacular spaces for creativity, when combined with an understanding of the representational space provided by theatricality, has the potential to re-vitalize William Morris's egalitarian ideal of creative practice for the twenty-first century. For theatre education, the recognition that creativity has a spatial, relational and temporal dynamic has a number of consequences. It affirms the importance of learning environments that value both the everyday processes of improvisation and the significance of tradition and cultural memory. This effectively challenges the binary opposition between the 'transmission model' of education and personalized learning. This outmoded polarity assumes that passing on cultural memories and traditions are necessarily authoritarian rather than interpersonal and improvisatory. These theories of creativity acknowledge the value of cultural histories and artistic traditions, and reassert the social dynamic of theatre education by inviting questions about the politics of cultural spaces and the values ascribed to creativity and contemporary cultural life. It brings the kinaesthetic imagination into the context of education, recognizing that creativity is generated in the performance of everyday life as well as in the embodied and aesthetic practices of theatre. This pedagogical approach revitalizes Lefebvre's materialist description of the everyday space of childhood, recognizing 'its hardships, its achievements, and its lacks' (1991, p. 362).

The next part of the book takes forward the idea of creativity as cultural improvisation, and suggests that the materialism of place a way to understand contemporary ways of life. Young people's cultural geographies and their experiences of public and private places are, I suggest, symbolic of how they are valued in society and a contemporary mark of social justice. For that reason, the chapters follow a geographical narrative, addressing how questions about home, nation, internationalism, and the spatial metaphors of science have been explored in theatre education, before returning to the symbolism of theatre as a cultural space in the final chapter of the book. Perhaps most importantly, by reconceptualizing creativity as cultural improvisation I hope to loosen discussion of its practices from the clutches of economic instrumentalism, and open the way to recognize that creativity embodies a range of personal, cultural and social practices.

6

Dramatizing Home: Places of Safety and Risk

The symbolic space of home

The twenty-first century's preoccupation with travel and mobility has posed new questions about the symbolic space of home, both as a domestic dwelling and as a more abstract idea of somewhere where people feel they belong. Popular conceptions of the word 'home' tend to conjure images of stability, warmth and comfort but, as Doreen Massey suggests, the symbol of home as a place of unchanging comfort and familial stability frequently represents nostalgia for a lost or 'unspoilt' world in which 'the imagination of going home ... so frequently means going 'back' in both space and time' (2007, pp. 124–5). This means that the idea of home is often suffused with childhood memories, and suggests emotional attachments to places that may be both geographically and historically distant. Childhood memories are always selective and partial, however, and this means that home occupies a symbolic space that is complex and sometimes contradictory. In this chapter I shall investigate some of the tensions and ambiguities that surround dramatic representations of home in contemporary theatre education.

Current interest in the ideal of home as a powerful symbol of stability and belonging has coincided with the perception that home life has become dangerously fragmented. Nigel Thrift has claimed that mobility is the dominant structure of feeling in contemporary society, and this suggests that the stability of home and the durability of relationships have been thrown into question, not because mobility is a new way of life, but because it constitutes a new social aspiration in an era of globalization (1994, pp. 212–15). Commenting on how the imperative to keep moving has affected twenty-first century society, Zigmunt Bauman suggests that consumer societies have affected domestic relationships. He argues that the liquid life he associates with the twenty-first century culture of consumption has extended to liquid love, in which social networks are easily constructed and dismantled, relationships are disposable, and lovers carelessly 'move on' by simply refusing emails and deleting text messages (2003, p. xii). Contemporary life is caught between the pursuit of two values, freedom and security, he suggests, both of which are deemed necessary for happiness in a liquid society. Finding a constructive balance, rather than a compromise, between these two oppositions is, according to Bauman, fraught with anxieties:

> The problem, however, is when *security* is missing, free agents are stripped of their confidence without which freedom can hardly be exercised ... When, on the other, it is *freedom* that is missing, security feels like slavery or a prison. (2003, p. 36)

To counter this problem Bauman yearns for what he describes as 'good old fashioned commitment', although he rather forgets that while the traditional family structure provided solace and joy to many, it also left other people struggling in unhappy homes with relationships that were so enmeshed that people felt trapped, unable to leave or love, and paralysed by fears of rejection and social isolation.

So when was this period of 'good old fashioned commitment'? How did home become so deeply associated with the ideal of the family? Why does home and family remain such a potent ideal? Just as the social imaginary of childhood as a rural idyll was a convenient but well-meaning nineteenth century fiction, contemporary ideologies of home as a place of stability and comfortably localized identities are similarly based on a mythical image of the past. In industrialized countries the nineteenth century saw mass migration from the country to the city, and it was during this period that the nuclear family became increasingly revered both as a personal ideal and a symbol of a moral society. The privatized nuclear family came to represent the social stability that had been associated with smaller agricultural communities, and in the industrial revolution the family unit assumed increasing responsibility for children's well-being and discipline. As Jane Humphries points out in her essay on the working-class family, Marxist historians observed that the rise of the domestic nuclear family as a social norm served the interests of industrial capitalism particularly well, not least because it ensured that parents taught their children the kind of discipline required by the labour market (1982, pp. 198–9). This had significant implications for how home came to be understood, with personal and political consequences. During the twentieth century, as historian Norbert Elias identified in his book *The Civilising Process* (1978), the nuclear family became a self-regulating unit in which structures of power shifted from external, social constraints on behaviour to more informal processes of self-monitoring. It became expected, Elias argues, that moral values would be internalized through family relationships. The social and psychological converge in the idealization of the domestic space of home, therefore, representing a new biopolitics in which, as social psychologist Nikolas Rose argues, 'each normal family will fulfil its political obligations best at the very moment it conscientiously strives to realize its most private dreams' (1990, p. 209).

Home can be a place of refuge, a vernacular space in which intimate relationships are forged and played out, and in which people expect to feel safe and protected from the outside world. In his book *Capitalism, the Family and Personal Life*, Eli Zaretsky argues that the expectation that the nuclear family offers a sanctuary from the outside world can place immense strain on individual members:

> Under capitalism, almost all of our personal needs are restricted to the family. This is what gives family its resilience, in spite of the constant predictions of its demise and this also explains its inner torment; it simply cannot meet the pressure of being the only refuge in a brutal society. (1976, p. 141)

According to this analysis, although the intense emotional bonds that circumscribe familial relationships may guard individuals' well-being very successfully, there is also a risk that some members may feel constrained by the expectation that the family will meet all their emotional needs. Writing from a feminist perspective, however, Iris Marion Young argues in her 1997 essay 'House and home: Feminist variations on a theme' that although the experience of home can be oppressive to some, it is nevertheless an important site of identity formation. She argues that 'while politics should not succumb to a longing for comfort and unity, the material values of home can nevertheless provide leverage for radical social critique' (1997, p. 157). This radical critique rejects nostalgic fantasies of a lost home and conservative idealizations of family life, but following the African-American author bell hooks, Young argues that the 'homeplace' – a term hooks coined to describe an extended community of friends and family – can offer a safe and emotionally fulfilling space in which social identities can be fostered.

Dramatic representations of the home and family life in theatre education are generally focused on investigating the relationship between social attitudes and personal experience; theatre is particularly well placed to illuminate the social complexities of home, and the emotional interdependence that is associated with family life. Different kinds of dramatic interventions have been funded that respond directly to the needs of those who are 'at risk' in some way, including projects for young people who are homeless or refugees, many of whom have escaped unimaginable dangers in their homes or homelands. There are also theatre education programmes that explore domestic relationships, and the first case study in this chapter was part of a government-funded social welfare programme that aimed to encourage increased disclosure of family abuse. Home is a place of identity-formation, and this suggests that dramatic representations of home often act as metaphors for wider social and psychological concerns. This chapter will focus on the dramatization of home as a domestic space which, as Edward Bond suggests, attends to bigger social questions. 'Each moment of drama' he writes, 'contains both the kitchen table and the edge of the universe' (2009, p. xi). My aim in this chapter is to question how the politics of home and 'homeplaces' are represented and understood, a process which involves weaving together the fictional representation of imagined domestic worlds with theories of home and the family and analyses of the cultural geographies of childhood and adolescents.

Myths and monsters: Dramatizing family violence

The vision of home as a happy sanctuary is, of course, appallingly remote from the actual experiences of many children. In this section I shall consider the dramatization of family violence, using the example of Everyday Theatre, a theatre education programme. Everyday Theatre formed part of the provision of Applied Theatre Consultants Ltd, a company run by the theatre educator Peter O'Connor who is based in Auckland, New Zealand and I observed the programme in October 2006 in Whangarei, Northland. The programme was funded by the government Department of Child, Youth and Family in New Zealand and delivered in the institutional setting of publicly funded schools with the explicit and instrumental aim to prevent child abuse, neglect and family violence.[1] The success of a participatory theatre in education programme about family abuse relies on young people's willingness to explore the complexities and intimacies of home life, and to make connections between the fictional world of the play and lived experience. I am interested in applying readings of sociological and psychological theories of family abuse to this case study, not to test its credibility as a piece of theatre against the presumed authenticity of lived experience, but to try to understand how home life was represented dramatically in a programme that needed to be sufficiently informed about the psychological effects of abuse to portray emotions that were plausible and recognizable to the young participants.

Dramatizations of family violence are more regularly consumed by a mass market through the media rather than in the theatre, and in these accounts of cruelty the relationship between the privacy of home and public responsibility is often ambiguous. Nikolas Rose has offered an analysis of the central paradox that has dominated popular debates about violence in the home. On the one hand, he argues, there is widespread criticism of state intervention into the privacy of family life, and increased surveillance by social workers and others involved in child welfare is regarded as evidence of a 'nanny state' or, more seriously, as a breach of family rights. Conversely, individual cases of child abuse often become highly publicized as examples of the scandalous neglect of the social services. 'The tabloid and popular newspapers', Rose argues, 'are the ones most lurid in their representations of abuse, most judgmental in their depiction of the perpetrators as monster and devils, and most vehement in their demand for retribution' (1990, p. 201). This recognizable paradox represents, according to Rose, a central ambiguity about how the social role of the family is perceived, and this contradiction becomes most visible in times of crisis. It is when the pressure snaps, Rose suggests, that judgmental distinctions between 'normal' and 'abnormal' families are made. 'Normal' families, he argues, are regarded as autonomous and self-regulating, whereas 'abnormal' families are thought to deviate by, for example, cultivating delinquents and harbouring abusers. The counter-discourse of abnormality also provides an explanation for popular images of abusers as monsters or other uncanny imaginings of evil; the witch or monster, as 'a public spectacle of abuse' signifies, in Rose's psychoanalytic terms, a projection of deep fears about the demons that may lurk within the privacy of the family's home life (1990, p. 202).

It is within this complex political and social context that Everyday Theatre's educational programme about family violence took place. Young people will be acutely aware of media images of abusers and abused, as well as the perils of state intervention, and this suggests that young people whose lives are affected by family violence may find themselves confronting issues in school they would prefer to avoid or leave at home. Some young people fear that their family's privacy will be invaded by welfare agencies, suggesting that they have internalized the idea that the need for state intervention represents a failure to live up to the ideal of autonomy and self-sufficiency that governs discourses surrounding the family. In their study of children's disclosure of family violence, Marianne Hester, Chris Pearson and Nicola Harwin (2000) note that children's secrecy often helps them to cope with the situation; children also want to protect those they love, and fear that however difficult the family dynamic may have been, once the secret is out their homes will be irrevocably changed, and not necessarily for the better.

The challenge that the cast of Everyday Theatre faced, both in script-development and in performance, was how to avoid rehearsing judgmental caricatures of the abuser and abused which, while they might be recognizable tabloid stereotypes, would do little to raise more nuanced questions about familial loyalty, emotional ties and patterns of trust that make up this complex social terrain. John O'Toole, who assisted the devising process, describes how they wanted to 'help the audience avoid easy stereotypes and a villain/ heroine narrative' (2009, p. 487). Their answer was to create a dramatic situation that represented the family as a network of multifaceted relationships, a decision that drew attention to the family as an interdependent social system rather than a set of individual and autonomous social actors. The programme followed the two-part structure of classic Theatre-in-Education, with a short play performed to two classes in the school hall, followed by workshops for each class led by two actor-teachers. The performance provided the set-up for this complicated family network, and was structured as if the family were characters in an arcade game, both in the performance and workshop, thereby providing a protective aesthetic frame through which the students interpreted the issues. One of the arguments that has been put forward to explain why theatre is an effective tool for addressing sensitive subjects in educational contexts is that the aesthetic form creates a distance between the issue and the participants. This has been well theorized by Anthony Jackson in his book *Theatre, Education and the Making of Meanings* (2007), in which he argues that aesthetic distance in participatory theatre 'enables the audience to both believe and not believe at the same time' (2007, p. 140). Dramatically, the conceit of the arcade game served this aesthetic purpose, and it also offered a plausible reason for devices that encourage reflection, such as freezing the action, tracking the characters' thoughts or for replaying the action to allow actors to comment on events the audience had witnessed. Creating a family situation that allowed the students to explore the cracks in the family system enabled Everyday Theatre to re-situate domestic relationships in the public sphere, thereby taking account of poverty, class, ethnicity and culture, while also recognizing the very real pain and emotional hurt that follows family violence in the private and domestic confines of home.

The plot revolved around two children, Bernie and April, both of whom are being hit by their mother, Helen. Helen's former husband Tony had been an unreliable father, consistently breaking his promises to his children. Both Helen and Tony have new partners, Michael and Nicky, neither of whom were prepared to address the family's problems directly. The portrayal of Helen, skilfully played by Evelyn Mann, lay at the heart of the Everyday Theatre programme because it was through this role that the ambiguities and complexities of the family as a system were represented. Initially, when the audience first saw Helen hit her daughter, the action was unexplained and this instantly demonstrated that violence towards children is inexcusable. As the plot unravelled, however, a more subtle set of explanations emerge that shed light on how this situation had arisen. It became clear that Helen's anger had been provoked by seeing Tony and Nicky shopping when he had previously reneged on a promise to look after the children, meaning that Helen and Michael had to cancel a much-needed weekend away. Mann's interpretation of the role followed this trajectory, Helen was an unsympathetic character at first; she dominated the space both physically and vocally by taking a central position on stage and by talking at the other characters in an unnecessarily loud voice. When she complained, with justification, that 'Nobody's listening to me!' the audience was asked to see that not only had she isolated herself by her rigid attitude and aggressive manner, her behaviour also represented habitual patterns of interactions within the family as a whole that limited productive communication. Writing from a sociological perspective, John J. Rodgers recognized the importance of the dramaturgy of the voice in family dynamics, suggesting that shared language patterns, active forms of listening and other vocal signifiers are a prerequisite for constructing consensual systems of meaning. He suggests that observing hierarchies of communication is revealing:

> Family discourses include a number of competing voices which may be more or less absorbed or negated in the processes of family interaction. The question of 'speaking for' the family becomes a highly problematic issue. Indeed, the very idea that someone within a family can fully understand and articulate the feelings of all family members in 'normal' circumstances is doubtful; at a time of crisis or severe family breakdown, it seems unlikely. (1996, p. 15)

In the context of the Everyday Theatre programme, watching who speaks for whom, who dominated conversations and whose voices were being marginalized demonstrated the emotional affect of family communication to the audience. This suggests that the students' observations of the performativity of the family interactions (as well as what they actually say) placed them in a position where their knowledge (or 'emotional wisdom' in O'Connor's terms) gave them the authority to offer advice that would help the family to change their emotional script.

The aim of the workshop was, ostensibly, for the students to find the password that completes the arcade game, but the activities encouraged them to consider the situation from multiple points of view, aided by actor-teachers who often worked in role. This meant that learning to reflect on the emotions that motivate change was implicit in the workshop's aesthetic. If, as P. J. Ney (1992) suggests, violence, blame, fear and threats are paralysing, serving to maintain the family system as it is, which, of all the complicated emotions that surround family abuse, might be turned to more productive use? It is here that an understanding of shame, both as an embodied experience and as a theoretical concept, seems particularly apposite. Caroline Abraham found in her study *The Hidden Victims: Children and Domestic Violence* (1994) that shame is a word that is associated with abuse, and is often invoked by both the abused and abuser. The report commissioned about the work of Everyday Theatre *Children's Voices on Family Violence and Child Abuse* (Ministry of Social Development 2008) reached similar conclusions, where shame – or being shamed – is a word used frequently by young people to describe the feelings associated with disclosure. This fear was invoked in the play, when Bernie and April discuss whether they should reveal the abuse:

> *Bernie*: Yeah right, who would we tell?
> *April*: [THINKS FOR A MOMENT] Nicky, we could tell Nicky!

Bernie: No! [B GRABS APRIL'S ARM AGAIN AND TWISTS.]
April: Ow! Why not?
Bernie: No! cos she would tell Dad, and Dad would tell the school and everyone would know, we'd be really shamed. Keep it to yourself.

Fear of exposure is closely allied to the fear of shame suggesting that disclosing abuse, particularly in the public setting of school, would intensify feelings of failure as a family. These fears bind the children together, but their isolation also leads to tension between them. In her book *Blush: Faces of Shame* (2005), Elspeth Probyn argues that shame is emotionally powerful because it inhabits the place where personal identity and social values have become deeply enmeshed, and her distinction between guilt and shame illuminates the feelings associated with family abuse. She suggests that whereas guilt is related to specific actions and can be atoned quite quickly, shame has more lasting effects. Shame is more agonizing and painful to admit than guilt; it enters the body more profoundly because it strikes deeply at our sense of self-identity. Probyn offers this perception:

> While both guilt and shame are excited by what others think about us, shame goes further. Shame is deeply related not only to how others think about us but also how we think about ourselves. Guilt is triggered in response to specific acts and can be smoothed away by an act of reparation. (2005, p. 45)

In Probyn's conceptualization, guilt creates a context for blame in which the 'guilty party' is expected to 'pay the price' of their actions by accepting punishment. Guilt relies on authoritarian judgments of right and wrong whereas shame, by contrast, cuts into a sense of selfhood and demands a re-evaluation of the values, beliefs and emotional relationships on which self-identity is built (2005, pp. 55–6). Blame seeks to control others through belittling them and generating guilt and fear, but shame inspires compassion.

Applied to family abuse, Probyn's analysis suggests that although the perpetrators' feelings of guilt might stop the violence in the short term, they would do little to address its underlying causes. Furthermore, she suggests, guilt can prevent the more painful but productive feelings of shame from surfacing (2005, pp. 45–6). It follows that, if one person is blamed for the suffering of the whole family, it is likely that they will all remain trapped in a cycle of guilt and retribution and, although the problem may be hidden, nothing is ever resolved. Shame is more inclusive than guilt, and is often felt by both the abused and the abuser – it is both self and other-regarding. Everyday Theatre's programme illustrated this aspect of shame through the character of Bernie, whose fear of shame indicates a concern for both himself and others in his family. In the workshop, the students were expected to address this problem by considering each character's feelings and motives. In one activity the students wrote a letter, text or email to a friend in role as one of the characters in the drama. Their writing in role as Helen, captured in my fieldnotes, is particularly revealing:

> *Student 1*: I don't want to be doing this but I am scared. I'm scared that if anyone finds out I'll lose my kids. I take it out on them but I shouldn't. I miss Tony. He used to help.
>
> *Student 2*: It's too much. I am tired and no-one helps me out and no-one listens. It's all very well for Tony. He can get away. I can't. I wish I could but I keep doing my best but I go wrong and hit the kids.

These two examples are fairly typical of the students' reading of Helen's situation. They understood that she was caught between two very different sets of emotions – a desire to do the right thing by caring for her children well, and a feeling of frustration that she was unhappy. This is where shame becomes a positive force for change. According to Probyn, when people allow themselves to feel shame, rather than blaming someone else, it is an emotion that can motivate the kind of self-reflexivity that is enduring, it is a 'switching point rerouting the dynamics of knowing and ignorance (Probyn, 2005, p. 105). Encouraging the students to reflect in role as Helen's role made space for them to understand this emotional ambiguity, a process that inspired their compassion.

The aesthetic of Everyday Theatre's workshop is built on the premise that the double framing of the drama within an arcade game protects students from the kind of self-exposure that is often associated with the 'shame' of family breakdown or abuse. Educationally, it was imperative that the students treated all the characters compassionately as any child affected by abuse would inevitably be listening very carefully to their classmates' contributions. Voicing their private fears, albeit through the fiction of a drama, would be a very brave step. Although each workshop I witnessed was differently nuanced, the protective aesthetic frame and tight structure led the students to express similar sentiments and reach remarkably similar moral conclusions. One moment I observed in a workshop is particularly significant in that it challenged this convention. There was an activity towards the end of a workshop where the students gathered in small groups, in role as social workers, to decide what should happen to

Bernie and April. They were given a number of options, such as sending them to live with Tony or their grandparents, or taking them into care. None of these appealed to the group I was observing, and one girl was particularly insistent that they should simply ask the children what they wanted to do. When this group came to present their ideas, she chose to be hot-seated and face actor-teacher Peter O'Connor's questioning, in role as Tony. As his questioning intensified, she broke out of role to justify her decision:

It worked for me, and I'm only 11.

The aesthetic of the frame had allowed her to live in the fiction long enough to break it.

This made the aims of the education programme visible. It brought the fear of exposure and the shame with which disclosure is often accompanied into the room and, in the process, the girl re-wrote the story. By offering an alternative solution (to listen to the children), these particular students showed that they had the capacity to understand the complexity of adult emotion and to understand that it is possible to change situations when families learn to listen. Perhaps most pertinently, the girl's confident intervention suggests that young people can be resilient and flexible and that painful circumstances can have happy outcomes. Supported by this sensitive and compassionate programme, her actions suggest that there is no shame in telling your classmates that life sometimes involves facing difficult decisions. In the final moments of the workshop, this girl articulated its unspoken invitation – to bring her private experiences of home into the public space of the workshop.

It was this moment that showed the creative dynamic within the workshop. The programme's efficacy relies on moving from the representational space of theatre, and its structured theatricality, to the practices of everyday life. This transitional process of cultural improvisation extends beyond the product of the travelling theatre programme. Tim Ingold argues that 'a creativity that is inherent in the flow of life or consciousness' does not end with the completion of the artwork, whether this is a performance, a painting or, I would add, a theatre education workshop. If creativity is to be assimilated into everyday life, and enable young people to make imaginative choices about how to live, they will continue to process the work long after the actors have left the school. This way of thinking about creativity as cultural improvisation challenges distinctions between process and product as young people play their part, as Ingold puts it, in 'the never-ending and non-specific project of *keeping life going*' (2007, p. 48. Italics original).

Everyday Theatre is an example of an education programme that did not shy away from representing home as a place of physical danger. Preventing family abuse not only means changing family relationships; it also involves unfixing set ideas about the domestic politics of failure and success. Instrumentally, the programme offered young people safe and public space to rehearse their private responses to disclosure and abuse, and provided activities that were designed to help them to make creative and empathetic decisions about how to act. As a touring company who were spending only a few days in each school, the company needed to ensure that structures were in place with the relevant agencies that would support any children who subsequently disclosed abuse. The programme encouraged an ethic of care in which young people were invited to gain an expanded sense of themselves in relation to others, both emotionally and socially. Matching this sensitivity with the reality of disclosure depended on local systems of support, particularly if the young people continued to process the programme's dramatic content after the company had gone. The programme did not hide the scars of family abuse, and it showed that a fictional space can offer a safe place in which to face the uncomfortable feelings that can hold both abuse and social prejudice in place, and with this ambition lies ethical responsibilities.

Security and risk: At home and on the street

In proposing that drama contains 'both the kitchen sink and the edge of the universe', Edward Bond suggests that there is knowledge in childhood that adults 'may forget in the contrivance of survival' (2009, p. xi). It is interesting that many new plays for adults in the first half of the twentieth century were predominantly set in rooms where, as Baz Kershaw described, 'theatre grappled with the changing domestic world' (2007, p. 65). During the same period, theatre for young audiences, by contrast, found a spirit of adventure outside. Dramatizations of the child's playful world has been a central preoccupation for playwrights writing for children, of which *Peter Pan* (1904) is perhaps the most famous example. J. M. Barrie's Scottish imagination placed *Peter Pan* on an island where he mixed a Rousseau-esque arcadia with dangerous encounters with pirates, and this play represented a wider interest in dramatic portrayals of idyllic rural environments where children struggle to escape adult intervention in order to be free to play. Morag Styles has observed that in poetry written for children during the last quarter of the twentieth century there was a move from the protective and domestic comfort of the garden to the dangerous vernacular of the street (Styles, 1998). This move is also apparent in theatre for young audiences, where the set-change acts as a symbol of contemporary preoccupations and provides new ways of imagining young people's identities. To explore this further, I shall turn to plays written for young people to raise questions about young people's cultural geographies, and ask how the metaphor of the street raises political questions about the kind of 'homes' adults have created.

It is perhaps unsurprising that the dramatization of the domestic room has represented adult concerns. In his essay *Families and Domestic Routines*, the geographer David Sibley observes that the spaces children are allowed to occupy often symbolize adult visions of childhood, and are indicative, therefore, of different ways in which childhood is constructed and understood. Family relationships are often delineated spatially, he suggests, and this affects both the emotional resonances of each room in a house and the quality of domestic interaction. The dynamics of power are often symbolized through domestic spaces; arguments about teenagers' untidy bedrooms, for example, are often a metaphor for their desire for increased privacy and greater independence. Finding a productive balance between freedom and security is a particular challenge but, Sibley suggests, this process is a prerequisite for emotional health:

> the child's sense of boundary, anxieties about space and time or feelings about attachment to particular spaces, will be affected by the domestic environment as it is shaped and manipulated by family members. Clearly, the opportunities for control, or for giving children their own spaces, will be affected by the size of the home, the way in which space is partitioned, and the relationship between public and private space. (1992, p. 122)

Sibley's observations of home as a site of both security and conflict is balanced by his acknowledgement that young people's perceptions of home are likely to change as territorial power struggles slip into memory. He comments interestingly on the physical sensations children experience in relation to the material world, and he particularly notes the sense of anxiety, excitement, sickness and delight that many children experience in relation to particular places. He cites Juliet Kristeva's *Powers of Horror* (1982) to theorize this sense, describing how these physical and emotional sensations contribute to identity formation and, crucially, their relationships with others:

> Aversion and desire, repulsion and attraction, play against each other in defining the border which gives the self identity and, importantly, these opposing feelings are transferred to others during childhood. (1992, p. 126)

Young people affect strong relationships with public and private spaces, and their negotiation between different places, however uncomfortable, often demonstrates their resilience and ability to improvise as they experiment with new ways of being.

In his observation of the cultural geographies of young people, Stuart C. Aitken points out that public places where young people gather to make friends and express their peer culture may also carry an element of danger (2001, pp. 156–61). He suggests that the negotiation between public and private space is often integral to how young people construct their identities, and how they understand the boundaries between self and other. It is in this context that exterior spaces such as dens, streets, parks and other non-domestic places where some young people meet may acquire an emotional and performative significance, as they are places to escape from home and construct their own 'homeplaces' as geographies of resistance. Lefebvre makes the connection between spatial practices and adolescent rebellion:

> Inasmuch as adolescents are unable to challenge either the dominant system's impervious architecture or its deployment of signs, it is only by way of revolt that they have any prospect of recovering the world of difference – the natural, the sensory/sensual, sexuality and pleasure. (1991, p. 50)

The element of sensuous rebellion – or revolt, in Lefebvre's terms – is part of the dramaturgy of freedom that spaces outside the home can represent to young people. Conversely, however, young people on the street are frequently subject to the disciplinary gaze of adults, and groups of young people are often seen as a threat to moral order. One controversial solution that has been in operation in England and Wales is to use a high pitched sound that can only be heard by young people – known as the mosquito – to disperse 'trouble-makers' from public spaces, and particularly shopping malls where they are thought to deter shoppers. Civil rights campaigners argue that the imposition of this terrible sound constitutes a breach of young people's civil liberties, because it indiscriminately demonizes all young people. Public spaces offer some young people a sense of belonging that may be difficult at home, but the idea that they pose a threat to society has led to pernicious measures that are primarily concerned with protecting the culture of consumerism.

It is interesting that plays written for young people often invoke dens, wasteland, parks, rooftops and other secret spaces in which young people test their own and each others' boundaries as dramatic metaphor to show how their changing identities are improvised and mapped. Derelict urban spaces are often integral to the set and to the dramatic representation of ideas; the roof top of a towerblock in Philip Ridley's *Sparkleshark* (first performed in 1997) or the abandoned railway lot in Bond's *The Children* (2000a), for example, simultaneously represent places of refuge and danger to characters whose everyday lives take place in urban environments that are far removed from either the Morrisonian child-garden or the gentrified cultural quarters of creative cities. The cultural theorist Brian Massumi argues that derelict spaces can have a particular significance in the construction of young people's identity because they are 'the zone of indeterminacy that bodies-in-becoming make their own' (1992, p. 104). Although Massumi risks generalizations about how teenagers actually behave, the dramatic metaphor remains clear. In *Sparkleshark* a group of disparate young people gradually gather on a rooftop, using the space to explore their relationships and, in the process, to renegotiate their sense of self. The play begins with Jake, a boy who is described as 'geeky' because he enjoys writing stories, settling into an old armchair on the roof, 'his secret hideaway' where he can write his stories. He is escaping from Russell, who has been bullying him, and the rooftop offers him the kind of refuge from the outside world that is often associated with home. Jake's privacy is broken, however, first by Polly, who had been moved by reading a fragment of a story he had written, and then by other teenagers, including the bullies who use the captive site of the rooftop as an excuse to torment him. Each character begins with an identity within the group that is fixed; Russell is a bully but good looking, Carol is awkward, Buzz and Speed are Russell's henchmen, and the large but ungainly Finn is described as a monster. Jake is saved by his witty ability to tell stories, and the derelict space is gradually turned into a site of collective storytelling, through which the young people shed their habitual identities through the process of making friends. On one level *Sparkleshark* is a rather sentimental essay about the power of storytelling, but it is also testament to the ways in which the rooftop offers a 'zone of indeterminacy' in which young people can experiment with new identities. There are no adults in *Sparkleshark,* presumably in part because the commission from the National Theatre in London was for a play for young people to perform, but the absence of adults has the effect of creating a world in which their imaginations are independent of adult intervention. There is no sense that the characters are troubled by their families, and their developing friendship inverts the popular stereotype that gatherings of young people pose a threat to social order.

In some ways the rooftop in *Sparkleshark* is a substitute for home; the world the play creates turns out to be benign because the young people use the poetics of the derelict space to learn about themselves. Edward Bond's *The Children* (2000a), by contrast, dramatizes a journey that is much more sinister. The plot follows a group of friends on a journey to escape from home, but as each is gradually murdered by a man for whom they are caring, their isolation becomes increasingly apparent. This play represents itinerancy in which mobility constitutes a threat and the outside world is often dangerous, but the alternative is worse – a family that is damaged and a home that offers little sense of security. In writing this play, Bond encouraged the cast to improvise their lines, a process that, I observed, enables young actors to reflect on their own lives in relation to the play (Nicholson, 2003). On one level Bond's invitation to the young cast to improvise was a politic gesture; the children's improvisation implies that they have the capacity to change the 'script' of a society that has been determined by adults. In different ways and to different degrees, Ridley and Bond's teenage characters inhabit a troubled, socially deprived urban environment; their dramatic narratives celebrate the strength of friendship as an optimistic substitute for, or supplement to, family relationships. The unspoken invitation in both plays is to invite young audiences and actors to imagine how life might be different, and each dramatizes a political statement in which young people seek a better way to live in a world that has been compromised or corrupted by adults.

Questions of belonging

There are many childhoods, and the social and emotional meanings of home change according to time and place. Just as the social processes of industrialization changed the ways in which families were constructed and experienced, so too is globalization altering how homes, families and friendships are understood. It seems that contemporary dramatizations of home not only contest the idealization of home as a conservative symbol of moral order that derived from industrialization, they also raise questions about the commodification of friendship that some cultural commentators regard as a symptom of moral decay in a globalized, networked society. Although the contemporary world may be characterized by movement and mobility, whether real or imagined, for most people the impact of globalization is felt not through travel, but at home.

David Morley observed that at the end of the twentieth century there was, in fact, a very low level of mobility in the United Kingdom, with over half the population living within a five mile radius of their place of birth (2000, p. 14). Mobility is associated either with intelligentsia who travel to work by choice, or with those who are displaced through poverty, disaster or prejudice. Despite the appeal of the former, there is considerable prejudice against those who move because they are forcibly displaced or disadvantaged. Tim Cresswell's study of the cultural geography of mobility is significant here. He argues that the idea of 'home' as a place of moral stability has served the politics of both the Left and Right. Matthew Arnold's liberal conception of culture as sweetness and light became associated with conservative notions of a lost heritage and tradition in the twentieth century, and cultural critics of the political Right, notably T. S. Eliot, invoked a bounded sense of place to argue that people should stay morally rooted in a culture's history and tradition. On the political Left, Cresswell suggests, mid-twentieth century socialist writers Richard Hoggart and Raymond Williams furthered nostalgic vision of white working-class homes as places of harmony and stability, and this led them to regard the vernacular traditions of domestic culture as a form of resistance to rootless global capitalism and mass commercialization (2006, pp. 32–4). In both conceptualizations, Cresswell concludes, rootlessness represents deviance, threat and a lack of sustained moral values, whereas home symbolizes social order, unchanging cultural practices and a sense of belonging. This political and cultural idealization of home is clearly evident in prejudicial attitudes to those who are homeless, refugees or those new arrivals who are not part of the metropolitan élite.

Questions of belonging, emotional attachments to place, and ideas about what home means have always been subject to change. And although in many ways the recognition that there are multiple homes and ways to live represents a positive way forward, it can also be emotionally bewildering and inspires the kind of prejudice that leads families and communities to seek to demonize those whom they consider to be outside the 'norm'. One of the educational roles of theatre is to provide a transitional space in which young people can make emotional connections between the drama, as a fictional and symbolic space, and their own lives. Elizabeth Ellsworth draws on the psychological theories of D. W. Winnicott to examine the significance of transitional space in her discussion of the pedagogy of place, and suggests that it is a 'process that moves inner relations into a special relation to outer realities' (2005, p. 60). This means that creative encounters in transitional spaces will traverse the boundaries between self and other, as Ellsworth explains:

> The limits of our knowledge of self, of other, and of the world require us to put ourselves in relation while at the same time keeping ourselves separate. What we cannot know requires us to constantly traverse the porous boundaries between self and other, individual and social, personal and historical. (2005, p. 61)

Perhaps when theatre works best it creates environments where participants might 'know what we cannot know'. This has the potential to illuminate both the comfort and the disconcerting strangeness that might be found both at the kitchen sink and at the edge of the universe. It is this process of experimentation, according to David Morley, that enables us to explore the 'alterity in ourselves, and encounter ourselves as others' (2000, p. 264).

There is a delightful postscript that illustrates how quickly and wittily young people subvert disciplinary spaces constructed by adults. The mosquito sound was quickly turned into a mobile phone ring tone which allowed young people to use their phones during lessons without their teachers knowing. It is apparently available to download free from www.freemosquitoringtone.org, though I can't hear it.

7

'This Island's Mine': National Identity and Questions of Belonging

Bombings

I was not in London on 7th July 2005. The announcement that London would host the 2012 Olympics had just been made on 6th July, but any feelings of national euphoria snapped the following morning. News of the bombings broke slowly; the BBC interrupted their scheduled programmes to make tentative announcements about explosions in central London, and gradually a picture of four 'incidents' on London transport began to emerge. Londoners are used to bombs – many of us grew up with the constant threat of IRA bombings – but these bombs felt different; there was no warning, no clear target. It was just an ordinary rush hour, suggesting that war reaches the practices of everyday life as well as targeted against the architectural symbols of global capitalism. I called my sister who was due to leave London to meet me later that day, and I told her not to worry about being late if the transport was slow. It was clumsy, of course, and what I really wanted to know was that she was safe. London changed that day, symbolized by the lines of commuters walking home across the city while the transport system remained still and, in the weeks ahead, the half-empty carriages on the tube ferried passengers who seemed visibly frightened. Given Britain's participation in the war in Iraq and military involvement in Afghanistan, the news that the suicide bombers were linked to al-Qaeda was not a surprise. The fact that they were all British nationals, and that the leader Mohammed

Sidique Khan was a teaching assistant in a primary school in Leeds, was shocking.

Anti-Muslim hate crime in Britain had already increased in the years following the horrific attack on the Twin Towers in New York on 11th September 2001 and British involvement in the Iraq war. In the months after the 7/7 bombings it escalated, organized by racist extremists such as the British Nationalist Party (the BNP) and fuelled by the Right-wing press. A recent report by Jonathan Githens-Mazer and Robert Lambert commissioned by the European Muslim Research Centre 'Islamophobia and Anti-Muslim Hate Crime: A London Case Study' (2010) points out that much Islamophobic crime and the intimidation experienced by Muslims in London has been driven by nationalist bigotry, and based on 'the negative and false belief that Muslims pose a security threat' (2010, p. 11). Although the security threat may have been limited, there was a changing mood among some Islamic young people, as Eliza Manningham-Buller, head of MI5 at the time, acknowledged in her evidence to the Chilcot inquiry on 20th July 2010. She claimed that the actions of the British government had 'radicalised ... a few among a generation who saw our involvement in Iraq, on top of our involvement in Afghanistan, as being an attack on Islam'.[1] In response to this social division, political rhetoric since 7/7 attempted to wrestle the idea of national identity away from the nationalist racism of organized groups such as the BNP. In a speech to the Fabian Society in 2006, Prime Minister Gordon Brown argued that the idea of Britishness had long been equated with values of 'liberty to all, responsibility by all, fairness for all' which, he said, 'owe more to progressive ideas than to right wing ones'.[2]

Gordon Brown's attempt to organize national sentiment around the moral consensus associated with liberal ideas of citizenship was perhaps stronger on rhetoric than action, particularly when it was accompanied by increasingly strict anti-terrorist and immigration laws. And although Brown's invocation of Britishness was clearly an attempt to promote social cohesion, his words easily became associated with the prejudicial attitudes he sought to displace. In June 2007 the *Times Educational Supplement* carried a story about teenagers' attitude to Brown's campaign which might be summarized by one student's response: 'I don't see the point of all this Britishness. Isn't it just alienating us from other countries, cultures and peoples? We're being told we live in a multicultural society yet now they want to enforce something completely different.'[3] However understood, the fear of social fragmentation resulting from acts of violence has refocused political debate on national identity and what it means to belong to a nation in a world that is both increasingly homogenized through globalization and fractured through global conflict.

This chapter is concerned with national identity, and what renewed debates about nation and nationhood might mean for contemporary practice in theatre education. In *Theatre & Nation* (2010) Nadine Holdsworth asked the question 'What do we mean when we combine the term *theatre* with *nation*?' (2010, p. 6). She argues that 'the vast majority of theatre practices that engage with the nation, directly or obliquely, do so to respond to moments of rupture, crisis or conflict' (2010, p. 7). Holdsworth suggests that contemporary performance artists and theatre-makers have responded to these moments of crisis by contesting homogenous images of the nation and disrupting national iconography. This marks a move away from the Arnoldian view that the study of culture represents an education in the 'best selves' of humanity. On the contrary, she argues, 'theatre opens up a creative space for exploring the paradoxes, ambiguities and complexities around issues of tradition, identity, authenticity and belonging associated with the nation' (2010, p. 7). This suggests that when theatre *education* is combined with nation, a productive and creative space might be opened for young people to debate and dramatize these contested issues.

Because citizenship education has been introduced into the school curriculum, with various nomenclatures in different parts of the world, it seems important to distinguish between the two concepts of citizenship and nationhood. Citizenship is usually defined as a set of legal rights and civic responsibilities as a participant member of a democratic society, and although citizenship remains historically connected to the Nation-State, it is now often seen to extend beyond national boundaries and includes ideas of a global, cosmopolitan or even corporate citizenship. National identity, by contrast, relates to a matrix of spatial, material, performative and embodied identifications with nations and national cultures. Conjuring national identity as a unifying ideology is complex and problematic in many different parts of the world; Britain is a federation and part of Europe which means that my own national identity, for example, might be described variously as European, British and English. Many diasporic people have multiple allegiances to different parts of the world, and hyphenated terms such as British-Asian or African-American signify identification with multiple places as a marker of this dual heritage. Appadurai suggests that this hyphenation disrupts the idea of a homogenous national identity, thereby both troubling prejudicial nationalisms and signifying a transnational world in which loyalties may be divided (1996, p. 172). Debates about national identity, therefore, move the discussion away from the idea of home as a domestic space to the idea of a homeland – an extension of bell hooks' concept of 'homeplace' – in which everyone might find a 'culture of belonging' (2009, p. 7).

Imagining how national identity might become more equitable has been, of course, a preoccupation in theatre education for over a hundred years and, I argued in Chapter 2, the role of theatre in shaping national identity has received particular attention in times of mass migration and social fragmentation. The contemporary cultural anxiety surrounding the construction of national identity has been evident in theatre for young audiences in post 7/7 Britain; John Retallack's touring production *Hannah and Hanna* (Company of Angels, 2001) tackles the issue of social integration of young refugees, Mark Ravenhill's adaptation of Terry Pratchett's *Nation* (National Theatre, London, 2009) raises questions about island identity, and Carl Miller's *Red Fortress* (Unicorn, London, 2008) retells the story of the Alhambra in 1491 in ways that draw attention to the tensions and reconciliation between Catholics, Muslims and Jews. As Marvin Carlson points out, early theatrical responses to 9/11 in New York were primarily sentimental stories of heroes, but The New Victory Theater which specializes in theatre for children staged an inventive programme of plays from different nations, cultures and traditions (2004, p. 6). Contemporary mainstream theatre is also contributing to debates about national identity and, as I write in 2010, Jez Butterworth's *Jerusalem* (Royal Court, 2009) and David Greig's *Dunsinane* (RSC and Hampstead Theatre, 2010) are playing in London theatres, both of which use intertextual references to Shakespeare's plays to explore, respectively, contemporary English and Scottish identities. Australian playwrights, including Jane Harrison and Debra Oswald have explored the relationship between contemporary Australia, its colonial past and Aboriginal identities and, as theatre scholar Heike Roms points out, the renewed interest in site-specific performance often indicates an aesthetic and political interest in the dynamic between place, nationhood and cultural memory.[4] The educational practice invoked in this chapter is absorbed by this preoccupation, and although it is grounded in my own British context, I anticipate that the debates and issues I raise will have resonance elsewhere. The terrorist attacks on 9/11 in the United States and the bombings in London on 7/7 haunt this study, however different they were from each other in both scale and effect.

Working through the implications of these events, both emotionally and politically, suggests that there is a new urgency to debates about how national identity is performed and understood. In this chapter I shall consider how nationhood and national identity might be re-imagined in the twenty-first century, and explore some of the ways in which theatre education and cultural performance are contributing to this process, not as a vehicle for promoting nationhood as a marker of social cohesion in the way Matthew Arnold advocated, but as a way of raising difficult questions about nation, identity and belonging.

Learning national identity

So, how is national identity learnt? In his book *Nationalism and Modernism*, Anthony D. Smith traces the history of the Nation-State, and argues that it became consolidated as a political entity in the eighteenth and nineteenth centuries as a result of colonialism, industrialization and the expansion of global trade, which means that the idea of belonging to a nation is a relatively recent European construction rather than 'natural' or predetermined.[5] The conservative myth that that there is an authentic national identity, rooted in the history and culture of a particular people and place is not only an 'invented tradition' as Eric Hobsbawm claimed (1991), it also offers a partial and divisive concept of nationhood which serves to exclude those who have arrived more recently and whose personal or family histories do not cohere with this linear narrative of nationality. Writing about how these beliefs are perpetuated by conservative politicians and a commodified heritage industry, Tim Cresswell argues that the idea that there is an authentic national origin is a 'creation myth' that has assumed a quasi-mystical status (2004, p. 73). A sense of national identity is, therefore, an identity that is both culturally and spatially produced. It is learnt in childhood, and whatever social values are projected onto the idea of the nation, it remains sufficiently supple to inspire feelings of belonging among people who have multiple allegiances and histories.

From the various theories that address how national identities are assimilated, I would like to focus on two converging narratives that impact on the way in which national identity is learnt, imagined and produced, both of which impact on theatre and performance practices in education. One strand of thought suggests that belonging to a nation is encouraged through the cultural authority of an official language and heritage, the media and the organized institutions of governance, including the education system. Another strand of thought takes account of how national identity it is improvised and enmeshed in the cultural practices of everyday life. Both narratives take root in childhood, and understanding how national identities are learnt requires an awareness of how the dynamic between official and vernacular traditions is encountered. Both ways of thinking emphasize the cultural dimension of belonging to a place, and suggest that attachment to, and identification with, a nation's customs, habits, humour and traditions are integral to a sense of selfhood which changes over time. Learning national identity in childhood depends on a *range* of identifications, as Scourfield et al. point out in their study of children's identification with place (2006, p. 4), in which the process of socialization into a sense of nationhood from the top-down is interwoven with more informal affiliations with place that are often learnt at home.

Benedict Anderson's work on the link between the cultural improvisation of everyday life and nationhood as an official discourse is often used as the touchstone for debates about how national identity is learnt. Anderson argues that nation is an 'imagined community' rather than a fixed entity, which means that it is continually open to redefinition. His argument turns on how the development of print capitalism and an increasingly literate population in the eighteenth and nineteenth century generated a sense of national community through reading the same newspapers and novels. The theatre historian Bruce McConachie has argued that the period also coincided with the idea of an institutionalized national theatre, and the prevalence of the scripted play legitimated readerly bourgeois tastes which meant that the theatre provided a public forum for dissemination of ideas in a similar way to print media (2008, p. 58). The rise of capitalism supported these cultural practices, and created the conditions that fostered a sense of commonality and mutual identification with fellow countrymen which, Anderson suggests, produced a 'deep, horizontal comradeship' (1991, p. 7). In 1983, the date of the first publication of Anderson's book *Imagined Communities*, the idea that nationhood is an imagined political community represented a radical departure from essentialist constructions of nationhood, and his perception that national identity is constructed through shared cultural practices continues to offer a way of theorizing emotional attachments to specific countries. The power of print capitalism has waned, of course, and the new network society easily transports images and ideas across national boundaries through the internet and other digital media. The 'deep, horizontal comradeship' that Anderson associated with national identity has extended to transnational movements that cannot easily be contained within national boundaries, described by Appadurai as part of the mediascape of an 'imagined world' (1998, p. 33). More commercially, the imagined identity of different nations have been successfully branded by the heritage and tourist industries, and exported as part of an invented tradition of nationhood. Some conceptions of a national theatre are contributing to this market, McConachie argues, and it is easy to see how particular imaginings of nationhood might be easily turned into a niche-market for branded performances of national stereotypes (2008, p. 59). Notwithstanding its limitations, the idea that nationhood is an imagined community has been widely adopted as a critical lens through which to analyse theatre and performance because it explains, to borrow Jen Harvie's words, how structures of power can be both 'oppressive and enabling' (2005, p. 2).

The anthropologist Michael Herzfeld questions Anderson's perception that national identity is learnt from the 'top-down' through institutional practices, newspapers and other cultural artefacts rather than created through 'the symbolism, commensality, family and friendship' that constitute the affective texture of social relations (2005, p. 6). He relates these everyday embodied practices to national identity, describing them as part of the 'cultural intimacy' that defines a sense of belonging. Smith similarly recognizes that the vernacular, local and domestic narratives of ancestry and myth are instrumental in creating a sense of national identity. He suggests that this kind of collective identification is learnt by children 'at their mother's knee' as part of an inter-generational repertoire 'embodied in values, myths and symbols' that form part of a nation's varied traditions (1998, p. 187). These identifications change over time, however, particularly when migrants introduce new ways of living and, as their cultural patterning of domestic lives gradually moves from the home to the community, they become assimilated into the national psyche, creating a matrix of identifications that constitute national identity in pluralist worlds. Perhaps the most confident assertion that national identity is integral to the practices of everyday life derives from Michael Billig, whose book *Banal Nationalism* (1995) offers a persuasive account of the ways in which shared habits, familiar spaces and conventions evolve as part of the ordinary and unreflexive identifications with the daily habitus of a nation. Billig argues that sporting events, flag-waving, and other routine identifications with nationhood are good examples of banal nationalism although, as Tim Edensor argues, this might be extended to include less spectacular elements of everyday life such as ways of shopping, familiar brands of food and enjoyment of popular culture, things we scarcely notice have a national identity until they, or we, change (2002, pp. 110–12). For example, when Cadbury's chocolate was taken over by the US food giant Kraft in 2010, it was repeatedly claimed on vox-pox items on television news that selling children's favourite brand of chocolate was a sign that Britain was losing its national identity.

Whether national identity is a symbol of reactionary exclusivity or perceived to be pluralist and inclusive depends on not only how nationhood is imagined, but how culture is understood. National identity always suggests some negotiation between self and otherness, and whether this remains set in an idea of the past or is open to new shapes, forms and rhythms depends on conceptualizing culture as a process, as a site of multiplicity and displacement, rather than rooted and fixed. Doreen Massey famously describes places without fixed boundaries between 'us' and 'them' as 'progressive' (1997). A progressive sense of place, she argues, is open to change as a 'meeting place' of different social and cultural practices enacted in the ordinary and daily patterns of movement, production and consumption.[6] My suggestion is that although the education and cultural sectors may have institutional roles in perpetuating an imagined community of nationhood from the top-down, dramatic practice may also contribute to framing and challenging prejudicial nationalisms through the cultural intimacy and creative improvisation on which they rely for their efficacy and progressivism.

It would be easy to see text-led, building-based theatre as the readerly voice of the establishment, and devised and place or site-based performance as integral to a more vernacular everyday construction of national identity. My intention is, however, to resist and challenge this duality. The case study that follows is based on my own practice-based research with British Asian young people in Southall, West London in 2008 and 2009, in which we raised questions about the social and personal meanings of national identity by focusing on Shakespeare's play *The Tempest*. I chose to work on a Shakespeare play partly because he carries the weight of being the only playwright who is a compulsory part of the National Curriculum in England and Wales, and this perpetuates an official status that might seem to promote a national cultural élitism. I shall consider the significance of Shakespeare's status as national poet and an important part of an English heritage brand in the next section. My aim was to encourage young people to recognize that Shakespeare's plays can be interpreted in many different ways, not because their themes are universal, but because they are living texts with the capacity to speak to different generations in new ways. This led us to find ways to integrate their interpretations of *The Tempest* with a vernacular sense of place, and this process raised questions about belonging. The project took Shakespeare's play to a part of London in which 'Britishness' is regarded as a problematic and racist term, and to young people who did not consider Shakespeare to be part of their own heritage. Through this process I hoped to learn how the young people's complex matrix of identifications with different cultural histories and practices impacted on the work. By combining questions of national identity with pedagogies of place, I wanted to raise questions about how the affective and physical dynamic of theatre might contribute to what Elizabeth Ellsworth describes as a 'civic pedagogy that binds pieces of memory, experience, and anticipation into a cultural fabric' (2005, p. 85).

Shakespeare as national heritage and in national culture

So what place does Shakespeare have in British national culture? Tim Edensor commented that 'the staging of the nation for education and entertainment is a long-standing feature of national culture' (2002, p. 85). Shakespeare's enduring presence in the school curriculum, particularly in England, illuminates the ways in which nationhood and heritage have been conceptualized and understood. Although Matthew Arnold's perception that an education in 'the best culture of their nation' as 'the study of perfection' would cultivate the nation's 'best self' had liberal intentions, Shakespeare's status in the education system has acquired more conservative overtones. In his book *The Genius of Shakespeare* (1997) Jonathan Bate gives a spirited account of the ways in which Shakespeare has been regarded by the political Right as integral to cultural nationalism. Bate charts the ways in which Shakespeare came to be regarded as a creative genius in the eighteenth century, a move which elevated his status into a national poet and secured a lasting place for Shakespeare in the English education system. Bate's account draws attention to the link between national heritage and the study of Shakespeare's plays in more recent times; when school tests on Shakespeare's plays became statutory for all 14-year-olds in England and Wales in the 1990s a new government Department of National Heritage was simultaneously established.[7] These two moves were ideologically connected, Bate argues, as it was a way to secure 'the nation's sense of its own greatness' with Shakespeare at the 'epicentre of that heritage' (1997, p. 199).

This appropriation of Shakespeare's plays in the official education policies of the political Right has proved to be an irresistible challenge for teachers and theatre educators who are inspired by Shakespeare's plays, and this has affected both strategies for teaching and learning and the politics of interpretation, as Sean McEvoy has eloquently described in his book *Shakespeare: The Basics* (2000). Inspired by contemporary performance, classroom teachers and theatre practitioners have developed innovative and inventive ways of turning Shakespeare's work from a moralizing, desk-based study into a live and vernacular performance. Against this backdrop of creative teaching, however, there is still a mystery and mystique surrounding Shakespeare's work which influences young people's perceptions of Shakespeare, often before they encounter his plays, not least because many people have memories of studying his work in school that are not always positive. There are similar issues surrounding teaching ancient Greek plays in Greek schools – each nation has its own national iconography – and I felt that this background and context warranted critical investigation. I was interested in exploring the ways in which Shakespeare has become an iconic symbol of nationhood, and how the Shakespeare industry has contributed to this construction.

I want to start this account by taking up Herzfeld's notion that national identity entails a 'generous measure of embarrassment together with all the idealised virtues' in respect of Shakespeare as a heritage industry (rather than a playwright). Let's get the embarrassment over with first. Tourism is one of the main ways through which Shakespeare is known, and his place in popular culture has been secured internationally through mass pilgrimage to Stratford-upon-Avon, the birthplace of William Shakespeare and the home of the Royal Shakespeare Company. More visitors flock to sites associated with Shakespeare's spatial biography than go to the theatre, and regular features on the tourist trail include his birthplace, his tomb and his wife Anne Hathaway's cottage in the nearby hamlet of Shottery. Stratford is marketed as an image of a lost Englishness and Warwickshire has been branded as 'Shakespeare Country', invoking an idyllic Forest of Arden. The Shakespeare industry has extended to London, and a wittier, more urban Shakespeare is represented on the south bank of London, particularly in the re-constructed Globe Theatre. Outside the iconic shape of The Globe on the regenerated Bankside, however, there is little in the surrounding streets of Southwark to remind tourists of Shakespeare's life and it is with the olde-worldy-ness of Stratford's half-timbered buildings that he remains most associated in the popular imagination. Shakespeare is part of the brandscape of England, part of the mythology of a rooted national identity, and his status as a British 'National Poet' cannot be easily separated from this cultural imaginary. Herzfeld described this simulacrum of nationhood as 'the romantic folklore of the urban élite' (2005, p. 7).

Conventional academic readings of the Shakespeare industry are inevitably critical of the commercialization, suggesting that it depoliticizes his work and reduces his artistic complexity to an image on a mug.[8] This is often accompanied by a rather patronizing attitude to tourists (particularly Americans), where it is assumed that they are looking for authenticity, to become closer to the 'real Shakespeare' by gawping in amazement at the settle they believe Shakespeare really used to court Anne Hathaway or by drinking beer in a pub they imagine he once frequented. A more nuanced reading of the tourist imagination has been offered by theatre historian Nicola J. Watson, who argues that the tourist industry surrounding Shakespeare was not created by Stratford-upon-Avon, but by print culture. In her essay 'Shakespeare on the Tourist Trail', she traces the history of Shakespeare tourism from the eighteenth century, suggesting that Nicholas Rowe's edition of his plays in 1709 not only moved Shakespeare from stage to page, but that it also included biographical details that began an interest in his life. She describes the development of Shakespeare country as a 'biographically driven urge to imprint the virtual, readerly experience of Shakespeare onto topographical reality' (2007, p. 200). Her account of this history shows that the visual aesthetic that defined Shakespeare Country was widely distributed in illustrated books, particularly in the eighteenth and nineteenth centuries, and well-known landscapes, monuments and buildings came to represent the pastoral images they depicted rather than the other way round. The town's buildings were preserved to conform to this imaginary, Watson suggests, and The Birth Place Trust was established in response to an attempt to transport Shakespeare's former home to the United States in 1847. The building was 'aggressively restored to Tudor picturesqueness' in 1864, suggesting that the town is not 'unspoilt' but re-invented by the Victorian imagination (2007, p. 213). Watson concludes her convincing account of the relationship between print culture, urban preservation and Shakespeare tourism by suggesting that the experience of visiting a place is a 'negotiation between text and place' in which tourists 'seek to verify what he or she has learnt from prior representation' (2007, p. 223). Although Watson herself does not make the connection between the impact of print capitalism on the Shakespeare industry and Anderson's perception of nationhood as an imagined community, the parallels are striking. The image of Shakespeare as a national poetic genius coincided with the conservative image of Englishness that was offered in print, and this combination eventually turned Shakespeare into a successful brand. It is, however, important to distinguish between the economic exploitation of the Shakespeare brand and the appropriation of Shakespeare as a symbol of (white) British cultural superiority. Personally, I'm particularly troubled by Anne Hathaway tea towels and I am rather amused by Yorick beanies, but the ways in which Shakespeare is used by the Right-wing press to define an education in Britishness has some very worrying implications.[9] This extract from *The Sun* newspaper in 2003 illustrates this attitude:

> Schoolchildren are taught that the Empire was a racist, slave-mongering tyranny for which we should all be deeply ashamed ... How many pupils know, for instance, that it was the British Navy that brought about the end of the slave trade? We are told that mud huts and wood carvings are the equal of St Paul's and Shakespeare. (Richard Littlejohn, *The Sun*, January 2003)

If this is the imagined community that Anderson suggested the print capitalism promotes, then to say it is accompanied with more than a generous measure of embarrassment is an understatement. The challenge that faces theatre educators, therefore, is how to find a more inclusive counter-narrative for teaching Shakespeare within this divisive social context.

It is interesting that two of the major innovators in approaches to teaching Shakespeare are also significant tourist sites and imbrued in the heritage culture, The Globe in London and the Royal Shakespeare Company in Stratford. Their education programmes are, of course, differently inflected to engage with the particular strengths of the two theatres and the fact that they are differently funded. Both emphasize the importance of active approaches to learning Shakespeare's plays, both as participants and as audience members, and both refute the cynical suggestion that their education programmes are designed to increase box office sales. The Globe is inevitably implicated in the 'tourist stage' that Susan Bennett found on London's South Bank; the theatre is part of the streetscape that tourists come to see in this area of urban regeneration, and it contributes to the integration of high art, local community and tourist culture that Bennett recognizes as the South Bank's success (2008, p. 83). For those working in the theatre, however, the implications of the building are not always so commercially driven. Fiona Banks, head of education at The Globe, writes that the reconstruction of an Elizabethan playhouse placed everyone at the centre of learning, whether they were actors, directors, designers, audiences or those directly engaged in developing education programmes for schools and colleges. She makes the case that education programmes should encourage a sense of belonging to the Globe and ownership of Shakespeare's plays:

> Just as the audience in Shakespeare's original Globe would have come across a cross-section of society we seek to ensure that all students we work with regard the Globe as 'theirs' and access to Shakespeare as part of their cultural entitlement. (2008, p. 158)

Recalling the familiar Deweyan notion of learning by doing that had early inspired TIE practitioners, Banks suggests that active approaches to Shakespeare not only encourage practical encounters with the plays as texts for performance, they also encourage embodied and kinaesthetic learning. This way of working has become central to pedagogical approaches to Shakespeare, and the RSC has led an important campaign, Stand up for Shakespeare, in which theatre educationalist Jonothan Neelands has led a programme that places collaboration, activity and performance at the centre of the teaching and learning process. The research that accompanied the campaign revealed some interesting attitudes to Shakespeare, both from teachers and students, who were often wary initially of active approaches to the scripts but learnt that these methodologies significantly increased their enjoyment, empathy and textual knowledge of the plays.[10] These approaches to learning offer a good illustration of how theatre practitioners and teachers can learn from each other, and how practices from theatre can be adapted for use in education and how an understanding of the processes of learning can, in turn, help to shape practice in the professional theatre.

If the move from stage to page created the context in which Shakespeare's work became treated with reverence in education and his life became part of the tourist industry, the move back from page to stage might be seen as a way of popularizing and democratizing his work. If activity, dialogue, discussion and debate are contemporary markers of democracy, then perhaps they also indicate the kind of virtues that Herzfeld associated with national identity. Performing and embodying Shakespeare's plays always unfixes their meanings, allowing for new interpretations that speak to the contemporary world, thereby offering the cultural intimacy that, Herzfeld suggests, defines a sense of belonging. Seen in this light, physical and practical interpretation of Shakespeare's plays becomes not just a way of teaching, but a political statement about the place of Shakespeare in contemporary society.

The Tempest, Britishness and performing place

I had worked on *The Tempest* with young people in an earlier project where I focused the research on an investigation into citizenship, but it became clear that Britishness was a much more troubled concept in the minds of young people than citizenship. In order to address these questions I redesigned the project to focus on national identity and relocated the work to Southall, West London. My decision to work on *The Tempest* with a group of young people from this area of London, all of whom were third generation British Asian and Islamic in faith, stemmed from an interest in exploring whether young Muslims living in Britain today would find innovative ways to interpret the play's narrative of colonialism and revenge. *The Tempest* was first performed in 1611 and, as a Jacobean play, questions of British national identity were very current. Queen Elizabeth I had died in 1603, and her successor James VI of Scotland brought the first union between Scotland and England, Wales and a very disputed Ireland. The shift from English nationalism to British unionism was a painful process, and it was during this period that Shakespeare wrote *The Tempest*. Given this theatrical history, and in the light of the contemporary debates about what it means to be a young Muslim in a post-7/7 Britain, it seemed to me that there were further questions we might ask by working on the play.[11]

Southall might be described as a progressive place, in Massey's terms, with a particularly lively atmosphere on market day where the shops and stalls that sell a colourful range of imported clothes from the Asian subcontinent are mixed with the smells of spicy food and the banter of traditional costermongers with their barrows of fruit and veg. The Glassy Junction pub proudly boasts that it accepts Rupees, the Himalaya Palace cinema specializes in showing both Bollywood and Hollywood blockbusters, and Southall provided locations for the films *Bend it Like Beckham* (2002) and *Dhan Dhana Dhan Goal*

(2007), both of which used football as a metaphor for discussing cultural hybridity and national identity. The students who took part were self-selecting, a group of fifteen young people aged between 15 and 17, all of whom had been politicized to some extent by the anti-Islamic sentiment that followed 9/11 and 7/7. Many of their families had inhabited the same area of Southall, a district in West London that is under the Heathrow flight-path, since their grandparents' arrival from India, Pakistan and Bangladesh in the 1950s and 1960s. This was a gift to me as a theatre-maker and researcher as it opened new avenues of inquiry about their conceptualization of home and their identification with different imagined communities of nationhood. To the young people, of course, the 1950s and 1960s were ancient history, just as my grandparents' stories of the First World War seemed remote to me when I was a teenager, but this meant that all the students felt rooted to Southall – 'our hearts belong in Southall' as one of the boys said – thereby challenging Bauman's perception of a liquid society in which relationships with place are temporary. My decision to work in Southall was informed by its history as well as the liveliness of its diverse population; Southall was the site of a notorious demonstration against the National Front in 1979 in which the Anti-Nazi League activist Blair Peach was killed. The circumstances around his death were murky – it was widely believed that the weapon that crushed his skull had been wielded by a police officer, but there were no prosecutions. As I write in April 2010, the Metropolitan Police have only just published the report that admits responsibility, a full thirty years after his death. Southall is also only four stops on the train from my home village on the way to London, and it is the only station on that line in which the station signs are written in both English and Punjabi. All the students taking part were at least bilingual, and they particularly valued the range of languages regularly used in the shops and public spaces, and considered this both an ordinary part of their everyday lives and special to their home borough.

There were two parts to the project, the first phase was studio-based where we worked for an intensive period to explore the play's narrative and language, and the second took place on the streets of Southall and in an upstairs room near the library. The practice was planned to be responsive to the students' ideas and creative practice, and it was also structured to investigate the politics of place and identity, which I discussed with the students. I began by interviewing the students about their perceptions of Shakespeare and, to assist the process, I introduced ten statements about perceptions of

Shakespeare that were written on card (such as 'Shakespeare is the greatest British playwright' and 'Shakespeare should be banned in schools'). They were asked to sort these statements into rank order according to their level of agreement. I also gave them a series of images of Stratford and places associated with Shakespeare's biography, such as the streets of Southwark, Anne Hathaway's cottage and his birthplace, and asked them to put captions to the image. The interviews were recorded and transcribed. I was interested in hearing their attitudes rather than quantifying their responses, and what I learnt from these interviews was that they began the project with a distinct ambivalence about Shakespeare's place in national culture. All the students had studied Shakespeare in school, and although some had struggled with the language, the majority had enjoyed the experience. This did not, however, stop them from considering Shakespeare as a playwright whose work represented a cultural perspective that was remote from their own lives. One of the girls commented that his world was 'too pretty' and 'too English' to have 'anything to say in Southall'. Conversely, however, I was surprised that there was considerable disagreement with the statement that Shakespeare should be replaced in the National Curriculum by more contemporary playwrights. They saw Shakespeare representing of a culture that was not theirs but, in the words of one of the boys, 'will stay white if we don't learn it'.

It is not my intention to provide a detailed description of the drama workshops here, but I would like to select a few moments to illustrate their debates and practices. The work began fairly conventionally by focusing on the way Prospero insults Caliban in Act 1 scene 2, exploring physically and vocally such phrases as 'Filth as thou art' and 'abhorred slave' and 'thy vile race'. The students found it easy to empathize with Caliban's situation, and found Prospero's racist taunts both provocative and depressingly familiar. There was a turning point, however, that informed their dramatic interpretations of the play and challenged their perceptions of Prospero. I showed them two images of Prospero from past productions and asked them to describe the interpretation of his role and effect in words and movement. The first two pictures I showed them depicted Haviland in a production in 1904 and Mark Rylance at The Globe in 2005, both of which led them to describe Prospero as wise, authoritative and just, a perception that supported relatively conventional readings of Prospero as a benign and wronged Duke who asserts a benevolent spiritual power. In this interpretation, Prospero represents art over nature, philosopher over slave, civilization over chaos – an idea further fuelled by the mythology that the play is Shakespeare's autobiographical farewell to art. When the students returned to Act 1 scene 2 to realize this interpretation they found that although they could make it work theatrically, they remained so convinced that Prospero was a racist bully that their dramatic interpretation and their own political views were in tension. At this point I showed them two images from the British Asian Theatre Company's Tara Arts 2008 production that challenged their interpretation of the play (Figs 7.1 and 7.2). Prospero is clearly very angry, and his daughter Miranda is wearing a hijab.

These images prompted the students to become increasingly interested in the reasons for Prospero's anger, first, towards Caliban, and second in relation to his need for revenge for the loss of his Dukedom. They were first drawn to reconsider how Prospero's anger towards Caliban had been provoked because he believed that Caliban had attempted violate Miranda. These students understood, unlike others I have taught over the years, the complexity and ambiguity that surrounds this element of the play and they quickly identified the differences between the assumptions within the play and the liberal attitudes towards sexuality in the twenty-first century. Many admitted to struggling to reconcile the values of Islam and Western liberalism in this respect in their own lives, and understood how this tension might affect the interpretation of Miranda and Prospero in performance. The Tara Arts production, directed by Jatinder Verma, was alert to the cross-cultural implications of the play, and its potential to speak to a post-9/11 and 7/7 generation. The production invoked Islamic fundamentalism; Prospero is a man, exiled from a country he believes he should rightfully govern, who is holed up in a cave for 12 years plotting revenge on the world. The programme notes not only cited Osama Bin Laden, they compared Prospero to Said Imam al-Sharif, a prominent Jihadist who had renounced violence. We could all relate to the kind of anger that imagines revenge, and we drew up the plans Prospero might have made over the years, and charted how his feelings might have changed or softened over the years. The performance of Prospero's plots began with the students' witty explanation of intergalactic destruction of disaster movie proportions, but each year they mellowed until they were reduced to plans for a small, local tempest. This process became central to understanding Prospero's emotional journey and offered an imaginary glimpse inside his famous books. The parallels with 9/11 were startlingly clear. Offering the students different speeches and copies of the script, I asked them to find the

Figure 7.1 Prospero, played by Robert Mountford in Tara Arts' production of *The Tempest*. Photograph by Talula Sheppard.

Figure 7.2 Miranda, played by Jessica Manley. Photograph by Talula Sheppard.

reasons Shakespeare had given Prospero for not simply killing his brother and everyone on the boat. They found that it was Ariel who persuaded him against murder and Miranda who had softened his attitude to his former adversaries. The students returned to work on Act 1 scene 2 from this perspective. They recognized that Prospero felt excluded, deprived of his rightful territory, humiliated and vengeful. Would they act on his behalf? Would they attack their fellow countrymen on their own ground? It was a profound question. These insights prompted the students to make moral decisions about where their sympathies lay, and how to present Prospero to an audience. Rather than sanitizing Prospero's anger, they found ways to explore the effects of his feelings of revenge. This approach was intended to explore the distance between self and other, with the play serving to bridge the gap, in Ellsworth's terms, as a 'mode of transit to think relationally within that space' (2005, p. 85).

Working in the abstract space of a black box theatre allowed us to explore multiple interpretations of the play, but raising more precise questions about the relationship between the play and conceptions of national identity involved a change in venue. For the second part of the project the students suggested that we moved from the privacy of the studio to the public spaces of the streets, parks and other cultural land-marks of Southall. This followed Appiah's perception (1998, p. 94) that 'humans live best on a smaller scale', and by resituating *The Tempest* in Southall we aimed to see what questions it raised about place and (national) identity. We planned to record speeches from the play to accompany a walk around Southall that each audience member would follow individually on ipods and mp3 players. Using a sound recording spared the students from the embarrassment of a full-on Shakespearean street performance, but its main purpose was to encourage a sense of cultural intimacy with the audience as they negotiated the relationship between text, voice and place. Theatrically, sound created an intimacy with each walker that framed and gave shape to their experiences. Performatively, the sonic walk was intended to reframe, rather than dis-rupt, the geopolitics of the area.[12] The students were deeply attached to the places they chose, and the process of linking the route to extracts from *The Tempest* raised questions about their relationship to familiar sights and sites. Southall's cultural complexity and global sense of place, to borrow Massey's phrase, is inscribed in its streetscape and this was reflected in the Tempest walk, which started from the station, followed the road to the Gurdwara Sriguru Singh Sabham Sikh Temple, past the Glassy Junction pub and onto the shops on the Broadway, pausing at Beachcroft Avenue near the Town Hall where Blair Peach was struck, before finishing at the Central Jamia Masjid Mosque, a route that took us past a cemetery and through an underpass. Tim Ingold describes this kind of path-making as a 'taskscape', a term he uses to describe the creative ways in which patterns of daily movement associated with work, leisure and other regular activities are choreographed onto famil-iar places (Ingold, 2000). By asking audience members to pause, look around and listen at specific wayfaring points, we intended to highlight, in Edensor's words, the 'unreflexive constitution of spatial belonging' that contributes to an everyday sense of national identity (2000, p. 57).

The process of choosing extracts that both fitted the route and told the story revealed some interesting tensions in the play about author-ity, ownership and belonging. Prospero always accepted that he was a temporary resident on the island, but he still used his previous status as a duke to assume governance, whereas Caliban and Ariel both felt they belonged there. Caliban is a second generation islander, his mother Sycorax had been banished from Algiers; Ariel had lived there longer, but had been imprisoned in a tree by Sycorax until released by Prospero. The layers of ownership and conflict over territory represented in the play resonated with the students, all of whom felt that they had a stronger allegiance to Southall than the homeland of their grandparents, but they also understood the struggle to feel culturally accepted, particularly by those in positions of institutional power. As we mapped *The Tempest* onto Southall, we found street names such as Saxon Road and Viking Avenue that invoked a history of previous invaders, and it was this simple insight that clarified the students' political interpretation of the play. Not only did they learn that ownership of Prospero's island was multiply contested, they also recognized that the contemporary cultural anxiety about national cohesion was far from new. They chose to tell the story of *The Tempest* through the speeches of Caliban, Prospero and Ariel, with at least one performer stationed at each stopping place, either to draw attention to the streetscape or to carry out an everyday action that both framed and illuminated the audio recording. Stopping at the junction of Saxon Road to listen to the speech 'This island's mine' in which Caliban describes his feelings of betrayal was a moving experience, especially as the voice I heard was distinctly that of a young, British-Asian Londoner. Walking to the place where the teacher Blair Peach was attacked by the police similarly meant that Caliban's speech acquired a new resonance once it was relocated on the Southall streets:

> there thou mayst brain him,
> Having first seized his books, or with a log
> Batter his skull, or paunch him with a stake,
> Or cut his wezand with thy knife. Remember
> First to possess his books; for without them
> He's but a sot, as I am, nor hath not
> One spirit to command: they all do hate him
> As rootedly as I.
>
> Act 11, scene ii, lines 86–93

To hear this speech spoken very angrily, and to see a young performer quietly holding Blair Peach's image, was to witness a moment where history and the present came together. Although I am sure that Shakespeare purists would have challenged our eclectic interpretation, we all understood the layers of anger in the play about cultural and educational superiority and the claims to territory that had arisen through the words of Caliban, as a second generation inhabitant of the island. It suggested that nationhood and a sense of belonging was imagined and re-created in practice and through affect, rather than through an assertion of prior ownership. This led to discussions about how to play Prospero's final speech, which they wanted to situate in the street near the mosque. His journey through the play provided a context for the students to discuss their own relationship to the place and where they felt they belonged. We worked on Prospero's final speech together, trying out different interpretations, and they decided to record a collective version of Prospero's final speech that balanced anger with acceptance. They played the speech for forgiveness and reconciliation, a sentiment that seemed apposite in a context in which the desire for revenge for some deep injustices might easily turn to violence. Their sense of national identity was implicated in their faith as, one of the students explained, quoting both Caliban and Prospero's final speech: 'This island's mine, and the Qu'ran teaches that prayer "frees all faults". So long as these two hang together it's good as a place. But it's brittle'.

Lefebvre suggests that for people to be recognized as active social beings, they must produce space for themselves (1991, p. 416). When I returned to interview the young people a few weeks after the project they said that it had changed their relationship with familiar places, particularly as they couldn't help hearing Shakespeare's words as they passed each wayfaring place on the Tempest walk. So what did the project achieve? It had never been my intention to use Shakespeare to promote social cohesion, and my ambitions were more localized and open-ended. Educationally, the students had obviously learnt about the play, but this had also seeped into their bodies, memories and everyday lives as the play became inscribed with personal meanings. Working with the protection of a script enabled the students to negotiate the space in between self and other, between the aesthetics of performance and their social and cultural understandings. Ellsworth suggests that straddling the paradox between 'being simultaneously in difference and in relation' facilitates creative learning (2005, p. 89). In this context, framing everyday places theatrically invited the students to interrogate their 'unreflexive identifications' with places and practices, to borrow Edensor's phrase, and the negotiation between text and place encouraged them to re-imagine their sense of belonging. The students told me that working with Shakespeare on the streets of Southall did unfix his work from its association with British cultural elitism for them, and the process removed the play from the remoteness of an archive and into their embodied repertoire and creative improvisation of everyday cultural practice.

Dramatizing the nation in contemporary theatre

There is a delightful moment in Fin Kennedy's beautiful play, *Mehndi Night,* in which the London-born Muslim bride confesses that she

likes Shakespeare. Her sister Salma's reply, 'Yes, but you're weird' prompts a debate about the role of drama for British Muslim young women (2010, p. 23). Salma's argument with her younger sister rests on her view that: 'It's not our culture, this music and drama', to which her sister responds, 'Cultures are changing now, merging' (2010, p. 25). Globalization, migration and the effects of diaspora have forced a reconsideration of national and cultural identities and, although I have chosen to focus on the symbolic capital of Shakespeare in this chapter, it is perhaps even more significant that in the first decade of the twenty-first century there has been a proliferation of new plays that debate political questions of culture and nationhood, and this work is changing the national dynamic. Perhaps most significantly, as both Jen Harvie and Nadine Holdsworth have pointed out, theatre is demonstrating that there is not one coherent 'British' identity, but that national identities are multiple, changing and varied (Harvie, 2005; Holdsworth, 2010). It is interesting in this context that, unlike the Comédie Francaise that stages plays that celebrate the great works of the French cultural tradition, British National theatres are instrumental in commissioning and promoting new work. National Theatre of Scotland founded in 2006 is not building-based, nor is it charged with promoting an imaginary stereotype of heritage Scotland but generates a vibrant, contemporary programme that includes as many people as possible in site-specific performance, village halls, schools and community centres as well as entertaining and challenging audiences in more conventional theatre spaces both within Scotland and beyond. The National Theatre in London, though more conventionally building-based, has a long tradition of staging new plays, and new work also forms an important part of the RSC repertoire. Theatre education has a major role in reaching people who may not be considered conventional theatre audiences, and this brings an opportunity to wrestle national identity away from the clutches of nationalist prejudice by presenting young people with theatrical experiences that invite a range of identifications, thereby challenging perceptions of a fixed or unifying national culture.

One of the means through which this might be achieved is through encouraging the voices of young playwrights and theatre-makers. There is also a strong history of encouraging playwrights from a range of cultural backgrounds to write for young audiences that was particularly evident in the Federal Theatre project in the 1930s United States, and this tradition continues today. The black British playwrights Roy Williams, Angela Turvey and Winsome Pinnock received commissions to write for young audiences early in their careers and in Australia, as John O'Toole and Penny Bundy have observed, the Aboriginal playwright Jack Davis honed his craft by working in TIE (1980, p. 138). Theatre companies who work with young people are well placed to produce work that reflects the full diversity of a nation's identity, and the commitment to nurture new talent has introduced some lively apprenticeship schemes for young adults. The Royal Court Theatre in London has various schemes that specifically aim to support young black and Asian playwrights. One programme, Unheard Voices, was established in 2009 to encourage Muslim writers aged between 18 and 25, and supported Alio Bano in writing her award-winning play *Shades* (Royal Court, London, 2009) about the Muslim dating scene. If perceptions of national identity and national cultures are to change in response to changing social circumstances, theatres as cultural institutions will provide opportunities for theatre-makers and audiences to explore a new imaginary of nationhood and a dynamic sense of belonging to a place.

Both theatre and national identity depend on an ability to identify with others, at least partially, but new ideas about national identity are most productively generated when the symmetry between the spectator and performance is disrupted. This returns the debate to Appadurai's insight about the relationship between the imagination and social life, in which theatre can offer an alternative to conventional and packaged mediascapes of nationhood. Working through the aesthetic frame of theatre can hold this cultural anxiety long enough to look at the issues it raises, and drama, theatre and performance can provide young people with a symbolic space to explore alternative narratives of national identity. Theatre *education* can provide a further context for learning a sense of national identity that recognizes that it is inclusive, multiple and plural. To apply Ellsworth's description of this approach to learning to theatre education, theatre offers 'designed spaces and times' that 'both facilitate and alleviate the peril of putting oneself in relation (2005, pp. 89–90). In terms of *national* identity, which has become more pressing and prescient since 9/11 and 7/7, this holds both the mundane and the spectacle associated nationhood and nationality simultaneously, allowing the official map to meet everyday narratives, and to allow itself to change and be changed in the process.

8

International Spaces: Global Citizenship and Cultural Exchange

Global citizenship and the facebook generation

In the previous chapter I argued that performance frames and re-embodies national identity, and I suggested that locating questions of belonging in the vernacular spaces of everyday life allows young people to explore their allegiances and attachments to wider imagined communities through the symbolism of theatre. This way of working aims to stop racist and fundamentalist movements gaining ground or achieving official statehood by accepting that national identities, like other forms of identity, are not fixed but progressive, multiple and open to change. It is, however, equally clear that collective identification with the imagined community of the nation-state has its limits in the twenty-first century, and that loyalties extend far beyond national boundaries. Although citizenship is still a legal status that is primarily structured within the nation-state, globalization has forced a reconsideration of how collective habits, thoughts, feelings and values have become increasingly deterritorialized. In this chapter I shall consider how debates about citizenship have moved from the nation to the social imaginary of the world, and consider the implications of global citizenship for theatre, education and performance in the twenty-first century.

It is undoubtedly the case that the world is increasingly interconnected, but what is less clear is how personal relationships, civic values and cultural identities will be affected by this sense of mobility in the future. Zigmunt Bauman's picture of 'liquid love' in a liquid society suggests that the facebook generation move swiftly from one set of friends to another without forming deep emotional bonds. 'In a network', Bauman regrets, 'connecting and disconnecting are equally legitimate choices and carry the same importance' (2003, p. xii). One argument is that social networking sites have commodified friendship in ways that suit knowledge-based economies, where networks are easily formed and readily discarded. This is, perhaps, an unfair representation of the very real and sustaining friendships that are supported by increased ease of communication, but it is also the case that the needs of global capitalism are served well by a network society and an affluent, mobile workforce who are skilled at forming temporary social bonds. The fast-changing knowledge economy is in a permanent state of transition and transformation and there is a risk that a secure sense of loyalty, emotional ties and structured accountability that is associated with what Bruce Robbins calls 'old fashioned citizenship' is eroded (1998b, p. 11). More worryingly, Benedict Anderson suggests that the combination of mobility and global interconnectedness has generated the phenomenon of 'long-distance nationalism' in which those who have relocated to affluent countries 'play identity politics' by funding extremist propaganda and weapons in situations of conflict on the other side of the world. 'This citizenshipless participation is inevitably non-responsible', Anderson comments ironically, as 'our hero will not have to answer for, or pay the price of, the long-distance politics he undertakes' (1992, p. 13). It is within this political climate that theatre-makers, both within education and beyond, are seeking new ways to bridge social and cultural division.

Of all the many ways in which theatre-makers are striving to build constructive dialogues within and between cultures, I have chosen to focus in this chapter on the educational practice of cultural exchange. There have been educational exchanges between European countries for a very long time, often for the purposes of language learning, but schools and cultural organizations are now looking further afield as a way to challenge young people to extend their personal and cultural horizons.[1] The vision of equitable cultural exchange across national boundaries is, perhaps, a new twenty-first century utopianism, and the facebook generation has come to expect increased long-haul international travel. The cultural sector has also generated interest in theatre, music and dance from distant parts of the world, and international theatre, dance and music festivals (WOMAD is a good example) and have long brought together artists in innovative ways that challenge audiences' expectations. In relation to theatre, the politics of cultural exchange have been famously interrogated by the Indian theatre director Rustom Bharucha, who describes interculturalism as 'the least recognised struggle of our times' (2000, p. 160). Bharucha convincingly argues that all exchanges between practitioners in the developing world and globalizing nations are inevitably predicated on uneven distributions of wealth and power. This means that intercultural exchange (he is describing the work of professional theatre-makers) is easily appropriated and commodified by Westerners, whether they are theatre directors, academics or cultural tourists. But the creative dynamic of meeting through the medium of theatre, he argues, can provide an important catalyst for unfixing prejudicial attitudes and confronting the realities of social injustice. It is this aspect of intercultural exchange and dialogue that perhaps speaks most directly to theatre educators, not least because it allows the possibility for the practices of everyday life to come together with the imagined and fictional worlds of theatre.

In this chapter I shall consider the specific role theatre has to make to an education for global citizenship. In his book *Theatre & Interculturalism* (2010) Ric Knowles points out that there is a long history of applying theatre to intercultural dialogue, but he warns that such an ambition 'raises issues about cultural imperialism, appropriation, and colonialism, even as it offers the utopian promise of a world where race and cultural difference do not matter' (2010, pp. 1–2). My struggle in the first part of the chapter is to address questions of politics and principle, asking how – and if – theatre might contribute to an education that challenges prejudice in an increasingly globalized world. There are already unequal levels of opportunity and uneven access to resources that many young people in the affluent countries take for granted – how might intercultural exchanges avoid perpetuating this inequality? The remainder of the chapter reflects on two examples of my own practice as research, *Performing Citizenship*, *Investigating Place*, a trilogy of projects that took me to South Africa and Japan before returning to work with the young people in London on nationhood which I discussed in Chapter 7. Debates about interculturalism and theatre, as Knowles points out, are located firmly in the Western academic discourse, and much of the argument in this chapter derives from explicitly acknowledging that position. In the academy, Kwon suggests, the success and validity of someone's work sometimes seems to be judged according to the number of frequent flyer points they have accrued (2004, p. 156), and I have often wondered how far international travel, damaging as it is to the environment, has been used by theatre educationalists to export their own ways of working to different parts of the world; certainly in the published output of much-travelled theatre educators, I have found very little reference to how their practice changed in response to local cultures or their ideas challenged by encountering unfamiliar approaches to teaching and learning.[2] In this project, I was interested in learning how my own practices and frames of reference reflect – knowingly or unknowingly – a perspective that is imbued in a particular a set of cultural assumptions. Perhaps most particularly, I am interested here in exploring how thinking globally, as well as locally, involves moving beyond the limits of identity politics, and challenges the myth of shared nationalistic 'origins' by inviting identification with people and places with whom there is no obvious or imagined sense of community.

Global citizenship and vernacular cosmopolitanism

The principles and practice of citizenship have received considerable critical attention recently, not least because liberal conceptions of citizenship as a legal set of rights and responsibilities defined and policed by the nation-state provide an inadequate or partial account of its potential efficacy on an international scale. Anxieties about how national identity is understood has not always led to an easy equation between citizenship and social justice; the British government, for example, introduced citizenship legislation in the early years of the twentieth century that served as a form of cultural policing, with citizenship and English language tests for new arrivals and citizenship ceremonies offered to those who pass. Notwithstanding these limitations, citizenship remains a potent way to conceptualize democratic public participation and, as I argued in *Applied Drama: The Gift of Theatre* (2005), for that reason it remains a significant concept for theatre.

One of the political thinkers who is often invoked in discussions of the relationship between theatre and citizenship is Hannah Arendt (1906–75). Arendt recognized the importance of public spaces to democratic participation, and she described the public realm as a 'space of appearance' which comes into being 'in the manner of speech and action' (1958, p. 199). This democratic space has to be continually reproduced if it is to maintain its potential for efficacy and equality because, she suggests, 'the political realm rises directly out of acting together' (1958, p. 198). Arendt's argument that citizenship is dependent on interaction has been revisited in the twenty-first century because it provides a way of theorizing participant citizenship that extends beyond homogenous or fixed national identities. Arendt herself regarded sameness as 'antipolitical' and it is her interest in maintaining a radical commitment to social equality and pluralism that gives her work contemporary resonance. 'The attempt to do away with plurality', she claims, 'is always tantamount to the abolition of the public realm itself' (1958, p. 220). Chantal Mouffe extended Arendt's arguments to the globalized society of the twenty-first century, arguing that 'well functioning democracy calls for a vibrant clash of democratic political positions' (2000, p. 104). Eliminating antagonisms creates apathy, she explains, drives disaffection underground and creates the conditions for extremism or fundamentalism.

Finding ways to acknowledge pluralism in ways that will reduce extremism and discourage fundamentalism have, of course, acquired a new urgency since Mouffe published her work in 2000. One way to conceptualize the values associated with democratic citizenship that extend beyond national boundaries is through the idea of global citizenship, and, on first view, this sounds like an uncontroversial suggestion. There are, however, very different ways of thinking about global citizenship; the term is used by global capitalists as well as humanitarian organizations, with obviously different priorities and agendas. On the one hand, Microsoft founder Bill Gates advocates what he calls 'corporate global citizenship' which will extend what he sees as the 'genius' of capitalism to poorer countries.[3] Another computer giant, Hewlett Packard, similarly stresses its commitment to global citizenship as a way of aligning their 'business goals' with their 'impacts on society and the planet'.[4] Following in the tradition of self-interested philanthropy that supported the industrial revolution, both organizations offer 'social investments' grants to extend digital communication, thereby creating new markets for their products. From another perspective, Oxfam argues that education for global citizenship should underpin the whole curriculum in schools, and focus on ways of thinking about social inequality, the environment and the complex connections between the local and the global. Throughout its teaching materials, Oxfam emphasizes participatory approaches to teaching and learning and, in the spirit of progressive education, suggests that democratic participation in the classroom encourages young people to become active and responsible global citizens.[5] This approach to an education for global citizenship asks political questions about the asymmetrical power relations between rich and poor countries and, unlike Microsoft and Hewlett Packard, Oxfam obviously do not harness an education for global citizenship to the spread of global capitalism.

The ideas implicit in perceptions of global citizenship promoted by humanitarian organizations and many citizenship education programmes in schools are closer to cosmopolitanism than globalization. There has been a revival of interest in the ancient concept of cosmopolitanism in the twenty-first century, where it is seen as a radical opponent to globalization. Globalization is always motivated by the search for profit whereas cosmopolitanism, by contrast, is concerned with finding ways of thinking, feeling and acting ethically both within and beyond national boundaries. Deriving from the composite Greek word *kosmos – polites*, translatable as 'world citizen', cosmopolitanism refers to the moral philosophy that everyone, whatever their culture, ethnicity or beliefs, is worthy of equal regard and dignity. There is significant political and academic dissent about the different ways in which this might be interpreted, but it is this basic premise that informs debate. Although globalization and cosmopolitanism are both concerned with international interconnections, globalization is intent on making parts of the world *richer* (through increased consumption of homogenized products) whereas cosmopolitans want to make the world *better* by challenging social and economic division and resisting cultural homogeneity. So what are the implications of cosmopolitanism for the principles and practices of theatre education?

Of the different versions of cosmopolitanism that might inform theatre education, I find the versions put forward by the philosopher Kwame Anthony Appiah and the cultural theorist Homi Bhabha particularly persuasive. Appiah describes cosmopolitanism not as an ideology, but a sentiment, and this means that it is open to range of ideological perspectives provided that they conform to a broader framework of human rights. He sums up his ideal of 'rooted cosmopolitanism' in this way:

> We value the variety of human forms of social and cultural life; we do not want everybody to become part of a homogeneous global culture; and we know that this means there will be local differences (both within and between states) in moral climate as well. So long as these differences meet certain ethical constraints – so long, in particular, as political institutions respect basic human rights – we are happy to let them be. (1998, p. 94)

Part of the challenge in practice, of course, is defining what these 'ethical constraints' might be and how human rights are articulated. Yet it is because these ethical constraints are based on sentimental attachments to the rootedness of place as well as abstract ideas of social justice that they offer a helpful way of thinking about cultural exchange that is equitable rather than asymmetrical. First, this construction of cosmopolitanism recognizes that all moral and cultural identities are open to change as new cultural forms emerge, thereby acknowledging the effects and affects of cultural engagement with others from different parts of the world. Second, it also suggests that difference thrives where there is a broad commitment to sustaining institutional structures that are based on secure moral principles, yet also sufficiently flexible and porous to allow for their multiple interpretations in practice. Third, this radical openness to difference involves making connections, not only through shared identities, but also through caring about the wellbeing of strangers.

Appiah's perception of cosmopolitanism as ethical and emotional commitments to 'a world of strangers' (the subtitle of his book) prompts new ways to think about an ethic of care, and suggests how a sense of community might be imagined across national borders. Homi Bhabha further develops the question of how to relate ethically to strangers, and he rejects the idea, developed by Martha Nussbaum, that there is a pre-given, universal empathetic self on which cosmopolitan sensibilities for others depends.[6] Rather, Bhabha's 'vernacular cosmopolitanism' is built on narratives of history and selfhood that relate to crisis, displacement and suffering. He cites Richard Sennett's perception that kindness to strangers relies on affective identification with their difficulties. Care for others, Sennett writes:

> arises from recognising the insufficiencies of the self ... the fractures, self-destructiveness and irresolvable conflicts of desires within ourselves which ... will prompt us to cross boundaries ... Openness to the needs of others comes from ceasing to dream of the world made whole. (Sennett, cited in Bhabha 2001, pp. 42–3)

Facing the 'insufficiencies of the self' in ways that create openness to others is, for Bhabha, a political act that relies on a combination of imagination, narrative and performativity. Without the 'dream of the world made whole', it becomes possible to break the complacency he associates with Nussbaum's grander portrait of a common humanity and consider the political significance of the everyday and vernacular:

> For it is precisely there, in the ordinariness of the day to day, in the intimacy of the indigenous, that, unexpectedly, we become unrecognizable

strangers to ourselves in the very act of assuming a more worldly, or what is now termed "global", responsibility. (2001, p. 44)

Because this position is not based on projecting the humanist principle that there is a single, common humanity – and nor would we want everyone to be 'just like us' – that we have to face the delightful, painful and sometimes difficult negotiation of values and everyday practices that we do not share. It embraces difference, but knows that tolerance has limits.

Critics of Appiah and Bhabha's conceptions of vernacular cosmopolitanism argue, very persuasively, that they focus on addressing the conflicts that arise from cultural difference at the expense of addressing the very real political and economic inequalities driven by capitalism.[7] I think that is fair; I am not suggesting that the cultural politics of theatre education will bring down global capitalism. But I do believe that the pedagogical processes of intercultural exchange and theatre-making provide a rich, layered and transitional space to push against some of the boundaries of this inequality on a small scale.

Working together artistically does not involve exchanging one fixed world view for another, as Noël Greig points out in his book *Young People, New Theatre* (2008) in which he describes the methodologies used in the 'Contacting the World' festival. 'Contacting the World', based in Manchester, is a project that brings together young artists and performers from different parts of the world to make a new piece of theatre. Greig calls this theatrical interchange a 'partnership of difference', and shows how it is this very diversity that sparks creativity. As part of the process of collaborative exchange, Greig suggests a range of ways that young people might share their experiences, cultural memories and traditions, all of which generate source material for the play as well as insights into unfamiliar ways of living. In a section on 'hidden histories' he explains how young people share accounts of history that are normally hidden, and he acknowledges that although some of these cultural memories are painful, they are nonetheless stories that should be told. He cites an example of a shameful story of a community arts venue in London that has balconies which were once used by slave traders to select slaves, and the more uplifting case of a young woman in eighteenth century Brighton who, disguised as a boy, became a sailor and was awarded a medal for her bravery.[8] These stories were told to their twin, whose job it was to dramatize these cultural memories and perhaps interweave a story from their own community's hidden history with which it has some connections. This partnership of difference is robust; as Appiah comments, 'people often recommend relativism because they think it will lead to tolerance. But if we cannot learn from each other what it is right to think and feel and do, then a conversation between us will be pointless. Relativism of that sort isn't a way to encourage conversation; it's just a reason to fall silent' (2006, p. 31).

For intercultural dialogue to work both socially and theatrically requires everyone involved to be sufficiently open to learn from each other – to risk becoming 'unrecognizable strangers' to themselves. In terms that invoke performance theory, Elizabeth Ellsworth explains the pedagogic thinking that informs this kind of exchange as a transitional space:

> Being in relation opens up a space of difference between self and other, inner and outer realities. It opens up a third zone, a space that I can experience as both me and not me. (2005, p. 64)

Ellsworth explains that this pedagogical approach aims to shift the binaries between self and other, subjective and objective, inner and outer realities in order to avoid 'face-to-face opposition' and open the possibility of 'reordering of self and other' (2005, p. 64).Writing about 'Thirdspace', the cultural geographer Edward Soja also suggests that an emancipated space will resist rehearsing fixed binaries. Soja offers practical advice to anyone wishing to explore this Thirdspace, and his words might usefully inform theatre collaborations across cultures and places:

> Exploring Thirdspace therefore requires a strategic and flexible way of thinking that is guided by a particular motivating project, a set of clear practical objectives and preferred pathways that will help keep each individual journey on track while still allowing for lateral excursions to other spaces, times and social situations. (1996, p. 22)

This Thirdspace of 'real-and-imagined' places is centrally important to an ethic of cosmopolitanism, I would suggest, precisely because it offers a way to theorize the creative and unpredictable process of 'being in relation' to others.

In this chapter I shall discuss two different projects, one in South Africa and one in Japan, both of which illuminate some of the complexities of international collaboration in theatre education. In each case, I worked with sustained and ongoing programmes of educational and cultural exchange, which meant that my contribution was a small part of a bigger picture. I am particularly mindful of the role of the itinerant artists described by Kwon as 'a glamorisation of the trickster ethos that is in fact a reprise of the ideology of "freedom of choice"' which 'does not belong to everyone equally' (2004, p. 165). The sustained relationships that had been built up around both projects meant that there was room to experiment and, because of this, not everything went according to plan. But it is in moments of messiness when things seem to go wrong that we often learnt most – helping me to recognize, following Bhabha, the insufficiencies of myself – a feeling everyone involved recognized at different stages in the work. Of all the many challenges we faced I have chosen to focus on two elements of the work, language and mother tongue learning in South Africa and the relationship between play and learning in Japan. In different ways, both projects open debate about how drama enabled children to create real and imagined spaces that crossed cultural and political boundaries.

Citizenship, representation and theatre: Khayelitsha, South Africa and Slough, UK

The work that I was involved with in South Africa has long political roots. The drama project was developed in collaboration with the citizenship education co-ordinator at Creative Partnerships in Slough, Jan Fredrickson, whose anti-Apartheid campaigning and egalitarian vision for citizenship education has led her to build close associations with schools in the Cape Town region. Schools in Slough have been twinned with township schools since the first South African democratic elections in 1994, and there has been sustained dialogue between students and teachers through video conferencing, letters and regular educational exchanges. Funding for this collaboration has been garnered from a range of sponsors, including the British Council, DFID and local fundraising activities in the United Kingdom, with the clear objectives that the money raised contributes to an equal educational partnership rather than setting up a patronizing 'donor culture' from North to South. The collaboration is known as *The Hlanganani Learning Partnership,* Hlanganani is a Nguni word meaning 'the spirit of working together', and this summarizes the partnership's motives.[9]

One of the challenges for partnerships between schools is how to make dialogue meaningful, active and equitable between schools, particularly where only one partner has regular internet access and postal connections are costly for everyone. The drama element of the partnership was designed to extend links between primary schools and for the stimulus of the drama, a picture book called *Giraffes Can't Dance*, provided a shared context for conversations. In this particular project in 2006, undergraduate students in the department of drama at Royal Holloway, University of London worked with children in Slough, thereby gaining valuable classroom experience as theatre-makers in primary schools, and the teachers in South Africa worked on the same drama project with their classes in Khayelitsha, just outside Cape Town. Children of primary school age are too young to visit each others' countries and so the dialogue is sustained by regular exchange visits between teachers and, on this occasion, Jan Fredrickson and I visited South Africa halfway through the ten-week drama project. Notwithstanding this contact, the success of the work depended on the children's ability to imagine another part of the world. Encouraging children in the British school to learn about South Africa led us to confront issues of representation. Tom Collins, a student working on the project, created a slide show to help children in Slough imagine life in South Africa, but he found that he risked increasing the divide between cultures through both his use of technology and his choice of images:

> In my eagerness to entertain the children I used needless animation tools to make the pictures jump onto the screen and fade away. The children responded very positively to this use of presentation, but at what cost? Displaying pictures of poverty-stricken Africans on an expensive piece of equipment not only distracted the children, it also highlighted the gap between cultures and underlined my own misinterpretation of what it means to be a global citizen. (Tom Collins, 2006)

Tom's discomfort at the children's responses to images of South African children illustrates how his attempts to encourage the children's empathy easily slipped into generating their pity. Pity is an emotion that is often exploited by TV fund-raising campaigns and some charity rock concerts; there was considerable controversy in 2006 when there was a complete absence of African artists performing at the Live 8 concert in London, organized by Bono and Bob Geldof. Tom recognized that this mediascape represented the South African children as needy and apparently helpless, thereby undermining a more productive view of South Africans as active, participant, global citizens. This realization caused Tom to reconsider perceptions that had become familiar through years of media imagery, and refocused debates on representation, agency and power.

The children's story we had chosen to dramatize, *Giraffes Can't Dance,* takes place in the grassy plains of southern Africa and follows the struggle of Gerald, a lonely giraffe, who tries to dance in the same way as the other animals at the great Jungle Dance. His ungainly moves are mocked by the other animals, causing him to withdraw from the party. It is only when he is alone that he finds his own rhythm, and the story ends when the other animals have learnt to respect Gerald's style of dance. Theatrically, the British children were most interested in the affects of language on others, and in particular, on the ways Gerald responded to the animals' bullying. Gerald was represented by a large puppet, manipulated by the students, a decision that ensured that the children were not faced with the prospect of taunting each other. The emphasis on the ways in which words, gestures and actions are received linked language to citizenship education, as student Rachel Betts pointed out:

> The children chanted an African folk song in a thundering, loud and low tone of voice while stomping their feet ferociously on the floor; intimidating Gerald by invading his personal space, and leaning over him with clenched fists and menacing facial expressions. This mosaic of literacies used to create an atmosphere of violence and hostility meant that children were not just learning what language *is* (movement, dialogue, song and facial expression) but what it *does*; its effects, through experiencing how it made them feel. (Rachel Betts, 2006)

The children were asked to represent attitudes and actions they found unethical as *performers*, while also responding empathetically to the character of Gerald as *themselves*. This is a good example of relational learning, where the drama opens a 'Thirdspace' between self and other and thus allowed children to experience a space in which they are, in Ellsworth's terms 'both me and not me'. The fact that the children rather enjoyed the feet-stomping and chanting was, in itself, troubling to them because it suggested a lack of sympathy for Gerald, but locating themselves simultaneously both inside and outside the fictional frame of the drama meant that the children were required to confront ethical dilemmas represented in this transitional space.

The children in Khayelitsha were interested in the social role of dance in the story. In this interpretation the dramatic focus of the performance was the Jungle Dance, where Gerald the Giraffe felt clumsy and excluded, and the climax was Gerald's solo performance in the forest where he found his grace. The children had chosen to show the animals dancing in a Western style, using the restrained and formal choreography of ballroom dance. Gerald, by contrast, improvised his movements, using the rhythm and beat of African music, as an act of self-expression. This meant that the moment when the animals from the dance came to admire Gerald's solo performance had a strong political resonance. It implied that, by laughing at his style of dance, the animals had also been laughing at his culture. In the hands of these children, Gerald's dance became an affirmation and celebration of their cultural identity as South African citizens. Watching the children in the cavernous and echoing school hall, costumed in black plastic sacks that rustled as they moved, I became aware of how their creativity was an act of cultural improvisation that illustrated their relationship to the vernacular of their home culture.

I learnt from the children that their different dramatizations of the same story suggested two complementary conceptions of citizenship; one emphasized social identity and the importance of taking responsibility for excluded individuals, and the other foregrounded cultural identity and the collective right to cultural recognition. Their different interpretations illustrated Kathleen Gallagher's perception that the fictional worlds young people create in their drama is often in 'dynamic dialogue with the "realities" of their lives' (2007, p. 98). The children's reflections further illustrated how they negotiated this 'real-and-imagined' space. In South Africa, the children told me that they had tried out different forms of dance before they 'found out' that the central character had to learn 'English dancing' to try to fit in with the other animals. Their imaginary of England, I learnt, was a colonial white world of tea-dances and privileged, stiff-upper-lip formality, and they were very surprised to learn that there were black children in their partner school. In England, by contrast, the children had absorbed some of the mediascape of South African children as impoverished victims, but both the exchange and the drama provided a context for learning about South Africa that challenged this perception.

The drama invited the children to identify with feelings of exclusion experienced by an individual character, and the students were able to build on the children's empathy by asking them to consider how it would feel to be excluded from a whole political system. This way of working invokes Bhabha's vernacular cosmopolitanism in that it invited emotional identification with a history of exclusion and displacement, but it also showed the strength and resistance of people who had been dedicated to ending Apartheid. Thabisa, one of the older South African students who assisted me as translator in the Khayelitsha school, felt that strongly challenging ignorance lay at the heart of the The Hlanganani Learning Partnership. Thabisa had visited England as part of the partnership and she recounted, shockingly, that she had often been asked questions by young people in secondary schools that showed that they held images of black South Africans that had been internalized, presumably, from a combination of old movies and racially stereotypical 1950s picture books. If nothing else, the drama created a productive space that allowed these imaginaries of each other's places to be challenged. The children's manipulation of theatrical metaphor made some of their assumptions visible, and their dramatic portrayal of the relationship between their real and imagined worlds provided rich insights into their beliefs and self-representation.

Language, citizenship and creativity

My visits to South Africa have offered an opportunity to explore the relationship between language, theatre and citizenship. Citizenship, as the right to equal recognition, is obviously highly politicized in South Africa, and most of the teachers involved in the exchange had been active in the struggle against apartheid. Access to political participation in a democratic society depends upon equal ability to speak which, in the Constitution of postcolonial and post-apartheid South Africa, includes official recognition of eleven different languages. We had a lot to learn from South Africa, therefore, where children have a right to learn in their mother tongue. In England, the official language of instruction is always English and, although there are systems of support for children who have English as an additional language, they are very rarely taught in their mother tongue. There have been extensive debates about the relationship between educational achievement and mother tongue teaching and, in theatre, about the use of colonial languages, but my focus here is on the significance of language in relationship to intercultural exchange based on cosmopolitan sentiments.

Most of the children and teachers in Khayelitsha have Xhosa as their mother tongue, with English as an additional or second language. In school, we observed, English gradually becomes the main language of instruction as the children get older, with the effect that the English language becomes associated with success in the public sphere whereas the mother tongue is associated with the more intimate and domestic spaces of home and childhood. This has an effect on how cultural practices and identities are shared and constructed, a point that is developed by Appiah:

> To share a language is to participate in a complex set of mutual expectations and understandings, but in such a society it is not only linguistic behaviour that is coordinated through universally known expectations and understandings. People in this society share an understanding of many practices – marriages, funerals, other rites of passage – and largely share their views not only of the social but also of the natural world. (2006, p. 99)

In a nation where there are multiple languages, it follows that there are also many different cultural practices and that eroding an indigenous or minority language is to undermine part of its cultural diversity and richness. It is interesting in this context that theatre educator Gay Morris describes how the University of Cape Town used TIE as a way to 'Africanise' their drama curriculum in the 1980s because its orality and improvisational qualities 'had a good deal in common with non-formal and traditional African performance forms' (2002, p. 289). On the other hand, and more recently, because English is the major language of globalization and commerce, it has become the preferred language of instruction for many middle-class black parents who regard it as the language of progress and, understandably enough, do not want their children to be economically disadvantaged. In a revealing study into the use of Xhosa by children around the Eastern Cape Province, Vivien de Klerk found that there were significant psychological and social effects of black parents educating their children in English, not least because the children's decreasing competence in Xhosa was deepening old inequalities, albeit on the basis of class or wealth rather than 'race' (2000, pp. 201–2). De Klerk also noted that there are different forms of English spoken by children, and this was much in debate among the teenagers I met. One girl, who attended a former whites-only school in an affluent area, was criticized by her cousin for 'not sounding African' when she spoke English, and her accent and intonation sounded more American than her cousin's African-English tone. Taken together, this means that the choice of language used in theatre education, both within the drama and within the wider learning process, signals a political negotiation between South Africa's cultural histories and its economic and political future.

Central to creating an equitable international exchange is a political understanding of voice, and the ability for everyone to be heard on an equal basis lies at the root of cosmopolitan citizenship. Mindful of this, on International Mother Language Day in February 2006 (a day inspired by UNESCO that goes utterly unnoticed in England), I led a theatre workshop for teachers in the school hall of Masapumalele primary school. The workshop was structured with elements of English but also encouraged improvisation in the teachers' mother tongue. The story I had chosen to dramatize was called *A-Man-Amongst-Men*, a morality tale about a boastful man, who was tricked by women and children and learnt humility. The story moved between different linguistic registers – the declarations of the boastful man, the conspiratorial gossip of women at the well who plotted his downfall, and the formal language of brave children. In dramatizing different elements of the story, I invited the teachers to move between different languages to evoke contrasting dramatic atmospheres. Perhaps unsurprisingly, and with immense good humour, the man's declaratory boasts were spoken in English, and the more domestic or intimate scenes (I was told) in different registers in Xhosa. Of course, my ability to interpret these moments is limited, but it was instantly noticeable that the drama carried out in their home languages was lively, highly physical and emotionally engaged, whereas the work in English was more stilted and formal. Jan Fredrickson, who witnessed the workshop, observed that there was increased vitality, humour and physicality when the teachers used their home languages. This perception that language and identity are enmeshed underlines the power of the vernacular, and asserts its embodied and potentially subversive qualities. The structure of the drama supported discussions about the ways in which different languages are used, and the teachers commented that dramatizing the relationship between context, language and register would enable them to explore the social significance of language with children. With older learners, including my university students who analysed the DVD of the workshop, the drama offered material to debate the political uses of language in one form of post-colonial theatre.

The political complexities of language, both in theatre and in the performative practices of everyday life, has been much debated and well documented. Many accounts take their starting point from Ngugi wa Thiong'o's famous *Decolonizing the Mind: The Politics of Language in African Literature* (1981) in which he argues that in pre-colonial Kenya drama was not an 'isolated event', enacted in the colonizers' language, but occupied a vernacular space that was integral to the fabric of everyday life (1981, p. 37). Christopher Balme, whose book *Decolonizing the Stage* (1999) takes its inspiration from Ngugi, draws attention to the ways in which the languages of movement, dance, space, music as well as orality inherent in many indigenous theatre forms link 'aesthetics, politics and the concrete context of performance' in ways that challenge western aesthetics (1999, p. 212). Applying these debates to intercultural theatre requires, as Knowles points out, a move away from 'the idealist and universalist' towards a 'more grounded focus on the localist and the historical' (2010, p. 42). This process requires creativity and imagination. My contributions to the cultural exchange required me to engage with a history and geography of struggles that were not mine, and enter local territories in which I was not an expert. My modest intervention was to find a place for theatre within an egalitarian, creative and cosmopolitan vision, and to articulate how dramatic activity might make a space for the kind of vernacular creativity that enabled us to reflect on, to borrow Sennett's phrase, the insufficiencies of ourselves. It is in recognizing the vernacular – the story – within dramatic action that fixed ideas about cultures, place and identities might be questioned and troubled. This way of working recognizes that cosmopolitanism relies on active recognition that there are multiple languages of personal engagement and civic participation, because, without that, intercultural exchange will never achieve the equality it seeks.

Play and citizenship in Japan

The idea that social and political agency can be achieved through experience of the arts has been, of course, a recurring theme in theatre education. Democratic participation relies on communication and, whereas many theories of citizenship ally political action with speech, Dewey was an early proponent of the view that the arts can serve as an instrument of political action. He argued that aesthetic communication provided a way to understand and transform experience, and this required participation in a rich mix of different cultural practices (Dewey, 1934). It has been argued that Dewey's interest in eroding cultural barriers through the arts made him an early advocate of cosmopolitanism (Waks, 2007). In the spirit of the times, however, his position was predicated on the idea that human nature is universally shared and universally benign. My interest lies not in defending his claims to universalism, but in investigating the cultural specificity of methods of teaching and learning that follow the Deweyan principles of learning by doing and learning through play. The deep cultural roots of my own educational assumptions, inflected by Deweyan pedagogies, became particularly evident in a project on theatre, education and citizenship that I led in Japan in 2008.

I had visited Japan in 2007 to give a series of workshops and lectures on theatre education and citizenship to teachers, theatre artists and academics, and although I found the experience rich and rewarding, I also felt unsure how far my work was appropriate to the very different educational and artistic culture that I had glimpsed there. With this in mind, when I was invited back to Japan, I asked if I might bring three students with me to work with some children for an intensive period of time. I was interested in finding out what I did not know and the only way to do this was through practice-based research. We were asked by arts manager Kaori Nakayama to lead a theatre project called 'Citizenship, our narratives' in Mihara, Hiroshima with children aged 6 to 14. The project was more difficult to fund than a lecture tour with an obvious public profile, but Kaori and I gathered money from diverse sources, including the Great Britain Sasakawa Foundation, Japan Foundation and the Kirin Welfare Foundation all of which support intercultural exchange though the arts. I chose three students – Liz Bemment, Flic Minshall and Ashling McGee – who had worked with me a lot in their undergraduate degree, each of whom had different artistic skills and all wanted to follow careers in theatre and education. Kaori recruited three young translators to partner the Brits, and we knew that this would be an opportunity for everyone to learn. Beyond that, it was unknown, and it felt risky.

None of us were expecting to learn quite so fast, and the biggest lesson came as a jolt on the very first morning. For the first few days of the project we stayed in an education centre in the mountains before moving down into the town to rehearse a performance for parents in an arts venue. We had never seen the performance space which felt scary, but we put that to the back of our minds and ploughed on with the process. We had planned some quick name games to start, and expected to move on fairly swiftly to some work that built on physical theatre techniques of storytelling in a playful way. Within minutes we were flummoxed. The children scarcely spoke above a whisper, showed no inclination to move their bodies except in very small movements, and looked at us with quiet respect, but increasing bewilderment. The low point came when a boy called Tsi (pronounced 'Tits') gave his name and we ran manically round the hall, waving our arms around and yelling 'Tits! Tits!!' in a desperate attempt to get the children to join in. The louder we shouted, of course, and the more we waved our arms, the quieter and more reserved the children became. Our translators gamely joined in, but it wasn't really going anywhere. We had been working less than an hour. Any performance at the end of a week together seemed like a complete impossibility. We were already hot and exhausted, and we hadn't even seen the funny side of shouting 'tits' to a roomful of bemused Japanese children. We took a break.

In the break Liz commented that we must look like aliens to the children, and we'd certainly become 'unrecognizable strangers' to ourselves. We decided that working as a whole group was perhaps the problem, and we would stick to our plan to break into smaller groups with around eight children to each pair of adults where we could work at the children's pace and develop relationships with them as individuals. With no time to reflect, I issued quick instructions: break your plan down into much smaller, manageable steps; keep up a reasonable pace but move on if something isn't working. If all else fails, do painting. When we met at the end of the day we were relieved we had not needed the painting option, but the drama had been slower than we had imagined and although the children seemed to have enjoyed it, they remained reluctant to offer their ideas. We walked right to the end of the lake to reflect on the day, out of the children's sight, and Flic rolled a cigarette. We were unsure how to proceed and decided to revisit our plans in more detail that evening.

The moment of revelation came as we walked back to the lodge. The same children who had hardly spoken all day were running round the grounds and round a very deep lake, completely unsupervised, shouting, yelling, jumping, diving in the water and throwing sticks. They were *playing*, and they were unrecognizable from the timid young people we had met that morning. We stood and watched, and it suddenly seemed very clear that the children made no connection between learning and play, and that play was an activity that they expected to do without adults present. They had been taught to show a dignified respect to their elders, according to the tenets of Confucian philosophy, and this felt a long way from the child-centred pedagogies of progressive education. There had been nothing dignified about the tits game, and we realized that if we were to harness this energy we needed to find a way to integrate their understanding of play into the drama more explicitly. It was unclear at that stage how we might achieve this, but it became increasingly apparent that there were very clear differentiations between the children's space and adult space, and they expected to behave differently in each setting. There were times during the week when that clear delineation shocked us. There was a heavy storm one evening and the children got ready for bed early, but when it lifted the older boys were given a box of matches and fireworks and told to take the younger children outside to set them off. We winced, of course, and muttered about risk assessments and the lack of adult supervision as the children jumped about in their flimsy nightwear with sparklers, but we also learnt that the children were used to playing responsibly without adult intervention and sometimes found their presence inhibiting. To our surprise we were also objects of curiosity, and when we woke up in the morning on our communal sleeping platform we saw a line of little faces that had been watching us sleep. Liz completed our unintended performance by greeting them with a sleepy 'bugger off' which shamefully but entertainingly exploited their lack of comprehension. Few western tourists travel to Mihara, we were told, and although the children had obviously seen a lot of white westerners on TV, we were their first live experience. In Lefebvre's terms, as workshop leaders we occupied an official, conceived space for the children, and as curiosities we filled a perceived space that represented a real incarnation of imaged people from the TV. Neither perception was particularly conducive to creating an alternative Thirdspace in which we might share new creative relationships.

We had considered education for global citizenship in our planning, and we had discussed the implications of working in translation, the choice of dramatic narratives and the ways in which we might symbolize the relationship between story and culture. We borrowed a metaphor from Salman Rushdie's story, *Haroun and the Sea of Stories* (1990), about a sad town that has forgotten its own traditional tales because everyone works in factories, and from which the children escaped from the town and travelled to different islands to rediscover their stories. Japan and Britain are both island nations, with a wealth of traditional stories that invoke their seafaring histories, and we used Rushdie's conceit as a narrative frame for stories about the sea. The moral and cultural significance of traditional tales has been well theorized in drama education, particularly by Joe Winston (1998), and we hoped that the children would feel cultural experts in performing their own stories. We brought dramatic forms from our theatre traditions, integrating promenade, installation and physical theatre. For example, Liz's group worked on a story about miniature people and, having played a game where they use their bodies to create objects, they suggested ways to represent the rice bowl boats and chopsticks oars physically with their bodies. Working physically enabled us to communicate without the need for dialogue, and this enabled us to encourage the children to make connections between play and learning. The child psychologist D. W. Winnicott described this kind of imaginative play where children create their own environments as a 'potential space' in which the symbolism of an imagined object marks the creative boundaries between me and not me (1971, pp. 128–9).

As the week progressed these imaginative children adapted to our methodologies, and they made increasingly inventive suggestions and took ownership of the space, both physically and vocally. When we moved the drama from the comfort of our mountain lodge to the abstract space of the rather formal arts venue – a decision that we probably would not have made ourselves – we found that the process of restaging the work around the venue required us to think about adult perceptions of children as well as the artistic content. The promenade was designed to position the audience as active participants in a performance event rather than consumers of a theatrical product, and the children led the adults through the building, inviting them into different spaces and, at one stage, shouting very loudly at the audience. Reciprocally, the adults who attended the children's performance in Mihara were invited to put the names of their favourite childhood stories in a box which the children opened in performance. Using this style of theatre was part of the cultural exchange; the change in dynamics between performance and audiences and the aesthetic transformation of the space derives very clearly from contemporary Western theatre practices. In a way, this performance became an exchange of both aesthetics and cultural practice, extending the process that Nicolas Bourriaud describes in his book *Relational Aesthetics* as a 'social interstice' (2002, p. 18).

It is, of course, easy to overplay the implications of a week-long drama project. But it does offer some interesting insights into our own cultural assumptions about the negotiation between space and play, two of the most significant and recurring themes in theories of drama and theatre education. Robin Alexander has commented that pedagogy is a cultural intervention that is 'deeply saturated with the values and history of the society and community in which it is located' (2008, p. 173). We had learnt how some of our pedagogical assumptions reflected our own values in the process of working, but how did this relate to citizenship education? We learnt in Japan that our dramatic methodology, and our sense of selfhood, was profoundly and unexpectedly dependent on Western perceptions of childhood and the educational value of structured play. It had revealed to us the cultural specificity of our own pedagogies and methods; we were privileged to work in Japan and to be challenged to think and feel beyond the familiar. The children commented that they had enjoyed hearing English, and found they liked improvising. Many of the adults who observed or participated said that they had not been able to imagine how children would contribute creatively to making a performance until they had witnessed the work. One man, who had been an actor in Kabuki all his working life told me that working with children had led him to redefine his relationship to art-making, and he had discovered a deeper satisfaction in working not for himself but for others, and this sentiment seemed to summarize part of the cosmopolitan spirit.

Cartographers of the imagination

At the end of his book *Liquid Life*, Zigmunt Bauman asks the question 'Can public space be made once more a place of lasting engagement rather than of fleeting encounters?'. His answer is ambivalent. Yes, he suggests, provided that the public practice of citizenship is no longer tied to the nation-state, but requires 'a new and global public space' in which it is acknowledged that 'all of us who share the planet depend on each other for our present and our future' (2005, pp. 152–3). Finding ways to connect with others in different parts of the world, whether this is through face-to-face encounter or as an imaginative journey, requires the map to be redrawn to recognize the complexity of global interactions and interdependences. This is, in itself, a creative act of cultural improvisation where, to use Ingold and Hallam's words, 'every idea is like a place you visit' (2007, p. 8).

   It is in the organization of exchanges, however, rather than the art-making process, that the uneven power relations that David Harvey described are often felt at their most acute. Part of the problem of creating ethical encounters that encourage global citizenship is that there is often an inherent inequality that is defined by globalization, and media images that exchange-artists and young people have consumed do not always foster symmetry in these real-and-imagined spaces of intercultural interaction. Cultural exchanges offer a real opportunity to make the imaged world real, and this means that expectations can be very high. This sense of anticipation is not without its problems, and there are numerous examples in the United Kingdom of artists from the developing world who have been prevented from entering the country by the heavy-handed policing of national borders. The artist Antony Gormley is currently leading a campaign against Home Office Immigration Laws that are damaging international cultural collaboration.[10] My own work has been similarly affected. I had hoped to conclude this chapter with some examples of practice from Malawian, Ugandan and Mali artists working in local schools, but nine of the eleven invited artists were refused visas. This is an education in the realities of citizenship, though not one that the organizers had anticipated or wanted. But it also serves as an active reminder of Doreen Massey's warning that Westerners sometimes take for granted their own mobilities in ways that people in other parts of the world cannot (2005, pp. 88–9). It reveal how international exchanges are subject to the same inequalities of territory, class and money that, Harvey points out, 'continuously deepen under an individualised free market' (2009, p. 168). But it is within this inequitable political landscape that an education for global citizenship takes place.

Bharucha describes intercultural theatre-makers as 'cartographers of the imagination' who have to accept that 'the intercultural map has shifting boundaries' (2000, p. 160). There is a long history of using theatre to bridge social and cultural divisions, and this involves both creativity and cultural improvisation, to borrow Ingold and Hallam's phrase, as participants meet values, realities and practices that are different from their own. Shifting boundaries may be an uncomfortable process, particularly if participants come face-to-face with assumptions and prejudices they had not recognized before. But if the imaginary of artistic space is understood in relation to the vernacular histories of places, as Bhabha suggested, there is the possibility of developing the kind of cosmopolitanism sentiments that might begin to shape understanding of the complexity of friendship and hospitality that Jacques Derrida associates with equitable living in an interconnected world (Derrida, 2000). Cultural exchanges based on cosmopolitanism will face these political questions head-on, and ask how people can learn to co-exist interdependently, not by fusing horizons, but by learning beside each other and with an awareness of both the insufficiencies of ourselves and the political power structures on which equitable exchanges depend.

9

Changing Worlds: Performing Science, Theatre and Public Engagement

This chapter is about the ways in which theatre can encourage public engagement with science and illuminate the issues raised by the rapid pace of scientific and technological change in the twenty-first century. When I describe the world in which I grew up my undergraduate students look at me in horror and amazement, as if I were a museum piece. The idea of existing without computers, without the internet or, worse, without mobile phones is incomprehensible. How on earth did I manage to organize my social life? Make arrangements? Go on dates? Write essays? When I explain that, when I was a student, there were some advantages to being able to call home only occasionally from public phone boxes, and that in the vacations friends wrote letters to each other, longhand and in pen, they look bemused but intrigued. There is an intimacy about these letters that they find engaging and, as the conversation turns to how to stop your mum becoming one of your facebook friends (and thereby seeing what you are really getting up to in the student bar), the idea of the weekly payphone conversations home suddenly seems rather appealing. Locating oneself within the narrative of technological change is one way to chart the impact of science on everyday life. Taking a longer view, and across generations, the social implications of scientific advance become increasingly evident. My father was fond of telling people that he had studied electronic engineering at Cambridge University before the transistor was invented. My great-aunt might have been spared the pain of childlessness if IVF had been available, and my great-grandfather may have not died in his 40s from diseases related to a working life as a coal miner had its health risks been comprehended.

Reflecting on the impact of science, looking back is perhaps easier than looking forward; imagining how science, mathematics and technology will affect the lives of future citizens seems so unpredictable to be almost futile.[1] As I suggested in Chapter 5, one response to the pace of scientific and technological change has been to re-focus learning on what has become termed '21st century skills'. These 'personal, learning and thinking skills' are differently inflected in different parts of the globalized world, but generally include attributes such as critical thinking, creativity, teamwork, self-management and reflection. This statement, made by Ben Williamson and Sarah Payton in a document put out by *Futurelab*, a British educational think-tank that promotes the use of technology, illustrated the motives for this approach to education:

> Innovative approaches to the curriculum at the present time have shifted some of the stress from subject knowledge to the acquisition of '21st century skills' and 'personalisation' which are seen as essential both for individuals' personal successes in learning and adult life, and for national economic development.[2]

This kind of pedagogic intervention aims to address the way in which the content of the curriculum quickly dates, and it is intended to prepare young people to be responsive to the speed of technological and scientific innovation. It is a pedagogical vision that Lyotard predicted, where students are taught to reproduce saleable skills and for which, he comments, 'students would still have to be taught something: not contents, but how to use the terminals' (1984, p. 50). But skills are in themselves empty of ethics, and deemed to be measurable, reflecting the dominant ideology of performance management that pervades both contemporary education and employment practice.

More optimistically, the need to inspire young people to become scientists, to understand the intervention science is already making on their everyday lives, and to produce a scientifically literate populace has generated a significant body of funded work in the arts that is designed to capture the imagination and encourage debate about science and bioethics both in educational settings and within the wider public sphere. Charitable bodies such as The Wellcome Trust in London and the Sloan Foundation in New York have recognized the importance of this work by offering regular funding to collaborative projects between scientists and artists. The strategic plan of The Wellcome Trust, a biomedical research charity, *Making a Difference: 2005–2010,* emphasizes the Trust's commitment to public engagement. The third of its Six Strategic Aims, 'Engaging society', articulates an intention to fund public engagement activities and research that will:

- **promote interest, learning and excitement** about biomedical science and its past, present and future impacts on society
- **stimulate an informed debate** to raise awareness and understanding of biomedical science, its achievements, applications and implications
- **inform our own – and wider national – debates, research plans and policies,** in relation to public interests and concerns, to balance the needs of the research endeavour with those of society. (The Wellcome Trust, 2010, p. 14)

Theatre is particularly well placed to contribute to public engagement programmes in science, where it is valued for its capacity to generate informed discussion by representing and questioning the social implications of scientific knowledge. In turn, there is also a new generation of scientists who are alert to the ethical and social implications of their work, described by Alan Irwin as 'citizen scientists', who are rethinking the importance of science in everyday life (Irwin 1995).

This chapter argues that new epistemologies are developing as a result of collaborations between theatre-makers and scientists that redefine the relationship between theatre, performance, public engagement and experiential learning. This epistemology is based on the premise that theatre not only has the potential to dramatize bioethical debates, but that collaboration enables scientists and artists to challenge outdated perceptions that the arts are intuitive, emotional and empathetic whereas the sciences are, in Tim Ingold's words, built on 'the sovereign perspective of abstract reason' and the 'cold logic' of scientific judgement (2000, p. 25), a view that became entrenched in twentieth century educational discourse. My aim is to reflect how new ways of working are alert to the social and ethical implications associated with the speed of technological change, and recognize the ways in which the construction of knowledge – in science and elsewhere – is related to contemporary structures of power. To begin this discussion, I am taking my lead from the work of the cultural theorist Paul Virilio, who argued that there is a need for ever more vigilance in a society that is relying increasingly heavily on science for its sense of advancement because, he argues, 'without limits, there is no value' (2000, p. 33). Making links between the arts and sciences he asks, 'If freedom of SCIENTIFIC expression now actually has no more limits than freedom of ARTISTIC expression, where will *inhumanity* end in the future?' (2000, p. 32. Capitals and italics original). This chapter aims to respond to this question, not least by challenging the popular perception that science takes place in the realm of facts, logic and rationality and the arts in the sphere of intuition, imagination and empathy. My suggestion is that a reply to Virilio's ethical questions is most productively framed not by focusing on educating for the skills favoured by the global market, but by realigning pedagogic practices on the poetics, aesthetics and ethical narratives that are inherent in both science and the arts.

Disciplinary encounters: Science, theatre and education

Theatre has a long history of debating scientific knowledge and themes, but perception of their incompatibility has not always made creative conversations between artists and scientists easy. The differences between the arts and sciences was famously described by C. P. Snow as a cultural divide in his much-cited essay, *The Two Cultures* (1959), which began as a lecture in Cambridge. In this lecture Snow railed against the misunderstandings between scientists and 'literary intellectuals' (as he called them), and argued that contemporary social snobbery and academic attitudes towards the sciences had deepened the cultural divide. Furthermore, he claimed, prejudice on both sides about the processes of academic research had led to an impoverished intellectual life. Although Snow's criticisms are undoubtedly British and rooted in the 1950s parochialism of Cambridge University, they affirm a longer history of cultural anxiety about the ethical boundaries of science and the moral authority of the arts that continue to have resonance. According to the cultural critic Stephan Collini, Snow was articulating a view of the distinction between academic disciplines that had been defined in Enlightenment philosophy and took root in the Romantic movement, in which there was an anxiety that 'calculation and measurement generally might be displacing cultivation and compassion' (2008, p. 5). By the time Snow was speaking in Cambridge, Collini argued, it seemed clear that the cultural divisions were perpetuated by educational structures that forced early academic specialization, by British social prejudice towards the sciences and manufacturing industries, and by government policymaking that forced an unhelpful and damaging distinction between intellectual inquiry and creative activity (2008, p. 43). Twenty-first century education still carries more than a remnant of this disciplinary polarization, and the need to develop more productive ways of thinking about practices in both the sciences and the arts is central to challenging this pedagogic story.

The animation of science in the public space of the theatre has often been predicated on the perception that dramatizing scientific content brings the arts and sciences into conversation with each other. In her book *Science on Stage: From Doctor Faustus to Copenhagen* (2006), Kirsten Shepherd-Barr offers an illuminating account of how scientific and medical themes have been represented, critiqued and interpreted by playwrights and theatre-makers at different historical periods, thereby ensuring that theatre has been 'one of the consistent and prominent sites of engagement between the two cultures' (2006, p. 15). Scholarly attention on science plays, Shepherd-Barr notes, has tended to focus on the treatment of scientific themes and issues, but she also observes that many plays use science as a theatrical metaphor. Through careful use of metaphor, she argues, the most innovative and successful science plays integrate dramatic form and scientific content without 'oversimplification or reduction' (2006, p. 7). Education is not the focus of Shepherd-Barr's thesis, but her work does illuminate the intervention theatre can make into scientific debate. Citing Stephen Greenblatt, she suggests that scientific ideas become 'destabilised and interrogated when placed in the framework of performance' which, for theatre-makers, is generally seen as 'liberating' whereas for scientists it is often seen as 'threatening to the whole idea of truth' (2006, p. 190). In his book *Theatre, Education and the Making of Meanings* (2007), Anthony Jackson observes that theatre was used to illuminate the social implications of science during the period 1936–47, when theatre-makers' urge to question scientific knowledge was often 'in response to specific social crises in which science is seen either to offer solutions or itself to be implicated in the crisis' (2007, p. 124). Using the examples of the destruction caused by the Atomic bomb in 1945, anxieties about AIDS in the 1980s and recent controversy over genetically modified crops, Jackson suggests that theatrical interest in science has often been determined by its perceived effects on everyday life.

Anthony Jackson's elegant account of theatre and science suggests that the recent shift of thinking from public *understanding* to public *engagement* positions the audience as active interpreters of science rather than passive recipients of scientific knowledge (2007, p. 125). He also observed that Brecht and Ewan MacColl, a member of the Workers' Theatre Movement, developed techniques to encourage audience participation in the 1930s and 1940s, an approach that was designed to 'transcend the messenger-receiver paradigm' (2007, p. 124), and stimulate debate about the social effects of science from a Marxist perspective. Both Brecht and the Workers' Theatre Movement influenced the methodologies of Theatre in Education (TIE), as I pointed out in Chapter 4, and there have been many successful TIE programmes that explore scientific themes and issues. A particularly good example of this approach to theatre and science education is offered by the London-based company Y Touring, whose work is often funded by The Wellcome Trust. Y Touring commissions new plays that encourage scientific debate in educational settings, including plays about ethics of clinical trials in *Star Fish* (2009) and medical privacy in *Breathing Country* (2010). Their approach, *Theatre of Debate®*, works very much in the mode of traditional TIE programmes, in which the performance of a play is followed by participatory activities, now updated by using podcasts and other online resources to stimulate discussion. Y Touring consults scientific experts in developing their work and their main aim is to stimulate informed debate about scientific issues, particularly in the 11–18 age range, rather than effecting creative collaborations between artists and scientists in their classrooms, rehearsal spaces and laboratories.

The capacity of theatre to raise critical questions about the social implications of science is widely understood, but it is perhaps around conceptualizations of the body and nature that theatre, science and education have converged more fully. In his study *The Player's Passion: Studies in the Science of Acting* (1993), theatre historian Joseph Roach argues that there are considerable parallels between the history of scientific thought and the history of theatrical theories, particularly those that pertain to the workings of the actor's body (1993, p. 15). He draws attention to the ways in which scientific knowledge about human behaviour have been accepted as 'natural', 'true', 'universal' or 'common sense', and argues that theories of acting have been consistently aligned to contemporary notions of the 'natural'. Drama and theatre education, in common with actor training, have been responsive to different scientific ideas about how people learn and what governs 'natural' human development and behaviour. This was perhaps most clearly evident in twentieth century educational practices, as I outlined in Chapter 3, where assumptions about what constitutes 'natural' play or the dramatic 'instinct' provided the intellectual rationale for a whole pedagogy, particularly in early child-centred models of primary education. More recently, both theatre-makers and educationalists have become drawn to research in neuroscience, and scientific research into brain activity has begun to provide justification for particular modes of teaching and learning. Neuroscience has proved just as irresistible to contemporary theatre-makers as psychological naturalism was to Stanislavsky; the British theatre director Katie Mitchell, for example, has applied the work of the neuroscientist Antonio Damasio to her understanding of the relationship between body and the emotions. Theatrical and educational theories have tended to mirror each other's responses to science with, as Roach observes, each generation priding itself on 'having attained the right answers about how the world has worked' (1993, p. 15).

What an analysis of both approaches to collaboration reveals is that interactivity between theatre and science is responsive to, and creative of, the metaphors and modes of thought that are available and current at the time. In terms of historiography, Roach points out, theatrical investigations into scientific thought should not be read as a steady march towards greater veracity or authenticity, but as an insight into how different world-views and ideas of human nature have been articulated and understood over time (1993, p. 15). For example, the myth of the left/right brain function, in which it was believed that one side of the brain is related to creativity and the other to rationality conveniently mirrored the classifications of nineteenth century Western philosophical thought that separated the arts and science into two opposing cultures.[3] Educationalist and neuroscientist Usha Goswami argues that these 'neuromyths' have endured in education long after they have been discredited scientifically, and have generated expensive, packaged educational products such as 'Brain Gym®' that is based on misleading and inaccurate science (2006, p. 2).

The disciplinary frameworks through which the sciences and the arts are conceptualized have social and civic implications, according to the anthropologist Bruno Latour, who similarly points out that separations between the arts and science have been damaging. In his book *Pandora's Hope: Essays on the Reality of Science Studies* (1999) he addresses the two-culture-divide, insisting that both sides need to change their attitudes:

> One camp deems the sciences accurate only when they have been purged of any contamination by subjectivity, politics or passion; the other camp,

spread much more widely, deems humanity, morality, subjectivity, or rights worthwhile only when they have been protected from any contact with science, technology and objectivity. (1999, p. 18)

To 'fight against these two purges', Latour makes a distinction between Science (with a capital 'S'), which presents the results of its research as if they were undisputed truths, and science studies, which addresses the practices of science-in-the-making. In contrast to Science, he argues, that assumes autonomy, objectivity and dispassion, science studies makes politics possible by opening science to questions of human value and recognizing that the science is better and more effective when it is made in collaboration with others. Developing new ways of thinking about how science and the arts can inform each other depends, therefore, not on perpetuating the cultural divide that permeated twentieth century thought, but on recognizing that each generation redefines its relationship to scientific knowledge. So, how might the relationship between science and theatre education be reconceptualized for the twenty-first century?

Paradigms, practices and epistemologies: Language and narrative

The idea that scientific knowledge is as susceptible to contemporary discourse as artistic practice calls into question the ways in which its epistemologies have been constructed and legitimated at different times and in different places. The work of Jean-Francois Lyotard is particularly associated with this debate, and his book *The Postmodern Condition: A Report on Knowledge* (1984) questions the post-Enlightenment grand narrative that says science represents 'the totality of knowledge' (1984, p. 7). In asking 'who decides what knowledge is, and who knows what needs to be decided? (1984, p. 9), Lyotard draws on Wittgenstein's theory of language games, and argues that the frameworks on which the truth-claims of science are made are based on linguistic practices and communicative interaction that have been legitimated as objective and universal by those who hold institutional and cultural power. Recognizing the role of discourse and language in the production and legitimation of knowledge means that, according to Lyotard, hierarchical divisions between two kinds of knowledge – the 'positivist kind' that is 'directly applicable to technologies' and the 'critical, reflexive, or hermeneutic kind' – can no longer be sustained (1984, p. 14).

One of the consequences of the Western philosophical habit of classifying knowledge into bounded academic disciplines has been that it generates particular cultural frames through which the world is imagined and understood. In turn, this has defined the social identities of scientists and artists, who tend to see the world through the lens of their particular professional experiences. Engaging in productive interdisciplinary conversations, therefore, involves more than superficial knowledge about another discipline, it requires openness to a different world-view and a willingness to change deeply felt perceptions. Following in the Wittgensteinian tradition that accepts the centrality of language in constructing social realities, Collini likens this process to learning a new language:

> [W]hat is wanted is not to force potential physicists to read a bit of Dickens and potential literary critics to mug up some basic theorems. Rather, we need to encourage the growth of the intellectual equivalent of bilingualism, a capacity not only to exercise the language of our respective specialisms, but also to attend to, learn from, and eventually contribute to, wider cultural conversations. (2008, p. 61)

Collini's metaphor of bilingualism to describe the process of interdisciplinary dialogue is echoed by the literary critic Gillian Beer in her study of representations of science in literature, *Open Fields: Science in Cultural Encounter* (1996). In an illuminating chapter, 'Translation or Transformation? The Relations of Literature and Science', Beer argues that scientific and literary discourses are not fixed entities, but continually inform each other and overlap. Rather than seeing this process of interaction as a negotiation between two separate dialects in which novelists, playwrights and poets act as translator for some of the more impenetrable technical language used by scientists, Beer suggests that 'transformation' is a more appropriate metaphor to describe how writers represent scientific concepts in literary form. Beer draws attention to the phrase 'writing up' that is used by scientists when they seek to disseminate the results of their research, whereas writers in the arts (whether researchers or creative writers) expect that the process of writing will in itself clarify ideas and create new meanings (1996, p. 183). By transformation, therefore, Beer recognizes that the process of moving from one form to another, whether this is from scientific experiment to scientific journal, or from the technical language of a scientific journal to a work of literature, is not an unmediated process of translation but also involves a lively and poetic activity of re-ordering, narrating, symbolizing and interacting with newly formed scientific concepts. This transformation has the potential to shed new light on scientific knowledge by revealing and illuminating its discontinuities and testing its limits. She describes this interaction in the following terms:

> New orderings of knowledge will be sprung within the tensions of form as well as of description, abutting, sometimes merging with, but always casting light upon prior constructions of meaning, their decay, their tenacity. (1996, p. 194)

Collini's call for bilingualism draws inspiration from Beer's suggestion that, in moving between scientific and artistic modalities 'we all learn stories from each other' (1996, p. 194). This emphasis on narrative as a process of meaning-making suggests that scientists, artists and audiences are not restricted to exchanging established bodies of knowledge, but are generating new narratives, new knowledge and new epistemologies in the process of collaborating in rehearsal rooms, galleries, museums, theatres and laboratories. This is a process, Beer describes, that can disrupt the scientific knowledge, through an 'ironic doubling of reference or the disturbing of authoritative story' (1996, p. 193).

The idea that new knowledge is created in language and through social interaction recognizes that both scientists and artists have a role in the moral education of its citizens. It is here that the work of the French philosopher Gaston Bachelard is worth revisiting. Bachelard, who worked at the Sorbonne in Paris in the interwar years of the twentieth century, is perhaps best known for his theorization of domestic space, *The Poetics of Space* (1958/1994). He had also been, however, a science teacher in schools and philosopher of science with a strong interest in pedagogy, and it is his work on the socialization of science that is particularly relevant here. Bachelard argued that the positivism of science pedagogy created a misleading picture of scientific research by suggesting that progress is linear and continuous with existing knowledge. In *The Formation of the Scientific Mind* (1934/2001), he argued to the contrary, suggesting that it is through the ruptures and discontinuities with previous ways of thinking that new epistemologies and ways of seeing are generated. This meant that, in Bachelard's pedagogy, dialogue took a central place. If positivist patterns of thought are an obstacle to scientific learning, it follows that interaction between people with different understandings of the world are needed to challenge established (or common sense) constructions of knowledge. Pedagogically, therefore, Bachelard argued that discussion was needed in order for young people to develop the kind of cognitive structures that support scientific thought. In her study of the scientific pedagogy of Bachelard, Cristina Chimisso summarizes this position:

> For him, scientific activity creates not only new theories but also new objects, and even new relationships between people. (2001, p. 95)

Bachelard believed that creating structures of knowledge that challenge contemporary orthodoxies is predicated on criticism of existing social and scientific practices. This meant, therefore, that its epistemology is infused with ethics.

So what role might theatre and performance play in this process of translation and transformation? Like Bachelard, Latour recognizes the significance of narrative and conversation in the process of meaning-making, and he also understands that both the sciences and the arts have aesthetic qualities. Science is not a 'realist painting', he argues, nor an exact copy of the world, but both science and painting 'link us to an aligned, transformed, constructed world' (1999, p. 79). This way of thinking opens the way for collaborations between scientist and artists in which the arts not only provide a vehicle for debate, but may also generate new scientific insights. Experiments with interdisciplinary residences have intended to supported this approach, for example the New York performance artist Laurie Anderson took a position as artist in residence at NASA in 2003, and the Institute of Contemporary Arts (ICA) in London appointed the neuroscientist Daniel Glaser as its first scientist in residence in 2002. One strand of the innovative company the Clod Ensemble's work is called 'Performing Medicine' where theatre contributes to the training of medical practitioners, and the collaboration shows ways in which theatre-making can shed new light on medical processes and practice.[4] The case study I have chosen as an example for this chapter is one that involved a hospital school, two primary schools and a theatre in London, thereby mixing theatre education with public engagement with science in a professional theatre. To analyse this practice, I shall draw on Bachelard's everyday poetics and Freud's perception of the uncanny to investigate how the juxtaposition of different experiences, languages, forms of knowledge and emotional connections has the potential to transform the materiality of scientific procedure into poetic imagery and encourage public engagement in its social and aesthetic questions.

The poetics of science: *For the Best*

One of the ways in which science is encountered in everyday life is through the experience of illness, and this case-study illuminates the boundaries between medical science, patient experience and interdisciplinary (or multi-agency) technologies of care. The project *For the Best* was conceived by performance artist Mark Storor with educationalist Anna Ledgard and it was funded by The Wellcome Trust as part of their aim to increase public engagement in biomedical issues. The project took place over a series of months from September 2008 to June 2009, during which period Storor worked as an artist in residence with children in the Dialysis Unit of The Evelina Children's hospital and in the schools they attended when they were not in hospital. The educational work inspired a devised production *For the Best* that was performed at The Unicorn Theatre, London's only purpose-built professional theatre for children, and it ran throughout June 2009. This was the third of a series of installation performances that Storor and Ledgard had developed, the earlier work being *Visiting Time* (2005) at Dorset County Hospital, *Boychild* (2007) at Southwell Park, Portland, both of which also explored interface between biomedical science and personal experience. *For the Best* represented a development of Ledgard and Storor's methodology and, as it was the most risky and ambitious in scope, Ledgard and Storor attended every performance.

Children on a renal ward are often long-term patients, which means that the experience of hospitalization has a profound effect on the children's family and on their schooling. They can lose touch with their original schools and friends, and so the project also aimed to foster connections between the children of primary school ages at the Evelina hospital school and the school they had left behind. The project was multifaceted and layered, involving a large number of people and agencies, including the teachers and children at the Evelina hospital school and two other London primary schools (Charles Dickens in Southwark and Worpole in Hounslow), the medical professionals, the funding bodies, the staff at the Unicorn Theatre, the cast, and, most importantly, the children in the Dialysis Unit and their families. The number of people involved presented complex practical, ethical and educational responsibilities and a significant part of Anna Ledgard's role as producer was to ensure that relationships were carefully built and positive. Storor usually worked with the children in hospital on a one-to-one basis, supporting them to tell their stories, often through poetry and the visual arts, and the texture of the performance was guided by the stories the children in the dialysis unit had imagined. One of the children, for example, assisted Storor in setting a series of challenges for his classmates at his primary school which took the form of an imagined journey in which the children negotiated a maze, encountered a tiger and tried to solve an impossible jigsaw. In the programme notes, Matthew Wong, one of the older children, described the process like this:

> Mark provides the artist, I provide the experience and together we make the imagination.

My own involvement was not as the project's evaluator; I had seen demonstrations of *Visiting Time* and witnessed *Boychild* and had developed considerable respect for the way in which Storor and Ledgard worked with participants in a multi-agency environment as well as the quality of the artwork.[5] Researching other people's work always tends towards the parasitic, and in this sensitive context I was particularly anxious not to disturb the delicate relationships the producer and artist were building in the hospital and schools and to follow the ethic of care that characterized the project. Given that children on dialysis already experience considerable adult intervention and surveillance, this meant that I did not witness the education programme at first hand, although the texture and sensitivity of this process was visible in the production and clear from the testimony I heard from the participants. Instead, I shall focus here on the work shown at The Unicorn although I recognize that, by focusing on public engagement rather the educational elements of the project, I am touching only on a small part of a project that was complexly conceived and beautifully crafted.

I had booked my tickets for the June performance in January. The performance was an installation, taking place not in a conventional auditorium, but it took the form of a journey through the backstage spaces, lifts, scene docks and dressing rooms before opening out onto the wide open space of the closed-in stage. In small groups, we began the journey by sitting on a line of chairs, as if we were in a hospital waiting room, with a small child (one of the children from the primary school who had been involved in the project) beckoning us into a darkened room where we listened in silence to a poem, written by one of the older children. Death, we are told, is simply a door in a room that we have yet to see, and won't until our eyes adjust to the light. The child knocked on a closed door, and it was at that moment that we began the painful, tender and utterly absorbing theatrical journey that left many of us so moved we could scarcely speak. The performance followed the story of a family whose son had been diagnosed with kidney failure, taking the audience through the domestic spaces in which his father still cleaned his redundant football boots and where everyday activities still needed to be performed, and on to the technological space of the dialysis unit. A nurse moved acrobatically around the boy, adjusting tubes on the ceiling and all around the walls, busily checking his blood. The family arrived to visit, and we watched a joyful celebratory party of muffins and custard, but the playfulness was haunted by the spectre of death, who was always present but whom no-one seemed to notice. Eventually we were all ushered into the lift and the mood changed. We were caught in the stinking and claustrophobic debris of the party and we were transported up, needlessly as it turned out, with the mother, father and sister as they tried to find the right floor in an unfamiliar building. The tension was palpable, and as we left the lift and moved into the expansive space of the stage to watch the children's surreal stories played out and to see the family's final, painful battle with death, we knew we were witnesses not only to an extraordinary theatrical event, but to the everyday story of lives that are lived in the shadow of a child's illness. At the end we were simply led from the intensity of the dark space of the theatre, through the misty corridor of the scene dock and left on the street, blinking at each other. It evoked the moment when something deeply personal and significant has happened, but we are still thrust back into a world that is, unbelievably and bewilderingly, just carrying on its daily business. Although it was so intensely poetic that it has continued to haunt my imagination, most of all I shall remember the feelings I had, and in particular that deep and familiar pull right in the middle of my chest that is reserved for only the most intense of life's experiences and for which there are no words. I was not alone. When we all managed to speak on the pavement again I told my companions that I was intending to write about the performance. Their response was almost unanimous. They wanted everyone they cared about to see the performance, but no, they wouldn't be able to write about it. How could you, they asked, after that? They were right, of course, and it felt, and still feels, like an impossible responsibility.

In a sense that is the point. It was the echoes and resonances of everything feared, loved, familiar and lost that caught me firmly in the gut, and it was the emotional connections with the family's broken world that threw both the patient experience and the effects of medical science into such relief. There is no point in trying to describe the entire arc of the performance, not least because on each of the three occasions I saw the performance it was a different moment that startled and moved me. What I will do is to select some theatrical moments that illuminated a world that is often hidden, and to use them to suggest how the dramaturgical devices and the production values of the performance created a world that engaged the public in the lived experiences of illness, and asked them to find the dramatic metaphor in disease. To assist my reading of this performance, I shall return to the phenomenology of Gaston Bachelard, though this time not to his philosophy of science, but to his more lyrical analysis of home, *The Poetics of Space*, first published in French in 1958.

Bachelard invokes the image of an ordinary house to explore the significance of domestic places and, in the symbol of the home, he finds a metaphor for humanity, a humanist phenomenology. He is interested in its intimacy, its imagined worlds and its memories, and in what stories lie beneath the geometric surface of the house's architecture. 'How can secret rooms', he asks, 'rooms that have disappeared, become abodes for an unforgettable past?' (1994, p. xxxvi). Bachelard links the poetic of the house to the imagination, seeking the dreams hidden in the shadows of cellars and garrets, and exploring how memories are tucked away in the drawers, chests and wardrobes. Writing about the daydreams contained in attics, Bachelard suggests that:

> The phenomenology of the daydream can untangle the complexity of memory and imagination; it becomes necessarily sensitive to the differentiations of the symbol. And the poetic daydream, which creates symbols, confers on our intimate moments an activity that is poly-symbolic. (1994, p. 26)

By linking the domestic space of the home to an inner imaginative world, Bachelard provides a way of conceptualizing its grandeur and its poetic imagery. In Freudian psychoanalysis, by contrast, memories of home are haunted by a sense of the 'uncanny' or 'unheimlich' (unhomeliness), a term Freud uses to suggest the fear associated with a place that at once feels homely and yet also uncomfortably disturbed by the shadows of a terrifying supernatural presence. Rachel Bowlby summarizes his position:

> in psychoanalysis the home is no place of harmony...the house is...irredeemably driven by the presence of ghosts, its comforting appearance of womblike unity, doubled from the start by intruding forces...untimely

and dislocated hauntings of other times and places and other presences. (2001, p. 309)

A sense of the uncanny disturbs the comfortable homeliness of Bachelard's poetic, as a way of recognizing the fragility of home as well as its comforts. Freud describes the uncanny in physical terms, as a fear of being mutilated that recurs in dreams and nightmares. This childhood fear is repressed, Freud argues, which is why it appears as traces of a half-forgotten sensation and lurks in the shadows of home life.

Art often investigates the uncanny, as Colette Conroy has pointed out, because it disrupts an audience's expectations and troubles their identification with other people's experiences (2010, p. 26). It is this tension between Bachelard's comfortable poetic of home and Freud's disturbing sense of the uncanny which were played out in *For the Best*. The audience moved between the comfort of the domestic spaces of the family's home to the technological space of the hospital, where the personification of death became an uncanny presence for the audience, but remained hidden from sight and unnoticed (or ignored) by the family. The ending took place in the ambiguity of the empty space of the stage, and this dramatized the full force of the uncanny, where we sat on the floor following the action around an installation of abstract images, the symbols of a life that had become fragmented. The final stages of the performance showed the family's physical battle with death, painfully illustrating Freud's view of the uncanny 'as something which ought to have remained hidden but has come to light' (1997, p. 217).

The production is illuminated by a reading of Bachelard's suggestion that specific rooms have particular emotional resonances, as the impact of the play relied on the dramatic contrast between home and the uncanny feelings of 'unhomeliness'. The installations in the corridors and dressing rooms of the theatre that audiences encountered early in the performance held domestic narratives – the shower where the father sat motionless with water dripping pitifully from his body and clothes, the temporary comfort of the kitchen in which the mother baked an excess of muffins, and the laundry in which the sister watched helplessly as soft toys churned endlessly in the drying machine. Each room acted as a metaphor for the emotional effects of illness on the family, and all had been created with the children at the Evelina hospital. Dialysis was, according to one child, like being put through a washing machine and coming out clean, and this simile was captured in the excess of teddies dripping in the laundry. Moving from the disturbed stability of the home to the representation of dialysis, which was staged in the scene dock, felt raw and exposing after the intimacy of domestic spaces. The boy sat in the middle of an open space, with long red tubes running from his arm. The nurse, who constantly asked him to sit still, busied herself with the technology of his care by climbing along the walls and across the ceiling, her acrobatic harness adding to the illusion of the machinery that was keeping him alive. The cast spoke quietly, almost in whispers, and as I strained to overhear their conversation, I realized how slowly time passed for children on dialysis. This moment of theatre captured an alternative to the everyday narrative of domesticity by magnifying the daily routine of a hospital and the tedium of this form of medical intervention.

The poetic imagery framed the narrative, but the performance also affected the senses. Not only did we physically travel with the family, the very different atmospheres created in each of the rooms seeped into the body, invoking our own memories and stirring the imagination. The comforting smell of baking muffins, a recurring image of the mother's increasingly desperate attempts to care for her son, gave way to the sickly sweet smell of custard that dripped over the debris of a family party and lingered unhealthily in the lift in which we accompanied the father, mother and sister trying to find the right hospital floor. Bachelard describes the physicality of space as a polyphony of the senses, in which the sounds, smells, temperature and movement of a space add to its visual dimension. Taking Bachelard's idea further, the architecture theorist Juhani Pallasmaa describes this encounter in terms of a bodily reaction to a building or space, and he extends this to an audience's sensory interactivity with a work of art:

> The encounter with any work of art implies a bodily interaction ... A work of art functions as another person with whom one unconsciously converses. When confronting a work of art we project our emotions and feelings on to the work. A curious exchange takes place; we lend the work our emotions, whereas the work lends us its authority and aura. (2005, p. 66)

Although Pallasmaa was describing the visual arts, this 'curious exchange' can only be enhanced by the liveness of theatre and the physical interactivity that this particular poly-symbolic performance invited. In *For the Best*, the fragility of the human body was magnified by the sensate qualities of the dramatic symbolism and the family's experiences were framed by a self-conscious and sometimes surreal physicality. For example, in the party thrown in the hospital lift, the mother wore ribbons threaded with miniature muffins around her wrists, her feet and across her breasts in an absurd attempt to both nurture and entertain her children.

As audience members, we brought our own experiences to the performance as a whole, and this meant that we each identified with the narratives of characters whose journey touched us. I found that I started by identifying first with the stories that were most familiar, and that this process magnified those that seemed most troubling or strange. The aesthetic quality of the production and the power of the theatrical metaphor relied on Storor's meticulous attention to detail. In such a sensuous and textured performance each fragment of the imagery was open to close interpretation, whether this is in miniature or magnified. It is particularly in miniature worlds, Bachelard argues, that all our senses are most stirred and our deepest feelings most troubled, giving a 'double life to a poetic space' (1994, p. 169). The precision of imagery in the stories the children had created with Mark Storor had this condensed quality, sometimes using the poetry of the fairy tale – the princess who lived in the land of sick and threw up scrabble letters, or the pools of light that illuminated the cabbages that represented another child's sense of his body and emotions being peeled away, layer after layer (Fig. 9.1). This intense and condensed world illuminated the values inherent in the piece, the principles of care it embodied and the emotional clarity of the stories it told.

For the Best placed medical science at the limits of our poetic imagination, and insisted that audiences and medical professionals engaged in its narratives. It was not an easy journey for audiences, and this was part of its emotional power; the audiences' 'bodily interaction' with the play made them confront their own fears of childhood illness and death. This experience was, perhaps, more disturbing for adults than for children; children live with a sense of the uncanny, but adults have often repressed their fears, making the performance particularly vulnerable to their projections. Some audience members who found the work disturbing suggested that it was gratuitous or irresponsible to dramatize such personal narratives in the public space of the theatre. Ethical questions of translation from the privacy of the hospital to the public stage need to be raised, and it is important to record that the parents, teachers, hospital staff and children were all clear that the experience was positive for the children and families, and Susanna Steele's evaluation gave detailed examples of how the children had benefitted from seeing their own stories recognized.[6] As Pallasmaa recognized, embodied encounters with art-works rely on 'projecting our own emotions and feelings onto the work', and this is amplified when some of our worse

Figure 9.1 The Princess in the land of Sick. *For the Best,* Unicorn Theatre. Photographer Andrew Whittuck.

fears, the illness and death of children, are represented on stage. The performance also received considerable critical acclaim from the press, with *The Guardian Newspaper* critic Lyn Gardner awarding it a rare five stars and it subsequently won the 2009 Theatrical Management Association's award for the Best Play for children and young people.[7] But what was the role of the performance at the Unicorn Theatre in public engagement in science or biomedical issues?

One of the elements that the performance and project as a whole illuminated was the emotional impact of illness on the family, who had to operate within a complex professional system and network of medical care. It turned patient experience into metaphor, and showed the values of life and death in a condensed aesthetic form. The juxtaposition of technological space with the domestic space brought the poetic of everyday life into the technical world of the hospital, reminding each audience member that there is another dimension and a deeper, emotional element to medical science. Bringing together the naturalism of daily existence and the surreal world of the imagination ruptured commonsense patterns of thought, in Bachelard's terms, suggesting that the mind might be receptive to the kind of emotional changes needed to develop scientific imagination. The medical staff involved in this project described how it reminded them that illness affects the whole family, and the need to integrate technologies of care with the insights of artists, teachers and other agencies.[8] The project exemplified the networks and connectivity that Latour identified as integral to good scientific practices and, by occupying a trans-disciplinary space, enabled two perspectives (or two cultures) to be mediated by a theatrical language that allowed audiences, as all good poetry does, to fill the gaps between the images and the words. Perhaps the word to describe the audience's experience is not engagement, but insistence. There was an energy that held audiences tight – at times painfully, but always comfortingly and tenderly. It did not try to shield anyone from the pain of illness, and the teachers who worked on the project were insistent that children should not be protected from the world that one of their classmates inhabited. Perhaps most importantly, this was a multifaceted process, in which everyone had the opportunity to learn in ways that extended their own horizons.

Theatre aesthetics and the poetics of science

I began this chapter by invoking Virioli's question, in which he asked where 'inhumanity' would be if science were left without ethical constraints. The question, it seems to me, begs further consideration about the social conditions in which knowledge is produced, translated, transformed and disseminated. As Alan Irwin argues, scientists' work may well be oppositional, and they are as likely to be inspired by resistance to existing ways of living and social concerns as artists. Irwin specifically cites research into environmental change as an example of scientific activity that is motivated by a desire to make a difference to the world (1995, p. 169). This research requires, Irwin suggests, a re-conceptualization of science, in which it is regarded not as 'a single enterprise following one set of goals or practices' but relies on bringing together different perspectives and world views. This anti-essentialist and sociological view of science has implications for how scientists position their work in relation to other forms of knowledge, as it recognizes the specificity of its world view. 'The question becomes', Irwin states, 'not *whether* science should be applied to environmental (and, of course, other) questions, but rather *which form* of science is most appropriate and in *what relationship* to other forms of knowledge and understanding' (1995, p. 170. Italics original).

One of the arguments in this chapter is that the application of theatre to science education is predicated on challenging the two culture divide that is a legacy of the Enlightenment separation between reason and emotion, value and aesthetics. In charting this history, Joe Winston has pointed out that an education in the arts and science relies not on a narrow conception of learning facts that can be measured, but on a shared perception of beauty. To ignore the aesthetic of science and mathematics, he argues, is to fail to understand that beauty motivates learning. Citing the work of the British theatre company *Theatre-Rites*, he illustrates his perception that beauty has the capacity to balance a desire for order with sensory pleasure. Winston suggests that this has pedagogical implications:

> an apprehension of beauty can change students' perceptions dramatically, allowing them to grasp the error or ignorance of their previous, common-sense understandings. (2008, pp. 37–8)

This insight returns the debate to Bachelard's poetic of scientific learning, and brings an understanding of scientists as well as artists engaged with the integration of ethics with aesthetics. Sian Ede, in her book *Art and Science* (2005), underlines this perception by observing that scientists are motivated by the aesthetic interconnectiveness of form and content, by imagining new patterns and creating new structures of thought (2005, pp. 15–16). It is a way of working that recognizes that science, as well as the arts, is inspired by emotion and passion, shaped by intuition, and finds expression in narrative and aesthetic forms.

Reconceptualizing the educational role of theatre and science has wider implications for education, therefore, as it brokers a new epistemology that illuminates the foundations of entrenched patters of Western thought. In recognizing the specificity of the relationship between ethics, aesthetics and intuition, Tim Ingold returns the debate to the ways in which different world views have shaped intellectual endeavour. In making a case for intuition in science, he argues:

> Intuitive understanding, in short, is not contrary to science or ethics, nor does it appeal to instinct rather than reason, or to supposedly 'hardwired' imperatives of human nature. (2000, p. 25)

He suggests that this insight should not lead to an alternative conception of science from a perspective of 'other' or non-Western 'indigenous' cultures. On the contrary, he suggests a 'poetics of dwelling' that recognizes how the specificity of place and dwelling is integral to understanding the ecologies of the world in which we live (2000, p. 26). The anthropologist Gregory Bateson describes this ecological meeting of mind and material environment as 'third-order learning', a term he uses to articulate the ways in which discontinuities and consonances that challenge familiar patterns can inspire learning (1972, p. 252).

Witnessing how science can be shaped and informed by knowledge from a range of perspectives invites people to find different points of entry into scientific narratives and different forms of identification with the ideas it represents. For example, the collaborations between environmental scientist and artists, musicians, writers and theatre-makers have initiated a cultural response to climate change in an ambitious programme called 'Cape Farewell' in which artists work alongside scientists on expeditions to the Arctic.[9] This not only stimulates ethical and political debate, it also creates new metaphors with which to understand the process of climate change. Cape Farewell illustrates Jackson's view that theatre about science is often inspired by crisis, and it also illuminates how both scientists and artists are implicated in posing radical social questions that show their passions and commitments. Baz Kershaw extends the argument further, arguing that the reflexivity that is required by some performance practices 'may most crucially challenge the dualism of modernism which have fuelled the ecological crisis, particularly those between body and mind, analysis and creativity, thought and action, spectator and participant, culture and nature' (2007, p. 316). He argues for 'ethically principled immersive participation' in performance that transforms spectators into participants. My suggestion is that this often places education (in its broadest sense) at the centre of the performative event and, as Kershaw argues, this offers everyone a chance to re-think their ethical responsibilities by becoming alert to human and non-human systems of nature and ecology. This impulse has broad implications for the pedagogical relationship between theatre and science, and promises a way to recycle the participatory aesthetics of theatre-in-education and the modernist avant-garde in ways that speak to the ethical concerns of the twenty-first century.

The challenge for conversations across disciplines is how to main-tain an even balance of power between the arts and sciences, in which the educational imperative extends, rather than diminishes, their cap-acity to move, excite and provide an imaginative vision of the future. This kind of collaboration between artists and scientists is perhaps best summarized by Gillian Beer, whose words on literature might equally apply to theatre: 'such enquiry must not be subordinated to current demands in our society for predetermined relevance, nor can its success be measured by discovering identity between the different domains. The questioning of meaning in (and across) science and lit-erature needs to be sustained without always seeking reconciliation' (1996, p. 195).

10

Learning in Theatres and Participation in Theatre: Cool Spaces?

I once heard a story about theatre practitioners from a major opera house who were contributing to the education programme of a high security London prison. Part of the project involved a performance of an opera in the prison, and some of the prisoners were delegated to work with designers to create a set in the prison exercise yard. The designers were enchanted by the bleakness, the severe institutional lines and the imposing high walls of the yard, and wanted to use this found space as the set with few alterations. The prisoners, by contrast, wanted to fabricate a garden with riot of colour, a fantasy away from their own daily realities. I was told that the designers had the good sense to go along with the prisoners' suggestions, and the yard was temporarily transformed. The prisoners were interested in using theatre as a means of escape, through which they might imagine an alternative world and inhabit a different place. A different story, also about creative spaces, was told by urban planning scholar Graeme Evans. Evans describes how, in 2006, a local newspaper in Salford near Manchester had asked some boys from the deprived East Salford Housing Estate ('hoodies') to visit a free exhibition of Lowry paintings that portrayed factory scenes and working class culture. Within minutes the boys had been refused entry to the gallery for no apparent reason and security had been called (2010, p. 30). Salford Quays is an area of urban regeneration that has gentrified the former Manchester docklands through the creative industries, and it appeared that on this occasion they were less than welcoming to young people who did not conform to their image of the latte-drinking creative classes. Twentieth century revolutionary theatre-makers would understand the challenges of making theatre in non-theatrical spaces, progressive educators would appreciate the appeal of a garden to those living in a grim, urban environment and social reformists Jane Addams and Henrietta Barnett would certainly recognize the social division that denies some people right of access to the arts. Taken together, they raise questions about ownership of creative practices and cultural products, and about participating in cultural spaces that might be described as 'cool'. But cool to whom?

In this final chapter I am interested in revisiting ideas about participating in theatre as a cultural institution. One of the great achievements that the theatre-in-education movement made to theatre practice is that it redefined the politics of participation, and found innovative methodologies that blurred the boundaries between audiences and performers. But as Kershaw points out, in the contemporary mediatized world, performance is everywhere (Kershaw, 2007). There is drama on radio, on television and at the cinema. Consumerism is performed in shopping centres and malls, and there are performances on the street, in museums and heritage centres. Theatre comes in multiple forms, it happens in a plethora of sites and places and there are many different ways in which performers engage with audiences. There has been some memorable experimental practice in found spaces in recent years, and arguably the seriously metropolitan 'cool crowd' are more likely to be seen at performances in semi-derelict spaces such as old swimming pools, disused factories and empty hotels than in conventional theatre spaces, thereby inverting the Workers' Theatre Movement's preference for working on the street. As young people have also come increasingly to expect that they will participate in a range of interactive websites, computer games and other performance events, it becomes less clear whether they are consumers or producers of cultural practice. Rather than finding ways to arrest this form of cultural engagement, the new imperative is to recognize that, in performative societies, social participation has been redefined.

Within this performative culture, there are questions about whether the theatre is, in Kershaw's words, 'hopelessly quaint and inadequate' (2007, p. 68). In its defence, live theatre has claimed a place for itself as a space of resistance to the packaged images of the globalized media, a position that reasserts the traditional belief in the efficacy of theatre for the twenty-first century. But liveness is not in itself necessarily resistant, some forms of participation can be highly coercive, and this suggests that it is time to reassess some of the principles on which the participatory strategies of theatre education have relied. In the past, egalitarian theatre educators objected to the theatre on the grounds that it encouraged political passivity, and they were critical of its narrowly bourgeois tastes. It is a perception for which theatres themselves can take some responsibility; theatre can be an exploitative commercial business. Although this approach to theatre education may have been justifiable at the time, however, it was predicated on a very specific view of theatre that now seems remarkably narrow. One consequence was that young people were often discouraged from learning about the processes of theatre-making for themselves, and experimenting with how different dramatic forms create meaning tended to be left to specialist drama courses. But there is now a more equitable space in education for young people to develop as artists, who understand that theatre-makers do not simply possess saleable creative skills, but they have a social role as cultural critics who use theatrical imagery, symbol and metaphor to communicate their ideas, thoughts and feelings. As a pedagogy, this way of working has the potential to erode tired distinctions between educating young *artists* who engage in experiments in theatre form, and young *citizens* who are interested in the dramatic representation of ideas. On the contrary, I think that in today's performative, global and mediatized societies, they are mutually embedded.

Throughout this book I have argued that the politics of place and the aesthetics of space have a particular importance in theatre education, and whether young people become uncritical cultural consumers or develop their own cultural capital and abilities as theatre-makers depends on how spaces in theatres and outside theatres are used. In this chapter I shall suggest ways in which participation is being redefined in twenty-first century theatre education, and how this is creating new opportunities for young people to learn alongside theatre-makers as fellow artists. In a society that is dominated by all kinds of performance in everyday life, learning to participate in many different forms of theatre and understanding the conditions and constructions of performance is, arguably, one of the most important elements of education. In many ways this involves looking backwards as well as forwards, and so I shall begin this discussion by revisiting debates about the politics of participation that dominated the development of twentieth century theatre education, asking how new insights into the spectator/ participant binary might inform educational practice. I shall then consider how Deweyan pedagogic principles remain visible in groundbreaking contemporary theatre for young audiences, before considering how theatres are encouraging young people's participation as artists and in theatre as a cultural practice. In each instance, traces of the past are evident in theatre education practices, revitalized, revised and adapted for young people living in contemporary globalized, performative societies.

The politics of participation

It was, of course, the influence of Brecht and the Brazilian theatre director Augusto Boal on theatre education that contributed to the belief that spectatorship is inevitably passive and therefore lacking in emancipatory potential or political energy. Brecht was famously critical of 'culinary theatre', a term he used to describe commercial entertainment, but it was perhaps Boal's declaration that spectator is a 'bad word' in his first book, *Theatre of the Oppressed* (1979, p. 154), that came to haunt theatre education. As I pointed out in Chapter 4, the perception that activity was inherently liberating initially provided a welcome alternative to authoritarian styles of teaching and to forms of theatre that sought to entertain rather than challenge. But as the idea took root, however, it marked a denigration of the spectator's agency, and an enduring but ill-grounded perception that the experience of spectatorship equates with intellectual, political and emotional passivity. It is time to redress the balance.

The philosopher who has become an influential figure in redefining the aesthetics and politics of participation in theatre is Jacques Rancière, whose work challenges the binary between participation (active and good) and spectatorship (passive and bad). In his essay *The Emancipated Spectator* Rancière argues that distinctions between activity and passivity in theatre are premised on a misleading opposition between 'looking and knowing' and 'looking and acting'. This makes a patronizing assumption, Rancière argues, that theatre is a vehicle through which knowledge is transmitted to ignorant audiences who are content to sit in front of a spectacle 'without knowing the process of production and about the reality it conceals' (2009, p. 2). Instead, he argues that seeing is itself an active process, and he couches his argument in pedagogic terms:

> Spectatorship is not some passive condition that we should transform into activity. . It is our normal situation. We learn and teach, we act and know as spectators who link what they see with what they have seen and told,

done and dreamed ... Every spectator is already an actor in her story; every actor, every man of action, is the spectator of the same story. (2009, p. 17)

The idea that spectators link what they see to their own knowledge and experience challenges methodologies that equate spectatorship with passivity. This suggests, in Rancière's view, that students were considered too ignorant to make sense of what they saw for themselves. He describes the oppositions on which this approach was built – looking/ knowing, looking/ acting, appearance/ reality, activity/ passivity – as 'allegories of inequality' because they assume that one is superior to the other. As Rancière points out, 'She observes, she selects, she interprets. She links what she sees to a host of other things that she has seen on other stages, in other kinds of place' (2009, p. 13).

Rancière's argument has appealed to scholars in applied theatre and theatre education because he explicitly relates participation to political questions of efficacy and agency, although the idea that spectators bring their own knowledge and experiences to the practice of interpretation has been a recurring theme in audience studies for many years. Two studies of young people's responses to seeing plays confirm the view that audience's interpretations are informed by previous experience. John Tulloch's study of teenagers' discussions of performances of Chekhov plays observes that they move in and out of different registers, utilizing 'expert' and 'everyday' vocabularies (2000, p. 89), and Matthew Reason's analysis of children's responses to performances in Scotland similarly draws attention to their active and creative engagement with the theatre event (2010, pp. 170–1). Both studies illuminate important aspects of the audience experience, but it is interesting that neither scholar considers how seeing theatre might inform the young people's creativity as theatre-makers themselves. Tulloch rests his analysis on students' discussion rather than other forms of creative response, and his assumptions about their experiences of formal education relies on outdated research. He cites Alan Sinfield's essay about Shakespeare in education, first published in 1985, without apparently questioning whether his analysis was still relevant in 2000, and he quotes uncritically Henry Jenkins' view, articulated in 1992, that young people are taught for authorial meaning and are discouraged from demonstrating their personal feelings. This is, of course, ill-informed and under-researched; even a cursory glance at the excellent work of Rex Gibson on teaching Shakespeare (1998), or Sally Mackey and Simon Cooper (1995) and Andy Kempe (1997) on teaching drama at examination level, would have shown Tulloch that his argument may have fitted his political agenda, that 'students who respond with "personal feelings" are getting their own back .... against the teacher's surrogate "red pen" ' (2000, p. 98), but has little bearing on how teachers actually teach. Matthew Reason's work is more sensitively nuanced, and he makes an excellent case for encouraging children to draw in response to theatre, but I wondered why he had not considered how their experiences of seeing plays might also be interpreted creatively in their own drama and dramatic play. Notwithstanding, their research shows how the agency of young spectators unfixes the theatrical product, and challenges outmoded oppositions between process and product by valuing the creativity that audiences bring to the theatre or performance event.

I vividly recall a moment in my time as a drama teacher when sharp distinctions between spectatorship and participation, or process and product, seemed unhelpfully restrictive. I had taken a class of fifteen-year-olds to see a performance of *Trafford Tanzi* by Claire Luckham (renamed *Totterdown Tanzi* for the local Bristol audience), a play set in a boxing ring that uses the metaphor of a boxing match to debate sexism. It was 1987, and it was many of the students' first experience of being in a theatre. The company had gone to considerable lengths to re-create the atmosphere of a boxing match, and the space around the black-box theatre had been transformed by hot-dog stands, sweet stalls and other paraphernalia of boxing matches I've now forgotten. I do remember the smell of frying onions, and the students' surprise that they were allowed to eat before the show and that they were encouraged to shout out when things got rough on stage. They were thoroughly involved in the issues at stake, and became very angry with the gender politics that were played out. Afterwards, when they had calmed down we talked about the debates the play had raised, and they were interested in how the actors did it. Some of them had been to boxing matches, and they wanted to know how actors managed to portray such a realistic fight without getting hurt. They were also interested in how the play had generated such energy that they had found themselves swept along by arguments, and wanted to learn why some of them had found themselves supporting positions that contradicted their own views. They wanted to apply their understanding of narrative construction to their own practice, to create a piece of theatre that would raise similar passions. I kept my notes on this scheme of work, and when I re-read them I found that I have been pondering the implications of their questions, in different ways, ever since.

The questions the students raised in response to *Totterdown Tanzi* were political and cultural as well as artistic; in common with many other students whose work I have witnessed since, they were interested in debating the issues represented on stage and harnessing its theatrical power in their own work. Contrary to Tulloch's assumptions, the students' personal responses prompted their desire to acquire further 'expert' knowledge of theatre production. My aim here is not to offer a detailed analysis of young audiences, nor to relate theatre-going to the drama curriculum, but to explore the ways in which participation might be reconceptualized to demonstrate the relationship between personal engagement, creativity and emancipated spectatorship. As Reason points out, the assumption that children are passive when they are quiet is just too easy, the 'transfixed audience' he argues, may be 'passive externally (publically) but internally (privately) very active – at work interpreting, engaging, analysing and constructing what is going on in front of them' (2010, p. 170).

Seamus Heaney commented that writers have to start out as readers, and if young people are to develop as informed practitioners they will also be encouraged to become emancipated spectators of all kinds of performance practices. Learning about the mechanics of performance is inseparable from debates about the ideas represented and, as the first TIE actors recognised in Coventry, the sensory experience of being in the theatre or site of performance, its smells, sounds, textures, tastes and aesthetic qualities, form part of the memory of the event. In recognition of the relationship between spectatorship and creative practice, experimental companies such as Frantic Assembly, Stan's Cafe, Lone Twin and Third Angel have adapted their own methodologies for work in schools that mirror and extend their approaches to devising performances, and they often work with young people over sustained periods of time. Learning environments that challenge and support young people artistically, emotionally, culturally and intellectually will invite their responses to theatre that are not only discursive and political, but also aesthetic and poetic.

The poetics of participation

In discussing the implications of Rancière's argument in her book *Theatre & Audience* (2009), Helen Freshwater points out that because his work is limited to the modernist theatre of Artaud and Brecht, he misses the ways in which more contemporary forms of theatre foreground the active interpretation and participation of spectators. Freshwater cites the Wooster Group as an example of a company whose work requires audiences to decide how images are read and understood, but there are also many examples of innovative approaches to participation in theatre education that are perhaps less well known (2009, p. 17). The education work of Stan's Cafe, for example, in *Plague Nation* (2004) brought their installation *Of all the People in the World* from gallery spaces to school halls; Blast Theory contributed to interactive educational exhibitions in the Science Museum in London and Fevered Sleep generate environments in their work for children and for adult audiences that often challenge relationships to the performance space.[1] It is important that highly successful experimental theatre-makers are continuing to find working with young people artistically exciting, suggesting that young people represent an important participant public. Their work also draws attention to ways in which audiences construct theatrical meanings, and this approach implicitly rejects the idea that a work has a single meaning or a linear narrative in favour of the poetic perception that there are multiplicity of available narratives and a plurality of audience perspectives.

The integration of the poetics of participation and pedagogic practice is very clear in the theatre of Oily Cart, a London-based touring company that began in 1981 with the specific intention of making theatre for very small children. Their repertoire has grown to include multi-sensory, interactive performances for children with complex disabilities, particularly those on the autistic spectrum, which they perform both in schools and in the theatre. Lyn Gardner, a leading critic on the Guardian Newspaper, is an admiring fan and describes their work as 'theatrically way ahead that of many of our most internationally celebrated companies, despite the fact that it works in a sector which is under-funded, under-celebrated and woefully under-valued'. Gardner made this comment about the inventiveness of the company in her review of *Pool Piece* (2008), in which the company worked with children with disabilities in a swimming pool, and from which, she reflects 'many site-responsive theatre companies would learn a great deal from'.[2] Oily Cart are adept at transforming everyday spaces into magical places, and in creating work that is led by the children, with whom performers usually work on an one-to-one basis, responding to their rhythms and mirroring their reactions. Their work is artistically and aesthetically groundbreaking, and leads the way in making playful theatre in which learning and participation are embedded in the art form itself, blurring the lines between audience and spectator, artist and learner.

On each occasion I have seen Oily Cart's work, I have been struck by the ability of the company to tune into each of the children's needs, often expressed pre-verbally or without language. Older children are carefully prepared for the experience with clear guidance about how they might like to act and react, and this process helps them to feel comfortable laughing, calling out or talking to the actors. *Something in the Air*, an Oily Cart collaboration with Ockham's Razor, had already opened at the Manchester International Festival in July 2009 and toured special schools before I witnessed the performance at the Unicorn Theatre, London in April 2010. In this production, children were gently transported into the air in flying chairs alongside their carers, where they were positioned to enjoy an acrobatic performance and magical moments of theatrical simplicity.[3] When I saw the performance, one of their favourite sequences seemed to be when bouncy red balls, of increasing size, were dropped from the flies and which were allowed to bounce beneath them on the stage. The sense of joy I observed in these children at this simple, well-timed act, illustrated the children's imaginative engagement in the performance. The moments in which objects gain a theatrical life, and require the imagination and humour of the audience to make meaning, is a characteristic of Oily Cart's aesthetic and educational play(Fig. 10.1).

Encouraging children's playful inter-activity with objects was integral to John Dewey's aesthetic philosophy, and was turned into theories of learning by the psychologist D.W. Winnicott. Dewey suggested that the arts bring together the child's internal subjectivity with the external world of objects and, in his words, allow for a 'complete merging of playfulness with seriousness' (1934, p. 279). Winnicott extended this principle in his book *Playing and Reality* (1971), describing the objects with which children play as 'transitional'. Transitional objects are integral to developing a sense of self, as they are used by small children to represent something that is 'not me' and, particularly through their creative play, they learn a sense of their own place in the world. Oily Cart's work illustrates this theoretical understanding, and this is evident in the ways in which children engage in their interactive performances.

Mabel Davies came with me to see *Drum* in February 2010, an interactive performance for very small children and babies, when she was two years old. Mabel later told me that she especially liked it

Figure 10.1 *Something in the Air,* an Oily Cart Collaboration with Ockham's Razor. Photographer Nik Mackey, www.topright.co.uk.

when she made ants and beetles jump under stars. No one in the cast had suggested that interpretation, and it was, in fact, a large, well-lit bass drum, strewn first with grains of rice and then with raisins that bounced when the children hit it. But I like Mabel's story better. It shows the centrality of her imagination to making the performance, and also suggests how the company's understanding of early childhood play has informed their work. Dewey's ideas about the integrity of the audience to the making of meaning provided the inspiration for avant-garde *Happenings* by John Cage and his fellow students at Black Mountain College in the 1950s, but the synthesis of play, learning and aesthetic engagement have, in my view, found deeper and more original expression in Oily Cart's work.

Cultures of participation

Matthew Arnold valued the study of culture for its capacity to unite society, and William Morris encouraged community-building through the practice of craft. The synthesis of these two positions led to the idea that participation in the arts promotes social cohesion, a perspective that has been tested and endured, in different ways, ever since.

And although some educationalists have held on to the view that the theatre is either a high art and therefore élitist, or a commercial venture that is necessarily exploitative, there has also been a significant paradigm shift in the cultural sector in which participation and learning is taking a leading role. With the exception of a few enlightened theatre managers at places like The Belgrade Theatre, Coventry, education was generally considered to be a peripheral activity, sublimated to the interests of the paying public and the artistic programme which remained firmly at the heart of the building. But in the most forward-thinking theatres in the twenty-first century, theatre managers are placing education and learning central to the ethos of the entire cultural organization.

There are many reasons for this change in priorities, not least that the regeneration of post-industrial areas into metropolitan cultural quarters have left many theatres wondering about the actual level of cultural participation of those who live in nearby areas of social deprivation. A cynical view would be that education programmes are motivated by self-interest on the part of theatres, where people have finally recognized that their own metropolitan tastes are limiting their markets or, as John Tulloch puts it, school parties ensure 'at least one mass audience per season' (2000, p. 88). But that is not how I see it; although there is a desire that young people attend the theatre in numbers, many people who now run education programmes in theatres have inherited the political spirit of the TIE movement and there is genuine commitment to find inventive ways to invite people from all sectors of society into their performance spaces. Steve Ball at the Birmingham Repertory Theatre, UK, who leads the Learning and Participation Programme, for example, brought his experience of theatre in health education to a groundbreaking collaboration with the local hospitals where all babies who were born in one week in October 2004 were given free theatre experiences with their families for the first 10 years of their lives. Many of these families would not normally consider theatre-going, and this imaginative project has extended the experience of theatre to people beyond its habitual reach. Steve Ball commented that the theatre staff has learnt a lot from these families, not only about the demographic of theatre-going, but about how the artistic programme might inspire young children and families.[4] Writing about her experiences at the Young Vic Theatre in London, Ruth Little confirms the view that learning is a reciprocal activity, and this attitude has infiltrated into the working practices of the whole theatre. She describes the approach to theatre education developed at the Young Vic:

> Teaching is defined as a two-way process which aims not only to stimulate the minds and imagination of young participants but also to give them the tools to contribute to the creative life of the company and its developing artistic practice. (2004, p. 20)

This emphasis on reciprocity places learning at the centre of the life of the theatre. Without a willingness to learn and engage in dialogue, all theatre becomes intellectually stale, artistically lifeless and emotionally moribund and enlightened theatres have learnt to listen to the voices of young people both as audience members and as fellow artists.

Part of the challenge is to build an education programme that is genuinely inclusive, and changing the titles of education departments to names such as 'Participation' or 'Learning' has helped to loosen the idea that the work serves only schools. But although this helps, and the aesthetic space of the performance can have a magic of its own in the hands of sensitive performers, one of the obstacles to young people's participation in theatre is that the architecture can be off-putting, particularly to those who feel that the theatre is outside their cultural experience. There is an obvious correlation between their social experience of the theatre as a building, the aesthetic of the theatrical space and the ways in which learning is constructed and experienced. Bringing young people into theatres can bring buildings to life at times when they might otherwise seem dead, but as the Saltford Quay 'hoodies' would testify, this relies on cultivating positive ethos towards everyone who enters the building and making them feel safe and welcome. The social meanings of space are always fluid and constructed in relation to its energy and liveliness, but for any group of people to feel part of that space, Lefebvre points out, they need to be recognized by others as integral to producing that space. Making space for learning in theatres not only requires new ways of thinking about participation and new aesthetic forms, therefore, it also depends on young people's ability to generate their own spatial meanings within the building. The Lyric Hammersmith in London is a good example of a theatre in which a commitment to young people's learning is driving the artistic vision and influencing the theatre's architecture – synthesizing Lefebvre's conceived and representational spaces – and suggesting how participation in theatre as a public place can enable young people to produce their own spaces in which to learn.

The Lyric Hammersmith is a theatre in west London that has a long history of producing theatre that attracts local audiences as well as theatre-going audiences from across London and beyond. Its situation in Hammersmith, away from the glamour of the West End, has provided a space for new and experimental work, including the first London production of Pinter's *The Birthday Party* on 19 May 1958. More recently, as well as producing their own work, the Lyric has staged new work by companies such as Frantic Assembly and Knee High in the main house which have a strong following among young audiences, and the theatre also supports a regular repertoire of performances for small children. The theatre's architecture reflects its varied performance history and its growth as a community resource. It is found on the corner of a shopping precinct and its shop-window facade reflects the angular lines of the modernist architecture of the square, but inside there is an ornate Victorian auditorium designed by Frank Matcham that was rescued by the local people when Hammersmith's opera house was demolished in the 1960s. There is also a smaller black-box studio theatre built in 1979, but perhaps the most noticeable aspect of the architectural design today is the wide open space of the first floor cafe and terrace where people meet and young people gather. This combination of the popular, the experimental and the local has meant that it is ideally placed to support an inventive programme for young people. The centrality of the programme for young people and its commitment to artist development has been recognized by the award of a major development grant of over £15 million in 2010, which will make it the first 'Teaching Theatre' for the performing arts in Britain. This will fund new buildings that aim to add to the architectural eclecticism and energy of the existing space.

The Lyric's history favours local involvement and artist development, but realizing this ambition requires the commitment of everyone in the building, from people working in security to the box-office staff and across the administrative and artistic teams. The Lyric is a good example of a sustained and multilayered approach to collaboration, and in common with many theatres there is a range of provision including a youth theatre, resources for teachers and students on the main house artistic programme and a range of social inclusion programmes. Young performers who live in the Hammersmith area may join the youth theatre, and the Lyric Young Ambassadors are a steering group that is consulted about all aspects of theatre's programme for young people. Work is structured for young people to encourage a clear sense of progression from one part of the programme to another;

those who are interested in careers in the theatre are not discouraged, but they are reminded that it is possible to work in theatres as carpenters, accountants, electricians, caterers, marketing and press officers, administrators or security guards as well as artists or performers.

There is also a commitment to encouraging young people who have found formal education difficult, and there is an alternative education offered at the theatre. This programme accepts referrals and support from partner organizations including youth offending teams, the Social Services and charitable organizations. Some young people who struggled with the disciplinary structures of school or college seem to flourish at the Lyric, gaining formal qualifications in literacy and numeracy as well as participating in theatre-making. When I interviewed two of the young people who had benefitted from this programme, it was noticeable that they had developed strong emotional ties to the theatre as well as the theatre practitioners with whom they had worked. I was fortunate to meet Farhana Ahmed and Sam Thompson in July 2010, both in their early twenties at the time, who told me about the long-term relationship they had enjoyed at the theatre. Neither had been particularly successful at school, and Sam told me that before he had joined the Lyric programme he had been involved with 'a bunch of idiots who were always in trouble', adding that 'if you hang out with idiots you become an idiot yourself'. He had already decided to make changes to his life when he was encouraged by a social worker to join the theatre's programme, but he admitted that he had never been to the theatre and assumed he would be out of place. Once he had taken the first step, he described that the positive atmosphere generated by the practitioners had made him value himself more, and that he had learnt to feel proud of his achievements. The informal attitude had also appealed to Farhana, who described the theatre as a 'cool space' in which she felt comfortable to become the person she had always wanted to be. The role of the theatre in forming a positive sense of self was evident throughout our conversation, and both young people recognized that there was something about working in a space that generated creative activity that made them feel that they could learn to *be* different. 'When people are pretending to change who they are as a job', Sam commented, 'you work out that you can change yourself'. Sam also commented that he had become more articulate since attending the Lyric's programme and Farhana added that 'there's always someone to conversate with', which meant that neither of them 'felt judged'. Farhana was more interested in following a career in the performing arts than Sam,

whose conversation focused on the personal and social benefits of the programme. Farhana particularly valued her experiences on the professional stage, and the very practical advice she had received from Lyric staff with an application for a training programme at the BBC, for which she was successful. Throughout our conversation, Sam and Farhana were keen to stress the sense of belonging they felt to the theatre, and how the environment had provided them with a safe space in which they could take risks, both personal and artistic.

In some ways this provision echoes the work of Jane Addams in Hull House and the Barnetts in Toynbee Hall, because it shows how local cultural institutions provide a point of stability and creative opportunities for young people who may not have seen themselves as theatre-goers or theatre-makers. Of course some programmes that set out to be inclusive and artistically engaging miss the mark; without risk there is no failure. Making space for creativity, in this conceptualization, does not lie in following fixed pedagogic models, but on cross-fertilization between people and places, and in making connections with images, ideas, stories and people. In this way a culture of participation can animate theatre buildings, and lively education and participation programmes mean that the work on stage represents only part of the creative work of the theatre.

On metaphors, map and stories: Unchartered territories

Learning never happens in the absence of bodies, emotions, memories, history and place, as Elizabeth Ellsworth describes, and for that reason the metaphors that guided this book are spatial and relational. Participation in theatre depends on interactivity, and my intention was to chart some of the ways in which theatre education has responded to the cultural geographies of young people. In the process of exploring the many different ways in which theatre can contribute to education, I have kept asking myself if, and why, theatre still matters to young people, even in this mediatized world. There is no one definitive answer to that question, and of course it would be naïve to assume that all young people respond equally to theatre events and practices. But they are all implicated in societies that place performance at the centre of social relationships, and in which consumer cultures have theatricalized consumption and are finding new ways to capture young people's imaginations and encourage them to part with their money. And perhaps that is the point; theatre education has always been fluently responsive to social, cultural and educational change, and it touches the heart of recent debates about the values of education in the twenty-first century and insists that we reconsider the place of theatre in the new millennium.

One of the consequences of living in a world that is increasingly interconnected is that young people's geographical imaginations have been stretched. Doreen Massey has observed that youth cultures across the world are now recognizably hybrid, and that young people construct their own cultural practices that are at once both local and global. This means that youth cultures are neither homogeneous and globalized, nor local and closed, but 'products of interaction' that change, meld and reform as they encounter new lines of cultural connection and different meeting places. Of course, this way of thinking about how young people constitute and imagine their own geographical spaces immediately calls into question the way in which I structured the spatial metaphors in this book. My decision to move from home to street, nation and global is not, however, a linear march towards greater internationalism or intended to suggest a hierarchy of scale. Rather, I hoped to illustrate how different cultural narratives merge, blend and influence each other as an act of cultural improvisation, in both everyday spatial relationships and in the representational space of theatre. The metaphor provides a structure for thinking about the different 'spheres of moral concern', as Appiah puts it, rather than representing essentialized social identities. It has long been understood that theatre offers young people a transitional space in which to shape, disrupt and interpret narratives, both fictional and real, and the methodologies and pedagogies of theatre education depend on interactivity. Participating in theatre can offer young people a chance to produce equitable spaces in which to work, in which they can be 'me and not me', thereby meeting the alterity in themselves and encountering themselves as others.

The process of uncovering stories about theatre, education and performance, both from the distant past and more recent events, always encourages reflection on the future. This book was guided by this impulse, but by the end of this study, I am left with an uneasy sense that there are too many stories that have been left untold, too many places unvisited and too many ideas and practices ignored. In part, that sense of incompleteness is also integral to the argument in this book, as it seems that as soon we know where we are going, as soon as there is a clear path to follow, another set of challenges present themselves that demand attention. Without that uncertainty, however, particularly in a globalized society where injustices are geographical as well as historical, there is a risk that we become uncritical consumers of mediatized images and fail to imagine alternative ways of living. In tracing some of these histories and geographies, however, I hope that I have raised some questions about what it means to act creatively in our homes, streets, communities, networks, nations and in a world that is interconnected and in education systems that are always in a state of flux.

Throughout this book I have suggested that the educative role of theatre presses questions about the value placed on theatre in society. One recurring theme is that the commercialization of theatre has never been respected by theatre educators, and this perspective remains evident in contemporary practices. There is a deep utopianism about theatre education that consistently imagines the world to be more equitable and more just, and its aesthetic practices are orientated towards social engagement and cultural understanding. The spatial metaphors in this book underline the fact that the new challenge to the twenty-first century is environmental and geographical, and that problems and solutions can no longer be contained within national borders. This insists on ways of thinking that are beyond familiar modes of thought. Writing about the challenges of climate change, Zigmunt Bauman summarizes this uncertainty in emotional terms:

> We feel, guess, suspect what needs to be done. But we cannot know the shape and form it will eventually take. We can be pretty sure, though, that the shape will not be familiar. (2005, p. 153)

My suggestion is that, in a modest way, the theatre can help imagine what that shape might look like. If theatre is an interweaving of memory and liveness and learning is constructed in negotiation and dialogue, theatre education offers a powerful place to encounter the unexpected, to extend horizons of expectation and to consider where we are positioned in the world. It is material and ephemeral, and recognizes that meaning is made not only in the symbols, metaphors and narratives of drama, but between spaces and places, in the gaps and the silences of reflection as well as in the movement and activity of practice.

Notes

2 Spaces to Imagine: Theatre and Social Reform

1. This account of this history of the gallery movement is given in Borzello, F. (1987) *Civilising Caliban*, London and New York: Routledge and Kegan Paul, chapter 1.
2. See the following websites for information about the work of Toynbee Hall www.toynbeehall.org.uk and Jane Addam's Hull House Association: www.hullhouse.org/aboutus/mission.htm, both accessed 23.3.2010. See also the work of Adventure Stage Chicago, a Settlement House theatre founded by Harriet Vittum during her period as head warden, 1907–47. Harriet Vittum was inspired by Jane Addams, and the auditorium still carries her name. www.adventurestage.org, accessed 13.8.2010.

3 Spaces to Play: Childhood, Theatre and Educational Utopias

1. See Carolyn Steedman's account of the work of Margaret McMillan in Steedman, C. (1990) *Childhood, Culture and Class in Britain: Margaret McMillan 1860–1931*, London: Virago; and Pinder, D. (2005) *Visions of the City: Utopianism, Power and Politics in Twentieth-Century Urbanism*, Edinburgh: Edinburgh University Press for an account of the garden city movement. For the Children's Country Holidays Fund see http://cchfreunited.org.uk
2. Juliet Dusinberre gives an account of the influence of genetics on the attitudes presented in children's literature and educational practice, where the relationship between genius and genetics is cited. See Dusinberre, J. (1987) *Alice to the Lighthouse*, London and Basingstoke: The MacMillan Press, p. 17.

4 Places to Learn: Activity and Activism

1. This perception endured into the late twentieth century among those following the Brazilian theatre director, Augusto Boal. See Boal, A. (1979) *Theatre of the Oppressed*, London: Pluto Press.
2. These accounts can be found in Samuel, R., MacColl, E. and Cosgrove, S. (1985) *Theatres of the Left 1880–1935 Workers' Theatre Movements in Britain and America*, London: Routledge Kegan Paul, pp. 205–57, and Goorney,

H. and MacColl, E. (1986) (eds.) *Agit-prop to Theatre Workshop: Political Playscripts 1930-50*, Manchester: Manchester University Press, pp. xxvii–xxix
3. The Federal Theatre Project had been started by President Franklin Roosevelt to provide state-funded work for unemployed actors, and ran from 1935 to 1939.
4. See Hubbard, Phil. and Faire, Lucy. Remembering Post-War Reconstruction: Modernism and City Planning in Coventry, 1940–1962 www-staff.lboro.ac.uk/~gypjh/history.html, accessed 4.11.09
5. For a further discussion of this history see Nicholson, H. (2009b) *Theatre & Education*, Basingstoke: Palgrave.
6. For a more detailed discussion of the ways in which identification and performance relate to drama and theatre education, see Nicholson, H. (2005) *Applied Drama: The Gift of Theatre*, Basingstoke: Palgrave, pp. 77–80.

Introduction to Part Two: Traces and Places

1. Anthony Jackson identifies the different modes of working as Young people's theatre (an umbrella term for all professional theatre for children, including TIE); Children's theatre (professional performance of a play for children); Youth Theatre (theatre made by young people); Education in theatre (theatre companies' contribution to knowledge about making theatre through backstage tours and so on); The set play 'workshops' or 'play days' (workshops to support teaching plays); Curriculum drama or drama in education (taught by drama teachers in school); Simulation games (games that are constructed to allow students to learn about real situations. See Jackson, A. (1993). ed. *Learning Through Theatre*. Second ed. London: Routledge, pp. 7–9. 'Process drama' refers to a teaching methodology in which the drama is structured by teachers, and in which both teachers and students work in and out of role to explore a theme or situation through unscripted improvisation. See O'Neill, C. (1995) *Drama Worlds: A Framework for Process Drama*' London: Heinemann.
2. Currently there are two leading international organiszations, IDEA, which aims to meet the needs of educationalists working in drama and theatre, and ASSITEJ, which supports the work of theatre for children and young people. Both follow in the tradition of Left-orientated politics, and have mission statements that state their egalitarian and emancipatory intentions.

5   Globalization and Regeneration: Re-branding Creativity

1. www.teachernet.gov.uk/management/atoz/c/creativityinschools, accessed 2.4.2005.
2. For a fuller discussion of their mission and motives, see www.creative-partnerships.com, accessed 2.4.05.
3. www.creative-partnerships.com/ 'What we believe', accessed 23.3.2010.

4. Leadbeater, Charles (2005) *The Shape of Things to Come: Personalised Learning Through Collaboration* www.standards.dfes.gov.uk/sie/documents/shape.pdf. accessed 25.5.2010.
5. The Personal, Learning and Thinking Skills Leaflet. http://curriculum.qcda.gov.uk/key-stages-3-and-4/skills/plts/index.aspx, accessed 5.8.2010.
6. www.mscd.edu/extendedcampus/toolsofthemind, accessed 14.8.2010.

6 Dramatizing Home: Places of Safety and Risk

1. This programme has received considerable critical attention, and is the subject of a themed issue of *Research in Drama Education: The Journal of Applied Theatre and Performance*, 14(4), November 2009. This issue also contains an a expanded version of my discussion of their work (Nicholson 2009a). See also O'Connor, P., O'Connor, B. and Welsh-Morris, M. (2006) 'Making the everyday extraordinary: a theatre in education project to prevent child abuse, neglect and family violence' *Research in Drama Education* 2006, 11(2), 235–46.

7 'This Island's Mine': National Identity and Questions of Belonging

1. This was widely reported on the BBC at the time, and was quoted at www.guardian.co.uk/global/blog/2010/jul/20/iraq-war-inquiry-iraq
2. This speech was available at www.fabian-society.org.uk/events/speeches/the-future-of-britishness, 10 October 2009.
3. Mansell, W. Is 'Britishness' flagging? in The TES on 29 June 2007 www.tes.co.uk. 1 March 2009.
4. Heike Roms offers a clear analysis of the different ways in which Welsh identity is being represented and constructed, see Roms, H. (2008) 'Staging an Urban Identity: Place and Identity in Contemporary Welsh Theatre' in Holdsworth, N. and Luckhurst, M. (eds) *A Concise Companion to British and Irish Drama*, Oxford: Blackwell, pp. 107–24.
5. This history is explained by Anthony D. Smith in his book *Nationalism and Modernism* (1998), chapter 3. See also the analysis of national identity in a biopolitical context offered by Hardt and Negri (2000) *Empire*, Cambridge, MA: Harvard University press, p. 96.
6. Massey's famous essay can be found in Massey, D. (1997) 'A Global Sense of Place' in T. Barnes and D. Gregory (eds) *Reading Human Geography*, London: Arnold, pp. 315–23. For a careful discussion of her position, see Cresswell, 2004, chapter 3.
7. The ways in which government departments are entitled reveals the priorities of successive governments; the Tories' Department for Heritage was later to be re-named the Department for Culture, Media and Sport by the

Labour government following their election in 1997, and by 2010 heritage had become linked to the leisure industries, with the appointment of a minister for heritage and tourism by the new coalition government.

8. This is a position developed by Douglas Lanier (2002) *Shakespeare and Modern Popular Culture*, Oxford: Oxford University Press and Michael Rosen (2007) *What's so Special about Shakespeare?*, London: Walker Books.

9. There is, of course, a geopolitical distinction to be made here about Britishness that includes Scotland, Wales and Northern Ireland and England.

10. www.rsc.org.uk/standupforshakespeare/content/key_findings.aspx, accessed 24.6.2010.

11. One of the causes of this anger was the Prevent Strategy, introduced by the British government in 2008 in a move to stop violent extremism through community surveillance. This programme radicalized some young Muslims because they felt it demonized Muslims. See www.communities.gov.uk/publications/communities/preventstrategy *The Prevent Strategy: Stopping People Becoming* or *Supporting Terrorists*, accessed 2.8.2009.

12. There has been considerable analysis of the performative potential of walking; see the work of companies such as Lone Twin, Wrights & Sites. The work has also been analysed by practitioner-researchers Phil Smith, Carl Lavery and Deirdre Heddon (2009) in *Walking, Writing and Performance: Autobiographical Texts*, ed. Roberta Mock, Bristol: Intellect.

8   International Spaces: Global Citizenship and Cultural Exchange

1. An extremely thoughtful account of intercultural exchanges involving drama has been offered by Kate Donelan. See Donelan, K. (2004) 'Overlapping spheres and blurred spaces: Mapping Cultural Interactions in Drama and Theatre with young people', *NJ (Drama Australia Journal)*, 28(1), 15–33.

2. This research practice was informed by the aesthetics and pedagogies of theatre education, rather than Theatre for Development (TfD). Although TfD may have educational objectives, the term is used to describe a set of practices in which theatre practitioners (often from the West) travel to disadvantaged communities (usually in the developing world) to address particular social agendas and issues (HIV/ AIDS, for example), frequently using methodologies inspired by Augusto Boal.

3. See Bill Gates' speech at the World Economic Forum in 2008. www.microsoft.com/Presspass/exec/billg/speeches/2008/01-24WEFDavos.mspx. The Bill and Melina Gates Foundation offers significant grants to

health and education in the developing world. See www.gatesfoundation. org, *accessed 2.2.2009.*

4. For information, see www.hp.com/hpinfo/globalcitizenship, accessed 13.10.2010.
5. These resources are supplied at www.oxfam.org.uk/education/gc/files/education_for_global_citizenship_a_guide_for_schools.pdf, accessed 12.1.2010.
6. This position is argued by Martha Nussbaum (1996) in her book *For Love of Country: Debating the Limits of Patriotism*, Boston: Beacon Press.
7. See Harvey, D. (2009) *Cosmopolitanism and the Geographies of Freedom*, New York: Columbia University Press, p. 115.
8. Greig, N. (2008) *Young People, New Theatre: A Practical Guide to an Intercultural Process*, London: Routledge, pp. 83–4.
9. Information can be found at www.hlangananilearning.com, accessed 14.6.2010.
10. See Vanessa Thorpe's article, *Top artists battle visa clampdown*, ww.guardian.co.uk/uk/2009/feb/22/immigration-arts-gormley, 29.3.2010.

9 Changing Worlds: Performing Science, Theatre and Public Engagement

1. See www.sirkenrobinson.com for an example of a witty speech about creativity where he puts forward the view that the pace of technological change is placing new demands on education.
2. Williamson, B. and Payton, S. (2009) Curriculum and teaching innovation: transforming classroom practice and personalization www.futurelab.org.uk/handbook, accessed 13.12.2009.
3. This is discussed particularly well by Iain Gilcrest, in McGilcrest, I. (2009) *The Master and His Emissary: The Divided Brain and the Making of the Western World*, Yale: Yale University Press.
4. For more information about their innovative programme, see www.performingmedicine.com and wwww.clodemsemble.com, both accessed 17.8.2010.
5. Anna Ledgard has written about 'Visiting Time and Boychild' in Levinson, R., Nicholson H. And Parry, S. (2008) *Creative Encounters: Science, Education and the Arts*, London: The Wellcome Trust. See also my account of 'Boychild' in *Theatre & Education* (2009).
6. Steele, S. (2009) *For the Best: Evaluation Report* Unicorn Theatre, www.unicorntheatre.com/for_schools/project_archive, accessed 13.8.2010.
7. Lyn Gardner, Review, *For the Best*. www.guardian.co.uk/stage/2009/jun/05/review-for-the-best-theatre, 2.7.2009.
8. This statement was made very clear by contributors to an evaluation symposium at City Hall, London in July 2009 chaired by Dr Richard

Wingate. Consultant doctors in the renal unit and hospital teaching staff argued that this kind of work is to be funded as a way of engaging medical staff in the emotional realities of living with illness, which is also documented in the Evaluation Report.

9. Information about Cape Farewell is at www.capefarewell.com, all accessed 26.8.2009.

10   Learning in Theatres and Participation in Theatre: Cool Spaces?

1. www.stanscafe.co.uk/plaguenation/index.html. For a discussion of this work see Parry, S. (2010).
2. www.guardian.co.uk/stage/theatreblog/2008/jul/14/oilycartstheatremakesasplash. 12. 3 2010.
3. This production is discussed by Dan Goodley and Katherine Runswick-Cole (2011).
4. Steve Ball, Conference Paper at Theatre Applications, Central School of Speech and Drama, April 2010.

Bibliography

Abrahams, C. (1994) *The Hidden Victims: Children and Domestic Violence,*. London: NHC Action for Children.

Addams, J. (1912) *The Spirit of Youth and the City Streets*, New York: The MacMillan Company.

Aitken, S. C. (2001) *Geographies of Young people: The Morally Contested Spaces of Identity*, London: Routledge.

Alexander, R. (2008) *Essays on Pedagogy*, London: Routledge.

Anderson, B. (1991) *Imagined Communities* (2nd. ed.), London: Verso.

Anderson, B. (1992) 'The New World Disorder', *New Left Review* I/193, May–June, www.newleftreview.org.

Appadurai, A. (1996) *Modernity at Large: Cultural Dimension of Globalization*, Mineappolis: University of Minnesota Press.

Appiah, K. A. (1994) 'Loyalty to Humanity', *Boston Review* XIX, 5 Oct./ Nov.

Appiah, K. A. (1998) 'Cosmopolitan Patriots' in B. Robbins and P. Cheah (eds) *Cosmopolitics: Thinking and Feeling Beyond the Nation*, Minneapolis: University of Minnesota Press, pp. 91–116.

Appiah, K. A. (2006) *Cosmopolitanism*, Penguin Books.

Arac, J. (1987) *Critical Genealogies: Historical Situations for Postmodern Literary Studies*, New York: Columbia University Press.

Arends, B. and Thackara, D. (eds) (2003) *Experiment: Conversations in Art and Science*, London: The Wellcome Trust.

Arendt, H. (1958) *The Human Condition*, Chicago and London: The University of Chicago Press.

Bachelard, G. (1994) *The Poetics of Space* (trans. M. Jolas), Boston MA: Beacon Books.

Bachelard, G. (1934/2001) *The Formation of the Scientific Mind*, London: Clinamen Press.

Balme, C. (1999) *Decolonizing the Stage*, Oxford: Oxford University Press.

Banks, F. (2008) 'Learning with the Globe' in C. Carson and F. Karim-Cooper (eds) *Shakespeare's Globe: A Theatrical Experiment*, Cambridge: Cambridge University Press, pp. 154–65.

Barker, H. (1997) *Arguments for a Theatre* (3rd ed.), Manchester: Manchester University Press.

Barnett, H. (1918) *Canon Barnett, His Life, Work and Friends*, London: J. Murray.

Barnett, S. A. (1884) 'Settlements of university men in great towns. A paper read at St John's, Oxford on 17th November 1883', Oxford: The Chronicle

Company. Reprinted in J. A. R. Pimlott (1935) *Toynbee Hall. Fifty Years of Social Progress 1884–1934*, London: J. M. Dent, pp. 266–73.

Barnett, S. A. (1898) 'University Settlements' in W. Reason (ed.) *University and Social Settlements*, London: Methuen, pp. 11–26.

Barrett, M. (1979) *Virginia Woolf: Women and Writing*, London: The Women's Press.

Bate, J. (1997) *The Genius of Shakespeare*, London: Picador Press.

Bateson, G. (1972) *Steps to an Ecology of Mind*, Chicago: University of Chicago Press.

Bauman, Z. (2003) *Liquid Love: On the Frailty of Human Bonds*, Cambridge: Polity Press.

Bauman, Z. (2005) *Liquid Life*, Cambridge: Polity Press.

Beer, G. (1996) *Open Fields: Science in Cultural Encounter*, Oxford: Oxford University Press.

Bell, C. (1976) *Art*, Oxford: Oxford University Press [1914].

Bennett, S. (2008) 'Universal Experience: The City as a Tourist Stage' in. T. C. Davis (ed.) *The Cambridge Companion to Performance Studies*, Cambridge: Cambridge University Press, pp. 76–90.

Bhabha, H. K. (2001) 'Unsatisfied: Notes on Vernacular Cosmopolitanism' in G. Castle (ed.) *Postcolonial Discourses: An Anthology*, Oxford: Blackwell Publishers, pp. 38–52.

Bharucha, R. (2000) *The Politics of Cultural Practice: Thinking Through Theatre in an Age of Globalisation*, London: The Athlone Press.

Billig, M. (1995) *Banal Nationalism*, London: Sage Publication.

Bilton, C. (2007) *Management and Creativity*, Oxford: Basil Blackwell.

Boal, A. (1979) *Theatre of the Oppressed*, London: Pluto Press.

Boler, M. (1999) *Feeling Power: Emotions and Education*, London: Routledge Books.

Bolton, G. (1998) *Acting in Classroom Drama*, Stoke-on-Trent: Trentham Books.

Bond, E. (2000a) *The Children and Have I None*, London: Methuen.

Bond, E. (2000b) *The Hidden Plot: Notes on Theatre and The State*, London: Methuen.

Bond, E. (2009) 'Foreword' to H. Nicholson *Theatre &Education*, Basingstoke: Palgrave, pp. ix–xii.

Borzello, F. (1987) *Civilising Caliban*, London and New York: Routledge and Kegan Paul.

Bourdieu, P. (1984) *Distinction: A Social Critique of the Judgement of Taste* (trans. R. Nice), London: Routledge and Kegan Paul.

Bourdieu, P. (1996) *The Rules of Art* (trans. S. Emanuel), Cambridge: Polity Press.

Bourriaud, N. (2002) *Relational Aesthetics* (trans. S. Pleasance and F. Woods), Dijon: Les presses du reel.

Bowlby, R. (2001) 'Domestication' in M. McQuillan (ed.) *Deconstruction: A Reader*, London: Routledge, pp. 304–10.

Bradby, D. James, L and Sharratt, B. (eds) (1980) *Performance and Politics in Popular Drama*, Cambridge: Cambridge University Press.

Brecht, B. (1965) *The Messignkauf Dialogues* (trans. John Willett), London: Methuen.

Burger, Isabel B. (1983) 'Creative Dramatics: An Approach to Children's Theatre' in Brain Siks, G. and Brain Dunnington, H. (eds) *Children's Theatre and Creative Dramatics*, Seattle: University of Washington Press, pp. 185–93.

Burnard, P., Craft, A. and Grainger, T. et al. (2006) 'Possibility Thinking', *International Journal of Early Years Education*, 14(3), 243–62.

Butsch, Richard (2008) *The Citizen Audience: Crowds, Publics and Individuals*, London: Routledge.

Carlson, M. (2004) '9/11, Afghanistan, and Iraq: The Response of the New York Theatre', *Theatre Survey*, 45(1), 3–16.

Carlson, Marla (2009) 'Ways to Walk New York after 9/11' in D. J.Hopkins, S. Orr and K. Solja (eds) *Performance and The City*, Basingstoke: Palgrave MacMillan, pp. 15–32.

Case, S. E. (2006) *Performing Science and the Virtual*, London: Routledge.

Castells, M. (1996) *The Rise of the Network Society*, Oxford: Basil Blackwell.

Chekhov, M. (2002) *To the Actor*, London: Routledge.

Chimisso, C. (2001) *Gaston Bachelard. Critic of Science and the Imagination*, London: Routledge.

Cohen-Cruz, J. (2005) *Local Acts*, New Brunswick: Rutgers University Press.

Cohen-Cruz, J. and Schutzman, M. (2006) *A Boal Companion: Dialogues on Theatre and Cultural Politics*, London: Routledge.

Collini, S. (ed.) (1993) *Matthew Arnold: Culture and Anarchy and Other Writings*. Cambridge: Cambridge University Press.

Collini, S. (2008) 'Introduction' in C. P.S now *The Two Cultures*, Cambridge: Cambridge University Press, pp. 7–73.

Conquergood, D. (2004) 'Performance Studies: Interventions and radical Research' in H. Bial (ed.) *The Performance Studies Reader*, London: Routledge, pp. 311–22.

Conroy, C. (2010) *Theatre & the Body*, Basingstoke: Palgrave Macmillan.

Coveney, P. (1967) *The Image of Childhood*, Harmonsworth: Penguin.

Craft, A. (2005) *Creativity in Schools: Tensions and Dilemmas*, London: Routledge.

Craft, A. Cremin, T. and Burnard, P. (eds) (2008) *Creative Learning 3-11 and how We Document it*. Stoke on Trent: Trentham Books.

Cresswell, T. (2004) *Place. A Short Introduction*, Oxford: Blackwell.

Cresswell, T. (2006) *On the Move: Mobility in the Modern Western World*. London: Routledge.

Csikszentmihalyi, M. (1996) *Creativity: Flow and the Psychology of Discovery and Invention*, New York: Harper Collins.

Debord, G. (1983) *Society of the Spectacle*, Detroit: Black and Red Press.

de Certeau, M. (1984) *The Practice of Everyday Life* (trans S. Rendall), Berkeley: University of California Press.

de Klerk, V. (2000) 'To be Xhosa or not to be Xhosa.. That is the Question', *Journal of Multicultural and Multilingual Development* 21(3), 198–215.

Deleuze, G. (1980) 'Introduction' in J. Donzelot *The Policing of the Family: Welfare versus the State*, London: Hutchinson Press, pp. i–xxiii.

Derrida, J. (2000) *Of Hospitality*, Stanford: Stanford University Press.

Dewey, J. (1888) *How to Teach Manners in the School Room*, New York: A.S.Barnes Company.

Dewey, J. (1934) *Art as Experience*, London: George Allen and Unwin Ltd.

Dewey, J. (1998) *Experience and Education: The 60th Anniversary Edition*, Indianapolis: Kappa Delti Pi Press [1938].

DFES (2004) *Every Child Matters*. www.everychildmatters.gov.uk., accessed 15.5.2009.

Donelan, K. (2004) 'Overlapping Spheres and Blurred Spaces: Mapping Cultural Interactions in Drama and Theatre with young people', *NJ (Drama Australia Journal)*, 28(1), 15–33.

Donzelot, J. (1980) *The Policing of The Family: Welfare versus the State*, London: Hutchinson Press.

Dusinberre, J. (1987) *Alice to the Lighthouse*, London and Basingstoke: The Macmillan Press

Dyer, R. (1992) *Only Entertainment*, London: Routledge.

Eagleton, T. (1983) *Literary Theory*, Oxford: Oxford University Press.

Ede, S. (2005) *Art and Science*, New York: I.B.Tauris.

Edensor, T. (2002) *National Identity, Popular Culture and Everyday Life*, Oxford: Berg.

Edensor, T., Leslie, D., Millington, S., Rantisi, N. M. (eds) (2010) *Spaces of Vernacular Creativity: Re-thinking the Cultural Economy*, London: Routledge.

Edwards, Robin and Usher, Richard (2000) *Globalisation and Pedagogy: Space, Place and Identity*, London: Routledge.

Elias, N. (1978) *The Civilising Process* (trans. E. Jephcott), New York: Urizen Books.

Ellsworth, E. (2005) *Places of Learning*, London: Routledge.

Evans, G. (2010) Creative Spaces and the Art of Urban Living' in T. Edensor, D. Leslie, S. Millington, N. M. Rantisi (eds) *Spaces of Vernacular Creativity: Re-thinking the Cultural Economy*, London: Routledge, pp.19–32.

Féral, J. (2002) 'Introduction', *Substance*, 31(2&3), 3–17.

Féral, Josette (2002) 'Theatricality: The Specificity of Theatrical Language', *Substance*, 31, 94–109.

Filewod, A. (2009) 'The Documentary Body: Theatre Workshop to Banner Theatre' in A. Forsyth and C. Megson (eds) *Get Real: Documentary Theatre Past and Present*, Basingstoke: Palgrave, pp. 55–73.

Finlay-Johnson, H. (1912) *The Dramatic Method of Teaching*, London and New York: Nisbet Press.

Flew, T. (2009) 'Creative Economy' in J. Hartley (ed.) *Creative Industries*, Oxford: Blackwell Publishing, pp. 344–60.

Florida, R. (2002) *The Rise of the Creative Class: And How it's Transforming Work, Leisure, Community and Everyday Life*, New York: Basic Books.

Florida, R. (2008) *Who's Your City?*, New York: Basic Books.

Foucault, M. (1991) *Discipline and Punish* (trans. A. Sheridan), Harmondsworth: Penguin Books.

Freshwater, H. (2009) *Theatre & Audience*, Basingstoke: Palgrave.

Freud, S. (1997) 'The Uncanny' in James Strachey (ed.) *Writings on Literature and Art*, Stanford: Stanford University Press, pp. 193–233.

Fry, R. (1981) *Vision and Design*, London: Chatto and Windus [1920].

Gallagher, K. (2001) *Drama Education in the Lives of Girls*, Toronto: University of Toronto Press.

Gallagher, K. (2007) *The Theatre of Urban: Youth and Schooling in Dangerous Times*, Toronto: University of Toronto Press.

Gallagher, K. and Booth, D. (eds) (2003) *How Theatre Educates: Convergences and Counterpoints*, Toronto: University of Toronto Press.

Gardner, H. (1997) *Extraordinary Minds*, London: Weidenfeld and Nicolson.

Gardner, H. (1999) *Intelligence Reframed Multiple Intelligence for the 21st Century*, New York: Basic Books.

Gibson, R. (1998) *Teaching Shakespeare*, Cambridge: Cambridge University Press.

Githens-Mazer, J. and Lambert , R. (2010) *Islamophobia and Anti-Muslim Hate Crime: A London Case Study*, Exeter: University of Exeter.

Goffman, E. (1959) *The Presentation of the Self in Everyday Life*, Harmonsworth: Penguin Books.

Goodley, D. and Runswick-Cole, K. (2011) '*Something in the Air?* Creativity, Culture and Community' *RiDE: The Journal of Applied Theatre and Performance*, 16(1), pp. 75–91.

Goorney, H. and MacColl, E. (eds) (1986) *Agit-prop to Theatre Workshop: Political Playscripts 1930–50*, Manchester: Manchester University Press.

Gorell Barnes, G. (2004) *Family Therapy in Changing Times* (2nd ed.), Basingstoke: Palgrave MacMillan.

Goswami, U. (2006) 'Neuroscience and Education: From Research to Practice?' Nature, Reviews, Neuroscience, AOP, published online 12 April 2006. http://ltsnpsy.york.ac.uk/plat2006/assets/presentations/Goswami/GoswamiNRN2006.pdf, accessed 16.7.2010.

Govan, E., Nicholson, H., Normington, K. (2007) *Making a Performance: Devising Histories and Contemporary Practices*, London: Routledge.

Greenwich Young People's Theatre (1987) 'The School on the Green' in C. Redington (ed.) *Six T.I.E Programmes*, London: Methuen, pp. 57–88.

Greig, D. (2006) *Yellow Moon: The Ballad of Leia and Lee*, London: Faber and Faber.

Greig, D. (2008) 'Rough Theatre' in R. D'Monte and G. Saunders (eds) *Cool Britainnia: British Political Drama in the 1990s*, Basingstoke: Palgrave, pp. 208–21.

Greig, N. (2008) *Young People, New Theatre: A Practical Guide to an Intercultural Process*, London: Routledge.

Gubrium, J. (1992) *Out of Control: Family Therapy and Domestic Disorder*, London: Sage.

Hardt, M. and Negri, A. (2000) *Empire*, Cambridge, MA: Harvard University Press.

Hargreaves, David. (2005) *Personalised Learning -3: Learning to Learn and the New Technologies*, London: Specialist Schools Trust, www.sst-inet.com.au/files/David_Hargreaves_-_Personalising_Learning_3_-_Learning_to_Learn.pdf, accessed 23.6.2009.

Hartley, J. (ed.) (2005) *Creative Industries*, Oxford: Blackwell Publishing.

Harvey, D. (1996) *Justice, Nature and the Geography of Difference*, Oxford: Blackwell Publishers.

Harvey, D. (2009) *Cosmopolitanism and the Geographies of Freedom*, New York: Columbia University Press.

Harvie, J. (2005) *Staging the UK*, Manchester: Manchester University Press.

Herts, A. M. 'To Make Good Citizens – The Theatre for Children'; Miss Alice Minnie Herts Outlines Interesting Plan for a Permanent Institution of National Scope. *New York Times*, 12 November 1911, Sunday Section: Magazine Section, p. 7 http://query.nytimes.com/mem/archive-free/pdf, accessed 5.11.09.

Herzfeld, M. (2005) *Cultural Intimacy: Social Poetics in the Nation State*. London: Routledge.

Hester, M., Pearson, C and Harwin, N. (2000) *Making an Impact: Children and Domestic Violence*, London: Jessica Kingsley Publishers.

Hobsbawn, E. (1991) *Nations and Nationalism Since 1780: Programme, Myth, Reality*, Cambridge: Cambridge University Press.

Holdsworth, N. (2010) *Theatre & Nation*, Basingstoke: Palgrave.

Holmes, E. (1912) *What is and What Might Be: A Study of Education in General and Elementary Education in Particular*, London: Constable & Company.

hooks, b. (2009) *Belonging: A Culture of Place*, London: Routledge.

Horsfall, T. C. (ed.) (1885) *Education under Healthy Conditions*, London: John Heywood.

Hubbard, P. and Faire, L. 'Remembering Post-War Reconstruction: Modernism and City Planning in Coventry, 1940–1962'; www-staff.lboro.ac.uk/~gypjh/history.html, accessed 4.11.09.

Humphries, J. (1982) 'The Working Class Family: A Marxist Perspective' in J. Bethke Elshtain (ed.) *The Family in Political Thought*, Amherst: University of Massachusetts Press, pp. 197–222.

Hunter, M. A. (2001) 'Anxious Futures: Magpie2 and 'New Generationalism' in Australian Youth-Specific Theatre', *Theatre Research International*, 26(1), 71–81.

Ingold, T. (2000) *The Perception of the Environment: Essays in Livelihood, Dwelling and Skill*, London: Routledge.

Ingold, T. and Hallam, E. (eds) (2007) *Creativity and Cultural Improvisation*, Oxford: Berg.

Irwin, A. (1995) *Citizen Science: A Study of People, Expertise and Sustainable Development*, London: Routledge.

Isaacs, S. (1929) *The Nursery Years*, London: Routledge and Kegan Paul.

Jackson, A. (ed.) (1993) *Learning Through Theatre* (2nd ed.), London: Routledge.

Jackson, A. (2007) *Theatre, Education and the Making of Meanings: Art or Instrument?*, Manchester: Manchester University Press.

Jackson, S. (2001) *Lines of Activity: Performance, Historiography, Hull-House Domesticity*, Ann Arbor: University of Michigan Press.

Jackson, T. (ed.) (1980) *Learning Through Theatre: Essays and Casebooks on Theatre in Education*, Manchester: Manchester University Press.

Jenks, C. (1996) *Childhood*, London: Routledge.

Kelly, V. (1997) *Our Australian Theatre in the 1990s* (ed.) Veronica Kelly, Amsterdam: Rodopi.

Kempe, A. (1997) *The GCSE Drama Coursebook*, Cheltenham: Nelson Thornes.

Kennedy, F. (2010) *The Urban Girls' Guide to Camping and Other Plays*, London: Nick Hern Books.

Kershaw, B. (2007) *Theatre Ecologies: Environments and Performance Events*, Cambridge: Cambridge University Press.

Knowles, R. (2004) *Reading the Material Theatre*, Cambridge: Cambridge University Press.

Knowles, R. (2010) *Theatre & Interculturalism*, Basingstoke: Palgrave MacMillan.

Kwon, M. (2004) *One Place After Another: Site Specific Art and Locational Identity*, Cambridge, MA: MIT Press.

Landry, C. (2008) *The Creative City: A Toolkit for Urban Innovators* (2nd ed.), London: Earthscan.

Lanier, D. (2002) *Shakespeare and Modern Popular Culture*, Oxford: Oxford University Press.

Latour, B. (1999) *Pandora's Hope: Essays on the Reality of Science Studies*, Cambridge, MA: Harvard University Press.

Latour, P. and Combes, F. (1991) *Conversations avec Henri Lefebvre*, Paris: Messidor.

Leadbeater, C. (2005) *The Shape of Things to Come: Personalised Learning Through Collaboration* www.standards.dfes.gov.uk/sie/documents/**shape**.pdf. 25 April 2010.

Ledgard, A. (2008) 'Visting Time and Boychild: Site – Specific Pedagogical Experiments on the Boundaries of Theatre and Science' in R. Levinson, H. Nicholson and S. Parry (eds) *Creative Encounters: New Conversations in Science, Education and the Arts*, London: The Wellcome Trust, pp. 110–31.

Lefebvre, H. (1991) *The Production of Space* (trans. D. Nicholson-Smith), Oxford: Basil Blackwell.

Levinson, R., Nicholson, H. and Parry, S. (2008) *Creative Encounters: Science, Education and the Arts*, London: The Wellcome Trust, pp. 30–47.

Little, R. (2004) *The Young Vic Book: Theatre Work and Play*, London: Methuen.

Lyotard, Jean-Francois (1984) *The Postmodern Condition: A Report on Knowledge* (trans. G. Bennington and B. Massumi), Manchester: Manchester University Press.

Mackey, S. 'Performance, Place and Allotments: Feast or Famine?' *Contemporary Theatre Review*. http://www.informaworld.com/smpp/title~content=t713639923~db=all~tab=issueslist~branches=17 - v1717.2. (2007), pp. 181–91.

Mackey, S. and Cooper, S. (1995) *Theatre Studies: An Approach for Advanced Level*, Cheltenham: Nelson Thornes.

Mamet, D. (1994) *A Whore's Profession: Notes and Essays*, London: Faber and Faber.

Massey, D. (1997) 'A Global Sense of Place' in T. Barnes and D. Gregory (eds) *Reading Human Geography*, London: Arnold, pp. 315–23.

Massey, D. (1998) 'Spatial Construction of Youth Cultures' in T. Skelton and G. Valentine (eds) *Cool Places: Geographies of Youth Cultures*, London: Routledge, pp. 121–9.

Massey, D. (2005) *For Space*, London: Sage Publications.

Massey, D. (2007) *World City*, Cambridge: Polity Press.

Massumi, B. (1992) *A User's Guide to Capitalism and Schizophrenia. Derivations from Deleuze and Guttari*, Cambridge, MA: MIT Press.

McCaslin, N. (1971) *Theatre for Children in the United States: A History*, Norman: University of Oklahoma Press.

McConachie, B. (2008) 'Towards a History of National Theatres in Europe' in S. E. Wilmer (ed.) *National Theatres in a Changing Europe*, Basingstoke: Palgrave McMillan, pp. 49–60.

McEvoy, S. (2000) *Shakespeare: The Basics*, London: Routledge.

McGilcrest, I. (2009) *The Master and His Emissary: The Divided Brain and the Making of the Western World*, Yale: Yale University Press.

Ministry of Social Development (2008) *Where Do You Go When Your World has Ended?: Children's Voices on Family Violence and Child Abuse*, New Zealand: The Centre for Social Research and Evaluation.

Morley, D. (2000) *Home Territories: Media, Mobility and Identity*, London: Routledge.

Morris, G. (2002) 'Reconsidering Theatre-Making in South Africa: A Study of Theatre in Education in Cape Schools' *Theatre Research International*, 27(3), 289–305.

Morton, A. L. (ed.) (1973) *The Political Writing of William Morris*, London: Lawrence and Wishart.

Mouffe, C. (2000) *The Democratic Paradox*, London: Verso.

Nevitt, R. (1992) *The Burston School Strike*, Oxford Playscripts: Oxford University Press.

Ney, P. G. (1992) 'Transgenerational Triangles of Abuse: A Model of Family Violence' in E. C. Viano (ed.) *Intimate Violence: Interdisciplinary Perspectives*, London: Taylor and Francis, pp. 15–26.

Ngugi wa Thiong'o (1981) *Decolonizing the Mind: The Politics of Language in African Literature*, Oxford: James Curry.

Nicholson, H. (2003) 'Acting, Creativity and Justice: An Analysis of Edward Bond's *The Children*' *Research in Drama Education*, 1.8(1), 9–23.

Nicholson, H (2005). *Applied Drama: The Gift of Theatre*, Basingstoke: Palgrave MacMillan.

Nicholson, H. (2009a) 'Dramatising Family Violence: The Domestic Politics of Shame and Blame' in *RiDE: The Journal of Applied Theatre and Performance*, 14(4) Themed Issue, edited by Peter O'Connor, pp. 561–82.

Nicholson, H. (2009b) *Theatre & Education*, Basingstoke: Palgrave MacMillan.

Nussbaum, M. (1996) *For Love of Country: Debating the Limits of Patriotism*, Boston: Beacon Press.

O'Connor, P., O'Connor, B. and Welsh-Morris, M. (2006) 'Making the Everyday Extraordinary: A Theatre in Education Project to Prevent Child Abuse, Neglect and Family Violence' *Research in Drama Education*, 11(2), 235–46.

O'Neill, C. (1995) *Drama Worlds: A Framework for Process Drama*, London: Heinemann.

O'Toole, J. (1976) *Theatre in Education: New Objectives for Theatre – New Techniques in Education*, London: Hodder and Stoughton.

O'Toole, J. (2009) 'Writing Everyday Theatre: Applied Theatre, or just TIE Rides Again? *RiDE: The Journal of Applied Theatre and Performance*, 14(4), 479–502.

O'Toole, J. and P. Bundy (1980) 'Kites and Magpies: TIE in Australia' in Tony Jackson (ed.) *Learning Through Theatre: Essays and Casebooks on Theatre in Education*, Manchester: Manchester University Press, pp. 133–50.

Pallasmaa, J. (2005) *The Eyes of the Skin: Architecture and the Senses*, Chichester: John Wiley and Sons.

Pammenter, D. (1980) 'Devising for TIE' in Tony Jackson (ed.) *Learning Through Theatre: Essays and Casebooks on Theatre in Education*, Manchester: Manchester University Press, pp. 36–50.

Parry, S. (2010) 'Imagining Cosmopolitan Space: Spectacle, Rice and Global Citizenship' *RiDE: The Journal of Applied Theatre and Performance*, 15(3), 317–37.

Pinder, D. (2005) *Visions of the City: Utopianism, Power and Politics in Twentieth-Century Urbanism*, Edinburgh, Edinburgh University Press.

Pollard, A. and James, M. (eds) (2004) *Personalised Learning: A Commentary from the Teaching & Learning Research Programme*, London: TLRP.

Probyn, E. (2005) *Blush: Faces of Shame*, Minneapolis: University of Minnesota Press.

Ranciere, J. (2009) *The Emancipated Spectator*, London: Verso.

Read, A. (1993) *Theatre and Everyday Life: An Ethics of Performance*, London: Routledge.

Read, H. (1943) *Education Through Art*, London: Faber.

Reason, M. (2010) *The Young Audience: Exploring and Enhancing Children's Experiences of Theatre*, Stoke on Trent: Trentham Books.

Rebellato, D. (2008) 'From State of the Nation to Globalization: Shifting Political Agendas in Contemporary British Playwriting' in N. Holdsworth and M. Luckhurst (eds) *A Concise Companion to British and Irish Drama*, Oxford: Blackwell 242–62.

Rebellato, D. (2009) *Theatre & Globalization*, Basingstoke: Palgrave.

Redington, Christine (1983) *Can Theatre Teach?*, Oxford: Pergamon.

Reinelt, J. (1994) *After Brecht: British Epic Theatre*, Michigan: University of Michigan Press.

Reinelt, J. (2002) 'The Politics of Discourse: Performativity Meets Theatricality' *Substance*, 31, 201–15.

Ridley, P. (1998) 'Sparkleshark' in *Two Plays for Young People*, London: Faber and Faber, pp. 63–126.

Roach, J. (1993) *The Player's Passion: Studies in the Science of Acting*, Ann Arbor: University of Michigan Press.

Roach, J. (1996) *Cities of the Dead: Circum-Atlantic Performance*, New York: Columbia University Press.

Robbins, B. (1998a) 'Comparative Cosmopolitanisms' in B. Robbins and P. Cheah (eds) *Cosmopolitics: Thinking and Feeling beyond the Nation*, Minneapolis: University of Minnesota Press, pp. 246–64.

Robbins, B. (1998b) 'Introduction Part 1: Actually Existing Cosmopolitanism' in B. Robbins and P. Cheah (eds) *Cosmopolitics: Thinking and Feeling Beyond the Nation*, Minneapolis: University of Minnesota Press, pp. 1–19.

Robinson, K. (ed.) (1980) *Exploring Theatre and Education*, London: Heinemann.

Robinson, K. (2001) *Out of Our Minds: Learning to be Creative*, Oxford: Capstone Press.

Rodgers, J. J. (1996) *Family Life and Social Control: A Sociological Perspective*, Basingstoke: MacMillan.

Roms, H. (2008) 'Staging an Urban Identity: Place and Identity in Contemporary Welsh Theatre' in N. Holdsworth and M. Luckhurst (eds) *A Concise Companion to British and Irish Drama*, Oxford: Blackwell, pp. 107–24.

Rose, N. (1990) *Governing the Soul*, London: Routledge.

Rosen, M. (2007) *What's so Special about Shakespeare?*, London: Walker Books.

Rushdie, S. (1991) *Haroun and the Sea of Stories*, London: Penguin Books.

Samuel, R., MacColl, E. and Cosgrove, S. (1985) *Theatres of the Left 1880–1935 Workers' Theatre Movements in Britain and America*, London: Routledge Kegan Paul.

Schonmann, S. (2006) *Theatre as a Medium for Children and Young People: Images and Observations*, Dordrecht: Springer Press.

Scourfield, J. Dicks, B. Drakeford, M. and Davies, A. (2006) *Children, Place and Identity: Nation and Locality in Middle Childhood*, London: Routledge.

Shepherd-Barr, K. (2006) *Science on Stage: From Doctor Faustus to Copenhagen*, Princeton: Princeton University Press.

Sibley, D. (1992) 'Families and Domestic Routines: Constructing the Boundaries of Childhood' in S. Pile and N. Thrift (eds) *Mapping the Subject: Geographies of Cultural Transformation*, London: Routledge, pp. 114–27.

Skelton, T and Valentine, G. (eds) (1998) *Cool Places: Geographies of Youth Cultures*, London: Routledge.

Slade, P. (1948) 'Children's Theatre' in *The Children's Theatre*, Birmingham: The Birmingham Educational Drama Association, pp. 4–5.

Slade, P. (1954) *Child Drama*, London: University of London Press.

Slade, P. (1999) 'Peter Slade Talks' *Research in Drama Education*, 4(2), 253–8.

Smith, A. D. (1998) *Nationalism and Modernism*, London: Routledge.

Smith, P. Lavery, C. Heddon, D. and Mock, R. (eds) (2009) *Walking, Writing and Performance: Autobiographical Texts*, Bristol: Intellect.

Soja, E. W. (1996) *Thirdspace: Journeys to Los Angeles and other Real-and-Imagined Places*, Oxford: Blackwell Publishers.

Soper, K. (1995) *What is Nature? Culture, Politics and the Non-Human*, Oxford: Basil Blackwell.

Stanley Hall, G. (1904) *Adolescence: Its Psychology and Its Relationship to Physiology, Anthropology, Sociology, Sex, Crime, Religion, and Education*, New York: Appleton.

Stanley Hall, G. (1914) 'Foreword' to Whitman Curtis, E. *The Dramatic Instinct in Education*, Boston: Houghton Miffin Company, pp. xi–xvii.

Steedman, C. (1990) *Childhood, Culture and Class in Britain: Margaret McMillan 1860–1931*, London: Virago.

Steedman, C. (1995) *Strange Dislocations*, London: Virago.

Steedman, C. (2009) *Labours Lost. Domestic Service and the Making of Modern England*, Cambridge: Cambridge University Press.

Steele, S. (2009) *For the Best: Evaluation Report*, Unicorn Theatre, www.unicorntheatre.com/for_schools/project_archive, accessed 13.8.2010.

Styles, M. (1998) *From the Garden to the Street: Three Hundred Years of Poetry for Children*, London: Cassell.

Swortzell, L. (1993) 'Trying to Like TIE: An American Critic Hopes TIE can be Saved' in A. Jackson (ed.) *Learning Through Theatre: Essays and Casebooks on Theatre in Education*, (2nd ed.), Manchester: Manchester University Press, 239–50.

Taylor, C. (1989) *Sources of the Self*, Cambridge: Cambridge University Press.

Taylor, D. (2008) 'Performance and Intangible Cultural Heritage' in T. C. Davis (ed.) *The Cambridge Companion to Performance Studies*, Cambridge: Cambridge University Press, pp. 91–104.

The Wellcome Trust (2010) *Making a Difference: 2005–2010*, www.wellcome.ac.uk.

Thomas, T. (1977) 'A Propertyless Theatre for the Propertyless Class' in Samuel, R. MacColl, E. and Cosgrove, S. (eds) (1985) *Theatres of the Left 1880–1935 Workers' Theatre Movements in Britain and America*, London: Routledge Kegan Paul, pp. 77–98.

Thompson, E. P. (1955) *William Morris: Romantic to Revolutionary*, London: Lawrence and Wishart.

Thompson E. P. (1963) *The Making of the English Working Class*, London: Gollancz.

Thrift, N. (1994) 'Inhuman Geographies: Landscapes of Speed, Light and Power' in P. Cloke (ed.) *Writing the Rural: Five Cultural Geographies*, London: Paul Chapman, pp. 191–245.

Tuan, Y-F. (1977) *Space and Place: The Perspective of Experience*, Minneapolis: University of Minnesota Press.

Tulloch, J. (2000) 'Approaching Theatre Audiences: Active School Students and Commoditised High Culture', *Contemporary Theatre Review*, 10(2), 85-104.

Vallins, G. (1980) 'The Beginnings of TIE' in Tony Jackson (ed.) *Learning Through Theatre: Essays and Casebooks on Theatre in Education*, Manchester: Manchester University Press, pp. 2–15.

Van de Water, M. (2006) *Moscow Theatres for Young People: A Cultural History of Ideological Coercion and Artistic Innovation, 1917–2000*, Basingstoke: Palgrave MacMillan.

Varty, A. (2008) *Children and Theatre in Victorian Britain: 'All Work, No Play'*, Basingstoke: Palgrave McMillan.

Virilio, P. (2000) *Art and Fear* (trans. J. Rose), London: Continuum.

Waks, L. J. (2007) 'John Dewey on Globalization, Multiculturalism, and Democratic Education' *Education and Culture*, 23(1), 27–37.

Watson, N. J. (2007) 'Shakespeare on the Tourist Trail' in R. Shaughnessy (ed.) *The Cambridge Companion to Shakespeare and Popular Culture*, Cambridge: Cambridge University Press, pp.199–226.

Weller, S. (2007) *Teenagers' Citizenship: Experiences and Education*, London: Routledge.

Whitman Curtis, E. (1914) *The Dramatic Instinct in Education*, Boston: Houghton Mifflin Company.

Whybrow, N. 'The State, Ideology and Theatre in Education' *New Theatre Quarterly*, 39 (August 1994), 267–80.

Whybrow, N. 'Theatre in Education: What Remains?' *New Theatre Quarterly*, 38 (May 1994), 198–9.

Wickstrom, M. (2006) *Performing Consumers: Global Capital and its Theatrical Seductions*, New York and London: Routledge.

Wiles, D. (2003) *A Short History of Western Performance Space*, Cambridge: Cambridge University Press.

Willett, J. (ed.) (1964) *Brecht on Theatre: The Development of an Aesthetic*, London: Methuen.

Williams, B. (1973) *Problems of the Self*, Cambridge: Cambridge University Press.

Williams, R. (1980) 'The Bloomsbury Fraction' in *Problems in Materialism and Culture*, London: Verso, pp. 149–69.

Williams, R. (1992) *Culture and Society 1780–1950*, Harmondsworth: Penguin Books.

Williamson, B. and Payton, S. (2009) *Curriculum and Teaching Innovation: Transforming Classroom Practice and Personalisation*, www.futurelab. org.uk/handbook, accessed 13.12.2009.

Winnicott, D. W. (1971) *Playing and Reality*, Harmondsworth: Penguin Books.

Winston, J. (1998) *Drama, Narrative and Moral Education*, London: The Falmer Press.

Winston, J. (2007) *Editorial: Themed Issue, Drama for Citizenship and Human Rights, Research in Drama Education*, 12(3), 269–74.

Winston, J. (2008) 'Mathematics, Science and the Liberating Beauty of Theatre' in R. Levinson, H. Nicholson and S. Parry (eds) *Creative Encounters: Science, Education and the Arts*, London: The Wellcome Trust.

Winston, J. (2010) *Beauty and Education*, London: Routledge.

Winter, W. (1908) *Other Days: Being Chronicles and Memories of the Stage*, New York: Moffat, Yard.

Woolf, V. (1979) A *Room of One's Own*, London: Harvester Press.

Young, I. M. (1997) *Intersecting Voices: Dilemmas of Gender, Political Philosophy, and Policy*, Princeton, NJ: Princeton University Press.

Zaretsky, E. (1976) *Capitalism, the Family and Personal Life*, London: Pluto Press.

Websites

www.performingmedicine.com, accessed 17.8.2010.

wwww.clodensemble.com, accessed 17.8.2010.

www.guardian.co.uk/stage/theatreblog/2008/jul/14/oilycartstheatremake-sasplash, 12.3.2010.

www.teachernet.gov.uk/management/atoz/c/creativityinschools, accessed 2.4.05.

www.communities.gov.uk/publications/communities/preventstrategy *The Prevent Strategy: Stopping People Becoming or Supporting Terrorists*, accessed 2.8.2009.

British Council, 'A Direction for a Changing Europe' p. 12, www.british-council.org/greece.

Bill Gates (2008). www.microsoft.com/Presspass/exec/billg/speeches/2008/01-24WEFDavos.mspx

www.creative-partnerships.com, accessed 2.4.05.

www.creative-partnerships.com 'What we believe', accessed 23.3.2010.

www.mscd.edu/extendedcampus/toolsofthemind/index.shtml, accessed 4.8.2010.

The Personal, Learning and Thinking Skills Leaflet. http://curriculum.qcda.gov.uk/key-stages-3-and-4/skills/plts/index.aspx, accessed 5.8.10

www.guardian.co.uk/global/blog/2010/jul/20/iraq-war-inquiry-iraq, accessed 23.7.2010.

www.rsc.org.uk/standupforshakespeare/content/key_findings.aspx, accessed 24.6.2010.

www.sirkenrobinson.com, accessed 13.5.2010.

The Wellcome Trust (2010) *Making a Difference: 2005–2010* London: The Wellcome Trust www.wellcome.ac.uk, accessed 26.5.2010.

Index